*THE BLACK HOLE
CHALLENGES
MANY OF OUR
BASIC IDEAS
ABOUT OUR
SURROUNDINGS
AND OUR
PLACE IN THEM ...*

About the author:
Dr. Jerry Pournelle holds degrees in engineering, psychology, and political science. He worked in space research and was active in both the Mercury and Apollo programs. He was also Chief of Experimental Stress Project in the Human Factors Laboratories at the Boeing Company and was involved in the qualification tests for the original astronauts.

Dr. Pournelle is the winner of the 1972 John Campbell Award, and now resides in Studio City, California, with his wife and four sons. His other books include *The Mercenary* and, with Larry Niven, *The Mote in God's Eye* and *Lucifer's Hammer.*

Fawcett Crest Books
by Jerry Pournelle:

BLACK HOLES   23962-4 $1.95

With Larry Niven:

LUCIFER'S HAMMER   23599-8 $2.50

BLACK HOLES
and other marvels

edited by

Jerry Pournelle

FAWCETT CREST • NEW YORK

BLACK HOLES

Published by Fawcett Crest Books, a unit of CBS Publications, the Consumer Publishing Division of CBS Inc., by arrangement with Futura Publications Limited

ISBN: 0-449-23962-4

Printed in the United States of America

10   9   8   7   6   5   4   3   2   1

To Steve Hawking, who brings wonder to the universe

ACKNOWLEDGEMENTS

Black Holes and Cosmic Censors
An earlier version appeared in *Galaxy Magazine*,
December 1974, copyright © Universal Publishing and
Distributing Company, Inc., 1975. Published by
permission of the author and the author's agent, Lurton
Blassingame.

He Fell Into A Dark Hole
Appeared in *Analog Science Fact/Fiction* March 1973.
Copyright © Conde Nast Publications, Inc., 1973.
Reprinted by permission of the author and the author's
agent, Lurton Blassingame.

The Hole Man by Larry Niven
Copyright © 1973 by the Conde Nast Publications, Inc.
Reprinted by permission of the author and the author's
agent, Robert P. Mills, Ltd.

Fuzzy Black Holes Have No Hair by Jerry Pournelle
Appeared in the January 1975 issue of *Galaxy Magazine*.
Copyright © 1975 Universal Publishing and Distributing
Company, Inc., 1975. Reprinted by permission of the
author and the author's agent, Lurton Blassingame.

Kyrie by Poul Anderson
First published in *The Far Reaches*, Joseph Elder, ed.,
Trident Press, New York. Copyright © 1968 by Joseph
Elder and rights reassigned to author. Reprinted by
permission of the author and the author's agent, Scott
Meredith Literary Agency.

CONTENTS

Preface   11

Black Holes and Cosmic Censors
   Jerry Pournelle   15

He Fell Into A Dark Hole   Jerry Pournelle   31

The Hole Man   Larry Niven   72

Fuzzy Black Holes Have No Hair   Jerry Pournelle   89

Kyrie   Poul Anderson   97

Killing Vector   Charles Sheffield   111

The Borderland of Sol   Larry Niven   132

Pluto is Black!   Robert L. Forward   182

Fountain of Force   Grant Carrington and
   George Zebrowski   190

Papa Schimmelhorn's Yang   R. Bretnor   201

Gloria   Gail Kimberly   234

Singularity   Mildred Downey Broxon   242

Two Poems   Peter Dillingham
   Cygnus X-1   290
   The Salesman Who Fell From Grace With
     The Universe   291

The Nothing Spot   Dian Girard   294

For the Lady of a Physicist   Michael Bishop   301

The Venging   Greg Bear   304

In The Beginning . . .   Jerry Pournelle   341

PREFACE

Jerry Pournelle

Science fiction ought to be fun, and certainly I intend this book to be entertaining.

I say that at the start, because although there's nothing wrong with informative stories—and I hope many of those in this book will be—the first requirement is that stories should entertain, and to the best of my ability I've tried to select material that meets that requirement, even though the subject is a bit far out.

Black Holes have become popular. A few years ago

there was almost no reference to them in scientific literature. Books on gravitation had no index reference to Holes, and if you wanted to find out about those peculiar things you had to go to very obscure works indeed. Then, suddenly, we found Black Holes everywhere we looked. They appeared in science fiction stories and science fact articles. There they were in our newspapers and on the television. The concept became downright popular, and you could even hear talk of them at cocktail parties.

It was inevitable, then, that someone would publish an anthology of stories about Holes. It was a bit less than inevitable that I should edit the book, but I do have claims. My first Black Hole story appeared way back when, before all the hooplah in the popular press, and I wrote several columns about them in my GALAXY Magazine column, "A Step Farther Out". I can't say I have a patent on Holes, but by gollies I did manage to get into print about them before Isaac Asimov, and considering the number of books he writes each week that's an accomplishment. At any rate, when this anthology was proposed I was asked to be editor.

For all their new popularity, Black Holes remain a theory. No one has ever seen one—indeed, by definition no one will *ever* see one—and all we know has been deduced from various mathematical theories. The primary concept of a Black Hole—an object near which gravity is so strong that nothing, not even light, can escape, thus making the object invisible—can be and was deduced from Newton; but the real theoretical work came only after Einstein.

Now I realize that there is probably nothing which can so easily persuade readers to abandon a book than a promise to explain the Einstein theory of relativity, so let me hasten to assure you that you won't find that here. What you will find is speculation; speculations ranging from the relatively (pun intended) serious to the frankly ribald; stories and fact articles on Black Holes. I hope you'll have as much fun reading them as I've had putting them together.

Jerry Pournelle
Hollywood, 1978

BLACK HOLES AND COSMIC CENSORS

Jerry Pournelle, Ph.D.

Most of this book is stories, and the authors of those stories—myself included—have worked very hard to explain what's going on in them. Thus I don't blame any readers who want to skip this section and get on with the fun of science fiction. However, for those who want to stick around, I'll try to give a painless introduction into black holes, cosmic censors, singularities, frozen stars, and other such matters of extreme gravity.

Although they're studied by high-powered mathematics and have their origin in some of the most complicated ideas ever spawned by humanity, black holes are rather simple things. You can easily imagine them through "thought experiments", which is just as well, because we can't actually do the experiments.

Take normal matter. We all know that's made up of atoms, and that there's a great deal of empty space in what seems to be a solid object. We also know that those atoms can be squeezed closer together, and when that's done we say the matter has become more dense.

One of the universal properties of matter is gravity. Although there have been stories about "negative matter" which has no gravity, or which repels normal matter, no one has ever found any, and to the best of our knowledge all matter—and all energy as well, since matter and energy are only two forms of the same "thing"*—has gravity. The more matter you pile together, the higher the gravity will be.

Now gravity is a rather curious thing. In the Newtonian universe, and in most other theories of physics, gravity is a "force" which attracts everything to everything else. It is not a very powerful force. In fact, if the universe consisted of one proton and one electron, the electromagnetic force attracting them would be 10^{40} (1 followed by 40 zeroes) times as great as the gravitational force pulling them together. Thus if one takes two protons, one finds that they are repelled by their electromagnetic force 10^{40} times as hard as they're attracted together by their mass. Still, in most theories, gravity and electromagnetic forces are not fundamentally different: both are "forces" and both act on bodies at a distance.

This essential similarily between gravity and electromagnetism is also assumed in Einstein's special theory of relativity. Special relativity is the theory that asserts that no material object, and no signal, can *ever* travel faster than the speed of light. There's a great deal of evidence

---

* $E = mc^2$ says Einstein, which is to say that matter and energy are but two forms of one entity; and this was proved rather dramatically by the Manhattan Project.

for the truth of special relativity, and no really good counter-theories lurk in the wings to take its place. When science fiction writers want to use faster-than-light travel, they're forced to all kinds of lengths: hyperspace, magic drives, etc. My own faster-than-light drive was designed by a California Institute of Technology astrophysicist/computer expert named Dan Alderson, and has been worked out in marvelous detail. I'll spare you the five pages of equations Dan used in developing the theory, and if you want to know more about my spacedrive it figures prominently in the story included in this book.

Although there's a lot of evidence for special relativity, the *general* theory of relativity is another breed of cat entirely. There are several contenders in that realm, and a number of scientists hope to overthrow general relativity in favor of something else. General relativity is a theory of gravitation—and it asserts that gravity is not a force at all. In *general* relativity, gravity is the result of distortions in the geometry of space.

Whether gravity fields "exist" in the same way that electro-magnetic fields exist, or merely result from geometry, most theorists accept that gravitational attraction is universal. The more matter one piles together, the higher the gravity.

Thus the interior of Jupiter is a very great deal more dense than the interior of the Earth, because there is so very much more of Jupiter. The atoms of Jupiter are squeezed closer together than are atoms of Earth-matter. Now let's suppose that we piled more and more matter onto Jupiter. What would happen?

Well, first, Jupiter would probably become a star. The hydrogen would begin to fuse to helium, releasing a lot of energy, and the pressure of escaping energy would keep the new star from collapsing. This is what keeps our Sun from collapsing into a small ball, and a good thing, too.

Eventually, though, the Sun will run out of hydrogen to "burn" into helium; or, to continue our thought experiment, suppose what we piled onto Jupiter wasn't rich in hydrogen, but some kind of matter that won't fuse: iron, let's say.

It should be obvious that this matter-pile we're working with will get denser and denser, and the space between the atoms will get smaller and smaller.

That happens in the universe, and we call the result white dwarfs: stars of collapsed matter. The late H. Beam Piper made good use of "collapsium" in his stories, although he didn't specify how it was to be generated. We know of at least one object in the universe made of this stuff: Sirius B, called the "Companion of Sirius" in older books. This is a star with very nearly the mass of our Sun, but with a radius not a lot larger than the planet Neptune—about a third the size of Jupiter. It is about 3,-000 times as dense as the Earth's core, and about 350 times as dense as the Sun's.

Things don't stop there. Suppose we go on piling on matter, taking pains not to add anything that will fuse into energy. At first we still have "normal" matter, made up of a nucleus—protons and neutrons—and an outer shell of electrons. If we keep piling on matter, though, gravity will eventually win the battle: the very electrons will be forced down into the nuclei.

When an electron and a proton get together they make up a neutron. We would thus have an object made entirely of neutrons, and we might call such a substance "neutronium".

The idea of stars made up of neutronium was deduced by the Swiss American astronomer Fritz Zwicky back in 1934. He was working with Einstein's theory of gravitation. A few years later the American physicist J. Robert Oppenheimer did more work with the theory. It said that if about one and a half times the Sun's mass is piled into one place, the collapse into neutronium is inevitable.

Sine there are a lot of stars far larger than the Sun, and some of them must burn out—there are a hundred billion stars in our galaxy and many are far older than our

Sun—then it follows that out there somewhere there must be neutron stars, stars which have collapsed into pure neutronium. Fritz Zwicky organized a search for them, but he didn't live to see the final result.

Let's jump ahead for a moment. Years after Zwicky and Oppenheimer worked with pencil and paper to produce the theory of neutron stars, British radio-astronomers detected something incredible: objects which radiated at very precise intervals. Cosmic clocks, so to speak. They gave off a pulse of energy every few seconds, and they were regular to hundredths of millionths of seconds. These were called "pulsars", and they were mysterious indeed. As late as 1971 the most authoritative textbooks could not be sure what they were.

Now, of course, it is "known" that they are neutron stars. When a normal star collapses, it retains its rotation; like a figure-skater drawing her arms close to her body to increase her rate of spin, when a star collapses it spins faster and faster. A check of the math indicates that it is *highly* likely that "pulsars" are precisely that, rapidly rotating neutron stars, and this became generally accepted a few years ago and is not doubted seriously.

However, there is more to Einstein's math than neutron stars. Suppose we pile on matter again: more and more matter, piled onto a neutron star. Is there not a point at which the neutrons themselves will collapse?

Yes; and what happens next is almost incredible.

The star is literally pushed out of the universe. Well, perhaps not; but in any event, we'll never be able to see what happens.

Let's approach this from another direction, one first thought of by the mathematician LaPlace long before Einstein.

Planets have gravity. We call the gravity field of Earth "one gravity", and we're used to it. Gravity is a very weak force. It takes the entire mass of the Earth to pull at you with one g, and you can overcome it simply by standing, or by jumping. If you were to jump hard enough, you could escape from the Earth entirely.

No one can jump that hard, of course, but we can build chemical rockets to do the job. Give an object enough speed, and it will leave the earth never to return. On Earth that speed is about 11 kilometers a second.

The surface gravity of a planet—or anything else—depends on both the mass and the radius of the planet. To be exact, the equation is $V\hat{e} = \sqrt{2GM/r}$, which you needn't remember. In that equation $V\hat{e}$ is the velocity needed to leave the planet entirely, M is the mass of the planet, r is the radius, and G is a long number called the "universal constant of gravitation". G does not change—we think. The important thing to notice is that there are two ways to increase the escape velocity.

You can pile on more mass, or you can decrease the radius. In fact, if Earth's radius were squeezed down to a fourth—but the mass stayed the same—the escape velocity would be twice what it is now.

We have also seen that as you pile on the matter, the matter gets squeezed together; it collapses. Thus we are increasing the escape velocity two ways. The planet is getting heavier, and it is getting smaller.

So, since it costs us nothing to do thought experiments, let's pile on the matter. More and more, letting our object collapse. Eventually we'll get a neutron star. What escape velocity might it have?

Well, the Companion of Sirius has a mass equal to Sol's and a radius a third that of Jupiter; that works out to 2,-400 kilometers a second escape velocity (compared to the 618 km./sec. at the surface of the Sun). This is a respectable number, but still not something we can't imagine. Now let's continue to pour on the matter and decrease the radius.

As we do, the escape velocity goes up. Eventually it might rise higher than the speed of light.

At that point we have denied ourselves any possible knowledge of what is going on. So far as we know, nothing in this universe can exceed the speed of light. Therefore no messages can come from our superdense object. Anyone visiting it will never return, nor can they ever tell us what has happened to them.

All this is interesting, but is it possible? Certainly the math suggests that if we could ever pile on enough matter to create an object so heavy that the surface gravity is very high, so high that the escape velocity is very high, so high that the escape velocity is greater than the velocity of light, we have made a strange object indeed: one we can never see nor ever know much about.

It is here that the mathematics gets complex. Can there exist something both heavy enough and small enough to create that condition? Theory says there can be.

The theory says that if enough matter is piled together, even neutronium will collapse. The neutrons are forced together, squeezed, and continue to collapse until—

There is no "until". The collapse is infinite. Nothing, no force, nothing we can guess at, can halt the collapse. The object gets smaller until its radius is—zero. Now that is patently absurd. How can there be an object in this universe that has a real mass, but no radius at all?

There can't be; which is why we say that a black hole is not really in this universe at all.

Understand, the object is real, all right. It's there. If we get close to it we can feel the gravity. But there is no way we can ever measure its radius, no way to know what has happened to it, no way to observe it; and there is nothing we know of to halt its continued collapse to zero radius. This is not a trick with numbers; by zero we mean zero, goose egg, *l'oeuf*, nothing at all; we do not mean "infinitesimal". And we can never see it or observe it, because if light cannot get out, nothing else can either.

That is what we call a black hole. Incidentally, the Russians call them "frozen stars", because the phrase "black hole" in Russian is an obscenity that means exactly what you think it does. (I am told that because the term black hole is common in western astronomy, some Russians are beginning to use it in their own literature, with what effect on lay sensibilities I don't know.)

A black hole, then, is a theoretical construct. The idea of an object you cannot see because its gravity, and thus surface velocity, requires greater-than-light speeds for data to emerge is inherent even in Newtonian physics; but the concept of infinite collapse is derived from Einstein's general relativity. The first speculations about invisible objects came from LaPlace back in 1799, but it wasn't until after Einstein's publications that a German astronomer named Karl Schwarzschild did serious work on the concept.

Schwarzschild called the zero point, the dimensionless mass down at the bottom of the hole, a "singularity". In Einsteinian terms space has become so curved that it closes in on itself—and once again the object is not, in a certain sense anyway, in our universe at all. It has literally pulled the hole in after itself, leaving very little behind.

Now although the matter in the hole has infinite density, and no radius at all, the region around it in which gravity is so strong that light can't escape is rather larger. Both the Newtonian and Einsteinian equations give the same radius for it, namely the region at which $r = 2GM/c^2$ where r, G, and M have the same meaning as before, and c is the speed of light.

If our Sun were squeezed into a black hole that radius would be on the order of three kilometers, and if the Sun ever collapses that small we'll never be able to see it again.

Black holes can be large or small. You can imagine a whole galaxy of a hundred billion stars squeezed down until it occupies a space about the size of a solar system, say a third of a lightyear across: at that point you would have a black galaxy.

An observer diving into a black hole would never know when he had crossed this line, which is called the *event horizon.* The term is self-explanatory: events happening inside the region bounded by the event horizon will always remain unknown to those outside it. The astronaut could go on sending signals to his friends outside, and as far as the astronaut could tell his messages would go up and out. Those outside the hole, though, could never under any circumstances receive the messages, or indeed receive any information about what's going on in there.

Indeed, the mathematics suggest something even stranger: that the outside observers would see their friend approach the event horizon; his messages would become slower and slower; and as he reached the event horizon (also called the Schwarzschild limit) his apparent motion would stop; he would remain frozen in time and space for eternity. However, we also know that matter can fall into a black hole and produce effects, so there is some ambiguity about this "frozen time", and there's no point in going into the paradox here.

Note something else. Although star-sized black holes would have very high densities, galaxy-sized holes need not. In the case of a black galaxy, the density at the event horizon would be quite tolerable, and so would the tidal stresses; an astronaut could indeed survive the experience—but he could never return.

In fact, if you consider the equation for a black hole's event horizon; plug into it for mass the current estimates of the mass of our entire universe (100 billion galaxies of 100 billion stars each); put in for radius the distance to the furthest object we can see; then the equation almost balances. This implies that we may, all of us, our whole universe, be merely a black hole inside someone else's universe.

The question almost balances, but not quite. There isn't enough matter in the universe: we are missing from 20 to 98% of the needed mass, depending on whose figures you use for M and r. Still, it is very close (as things cosmic go), and there are theories: the missing matter might, for example, be in black holes. How would we ever know? If for every galaxy we can see there's another black galaxy, we'd never be able to find out; and the equation might balance.

If there is enough matter to balance the black hole equation, then space around us is curved into a closed figure; we live in a closed universe. Eventually, in that case, all those galaxies receding from us will stop and come back, and the whole universe will start coming together again until eventually it's packed into a big wad at the center.

If we don't live in a closed universe, the receding galaxies will go right on receding forever. Cosmologists want badly to settle this question, but the experimental data are hard to come by.

One experiment might be to measure gravity waves and study gravitation. In theory, if we could detect and examine gravitational waves, we might be able to tell whether they result from a field and are thus similar to magnetism, or if they are merely a property of space and its geometry. This would give us a means of confirming or rejecting Einstein's general theory of relativity.

Unfortunately, gravity is an incredibly weak force, really quite puny, and because it's so weak—compared to electromagnetic forces, for example—it's very hard to play with. You can't turn on a "gravity wave generator" and fiddle with the resulting forces to see if they refract, or can be tuned, or whatever. You can't wiggle a mass to generate gravity waves, because you can't get a large enough mass to wiggle properly. It's not even possible to blow off an atomic weapon, thus turning some matter into energy, and measure the effect of the matter's vanishing; the effect is just too small to be noticed, and is hidden among the rather drastic side effects.

However, there are a number of theoretical ways that gravity might be generated by the universe. Stars collapsing into black holes or into neutron stars might do it, for example. The universe might be riddled with gravitational waves. They'd be terribly weak, and require delicate and sophisticated apparatus, but they might be detectable.

Some years ago Dr. Joseph Weber of the University of Maryland decided to build a gravity wave antenna. He took a large aluminum cylinder and covered it with strain gauges. The idea was that so long as the cylinder were acted on only by the steady gravity of Earth, it would be in a stable configuration; but if a gravity wave passed through it, the cylinder would be distorted, and the strain gauges would show it.

He had to compensate for temperature, and isolate it from vibration, and worry about a lot of things, but the technology had been developed: the antenna was built. It was incredibly sensitive, able to detect vibrations and distortions on the order of an atomic diameter. It was also able to detect student demonstrations outside the library, trucks rumbling along the highway a mile distant, and other unwanted events.

The solution to the noise problem was simple: build another copy of the antenna and place it 1000 kilometers away. Now hook the two together, and pay no attention to an event that doesn't affect both. Such "coincidences" should be due to a force affecting both antennae, and since even earthquakes take time to propagate—and their effects move much slower than lightspeed—the output ought to be reliable.

Unfortunately it isn't as straightforward as that. The instruments must be very sensitive, and thus there's a lot of chatter from them. By the laws of chance, some of this chatter will be simultaneous, or near enough so, and thus you are guaranteed some false positive results. The output of the gravity wave detectors, therefore, needs careful analysis to decide what's data and what's mere chance.

Weber immediately got results. He got a lot of results, far too many for chance—according to his analysis. Unfortunately there were far too many results for cosmologists to believe. What could be causing so much energy to be turned into gravity waves?

One argument went this way: something is producing those gravity waves, and we can't see enough happening out there to account for it; but if normal matter falls into a black hole, or stars collapse into black holes, that will produce gravity waves of the kind Weber detected. However: if we take all his events seriously, then as much as 98% of all the matter in the universe must be inside black holes, forever invisible to us. This seemed to many to be absurd.

On the other hand, some cosmologists welcomed the results. If 98% of the matter in the universe were inside black holes, there is more than enough matter to balance the equation, and the universe is closed. We do indeed live inside a very large black hole, and all those receding galaxies will indeed come back together again.

Others made no comment, but tried to build their own gravity wave detectors.

Meanwhile, a second and more startling result came out of Weber's shop. It appeared that there was a 12-hour sidereal cycle to the coincidences, and furthermore, that this cycle was related to the galactic plane. In other words, his results implied that a lot of gravitational wave energy was originated in the center of our galaxy.

Since we have a good estimate of how far it is to the galactic center, we could calculate how much energy it would take to produce waves of sufficient strength to be detected out here on our spiral arm. The result was dismaying. Far too much energy was needed.

Now the energy radiating from the galactic center could be sprayed out in all directions, in which case the figures were absurd. Alternatively, it might be "beamed" into the galactic plane, which still takes a lot of energy, but nowhere near as much as if it radiated in all directions. Thus there was speculation about what might be causing the "beam" effect.

The speculations were many, imaginative, and varied. They were also rather frightening.

We know that when a black hole forms the matter inside collapses all the way; *nothing* can stop it from becoming infinite in density. When gravitational forces have got to this point we call it a "singularity"; a point at which normal laws of physics do not apply.

Actually it's worse than that. Not only don't normal laws apply, but the general theory of relativity says that *no* laws apply. Strange things happen in the region of a singularity. Time is reversed. Conservation laws don't work. Causality is a joke: if you could get into the region of a singularity, you really could go back in time and assassinate your grandfather.

In fact anything could happen and science ceases to exist; and you don't even have to physically go to the singularity for this to take place. If you can observe one directly science has just gone down the drain. That bothers a lot of theorists and scientists, and rather disturbs me as well.

If there is a naked singularity—that is, a singularity not covered with an event horizon—then, at least in potential, there is no order to the universe.

Out of that might come ghosties and ghoulies and things that go bump in the night.

What then may we do to save science? Why, invoke censorship, of course. The kind of censorship invoked is called rather whimsically the "Law of Cosmic Censorship", which states that "There shall be no such thing as a naked singularity." *All singularities must be decently clothed with an event horizon.*

Given cosmic censorship, a number of interesting laws about black holes may be demonstrated: that they never get smaller, that if one is rotating it can't be sped up until the escape velocity is smaller than the speed of light, and a number of other rules that are collectively known as the laws of black hole dynamics.

Unfortunately, cosmic censorship deprives science fiction writers of some of their best stories.

It does it this way. If all black holes are covered with event horizons, it follows that you can't plunge into a black hole and come out elsewhere or elsewhen. Actually, if you plunge into a random black hole, all that could ever come out anywhere would be a stream of undifferentiated subnuclear particles; for all their fantastic properties, singularities do retain one feature, namely that gravitation in their region is rather high, sufficient to disassociate not only the molecular, but the atomic, structure of anything visiting them.

On the other hand, if a star about to collapse into black hole status is rotating fast enough, some solutions to the Einstein tensor suggest that the singularity formed will be a donut; you could dive through that and come out in one piece, provided the donut were large enough.

Large enough means galactic sized, I'm afraid; stellar size black holes will still get you too close to the singularity so that you can't use them for transportation. Furthermore, what you come out to on the other side is not, according to the equations, our universe at all. What it will be like, no one can say, except that it will have in it a copy of the black hole you dove through to get there.

So, turn around and dive back, of course; but that doesn't work. You go through and out again, all right, but into a third universe different from either of the other two. The black hole is still there, so try again—and come out in a fourth, and there behind you is that rather tiresome black hole again.

Is any of this real, or are we playing with ideas? No one really knows, of course. The most we can say is that the people who can solve Einstein tensors come up with that kind of result.

It's rather discouraging for science fiction writers. Here we thought we had a new way to get faster than light travel, what with black holes connecting us to another universe, or, just possibly, to another region of our own, and the very people who gave us the black holes go on to prove we can't use them.

Still, maybe there's a way out. Perhaps someone will find a solution. But they can't so long as the law of cosmic censorship is enforced, because singularities decently covered with event horizons can't come out and affect our universe.

Back to Weber and gravitation waves. One of the models constructed to account for the enormous gravitational energy generated in the center of the galaxy had a very large singularity lurking down there. Suns fell into it, and as they were eaten, gravity waves poured out. It was a rather depressing picture, our galaxy being eaten alive like that.

Then a number of other laboratories constructed gravitational antennae. Bell Laboratories, an English group, the Russians, all made gravity wave detectors. In each case their equipment was supposed to be an improvement on Weber's.

None of them found any coincidences at all. People began to wonder just what Weber had done, and to doubt his results.

In summer 1975, at the Cambridge Conference of experimental relativists, the picture changed again. The people who had built "improved" gravity wave antennae reported no results whatever.

(Weber continued to report results, but with a change I'll get back to in a moment.)

Meanwhile two other groups, one at Frascatti, Italy, the other at Munich, Germany, had built carbon copies of Weber's antenna. They got coincidences. Whatever Weber was observing, others have independently observed something similar now.

While all this was going on Weber did a re-analysis of his coincidences—using a computer rather than human judgment to define just what was a coincidence. The result was startling. He still gets events—but they are no longer concentrated in the galactic plane. The sidereal coincidences have gone away, and with them has gone the evidence for the large singularity eating the galaxy.

Moreover, Dr. Robert Forward, of Hughes Research at Malibu, California, has constructed his own gravity wave antenna. Since lasers were invented at Hughes Labs, it's no surprise that Forward's antenna employs them. He has three big weights at the apexes of a right-angle triangle.

Lasers measure the precise distance of each weight from the others. A gravity wave will presumably distort that triangle, and thus be detected.

Forward has "events" too. They seem to coincide with the kinds of things Weber gets but no serious attempt has been made to compare results.

For that matter, the Munich people have just got started. They were quite surprised, by the way; they'd thought Weber's results were some kind of artifact.

It appears, then, that some kind of gravity waves do travel about through the universe; at least something that can affect large aluminum cylinders hundreds of kilometers apart is operating here.

The next step is to see if these events have any relationship to the bursts of x-ray energy detected by Vela satellites. At the moment that's not possible, and of course there are a lot more gravity wave events than x-ray events; but if the x-ray events are accompanied by coincidences on the gravity antenna, we'll know a lot more about both. When the shuttle lets us take a telescope to space we can get the data.

We may then be able to decide what gravity is: a force, or a distortion of geometry. We may be able to learn more about black holes, and what happens inside them, and who knows, those trips to alternate universes could be a real possibility.

Until we get rid of cosmic censorship, though, we'll never know what happens to the volunteers who go exploring down black holes; and that leads into the first story.

HE FELL INTO A DARK HOLE

Jerry Pournelle

This story is the reason I am editor of this book. Some years ago my friend and partner Larry Niven published a story called "Neutron Star" which made use of what was then a new concept, neutron stars. He won a Hugo with the story, and also introduced the idea into science fiction.

I couldn't be absolutely first with Black Holes. There had been a few stories about Holes already published although I hadn't seen them. (Writers have very little time to read fiction.) Still, I would be among the first, and with any luck I'd be able to do for Black Holes what Larry Niven had done for neutron stars.

I set the story in my world of the CoDominium, which takes us from a few years hence into the far future. A number of my other stories—the best known being THE MERCENARY and THE MOTE IN GOD'S EYE (with Larry Niven)—make use of this "future history". The series assumes that the United States and the Soviet Union end the cold war by joining in an uneasy alliance. Their respective governments find it far better that there be only two Great Powers, even as rivals, than for there to be a number of independent power centers. As a part of this alliance structure they create the CoDominium Space Navy. They also try to control all scientific research, since new developments might threaten the CoDominium's supremacy.

As a result there is little basic or theoretical research, and nearly everyone has forgotten about Black Holes, until . . .

CDSN Captain Bartholomew Ramsey watched his men check out, each man leaving the oval entry port under the satanic gaze of the master-at-arms. After nearly two years in space the men deserved something more exciting than twenty hours dirtside at Ceres Base, but they were eager for even that much. CDSS *Daniel Webster* got all the long patrols and dirty outsystem jobs in the Navy because her captain didn't protest. Now, when these men got to Luna Base and Navy Town, Lord help the local girls . . .

Well, they'd be all right here, Ramsey thought. The really expensive pleasures were reserved for Belt prospectors and the crews of Westinghouse mining ships. Bart glanced at the screens displaying ships docked at Ceres. None of the big ore-processing ships were in Thorstown. Things should be pretty quiet. Nothing Base Marines couldn't handle, even if *Daniel Webster*'s crew hadn't been on a good drunk for twenty months. Ramsey turned away from the entry port to go back to his cabin.

It was difficult to walk in the low gravity of Ceres. Very inconvenient place, he thought. But of course low gravity was a main reason for putting a Navy yard there. That and the asteroid mines . . .

He walked carefully through gray steel bulkheads to the central corridor. Just outside the bridge entrance he met Dave Trevor, the first lieutenant.

"Not going ashore?" Ramsey asked.

"No, sir." Trevor's boyish grin was infectious. Ramsey had once described it as the best crew morale booster in the Navy. And at age twenty-four Dave Trevor had been in space eleven years, as ship's boy, midshipman, and officer. He would know every pub in the Solar System and a lot outside . . . "Never cared much for the girls on Ceres," he said. "Too businesslike."

Captain Ramsey nodded sagely. With Trevor's looks he wouldn't have to shell out money for an evening's fun anywhere near civilization. Ceres was another matter. "I'd appreciate it if you'd make a call on the provost's office, Mr. Trevor. We might need a friend there by morning."

The lieutenant grinned again. "Aye, aye, Captain."

Bart nodded and climbed down the ladder to his cabin. Trevor's merry whistling followed him until he closed the door. Once Ramsey was inside he punched a four-digit code on the intercom console.

"Surgeon's office, Surgeon's Mate Hartley, sir."

"Captain here. Make sure we have access to a good dental repair unit in the morning, Hartley. Even if we have to use Base facilities."

"Aye, aye, sir."

Ramsey switched the unit off and permitted himself a thin smile. The regeneration stimulators aboard *Daniel Webster* worked but there was something wrong with the coding information in the dental unit. It produced buck teeth, not enormous but quite noticeable, and when his men were out drinking and some dirtpounder made a few funny remarks . . .

The smile faded as Ramsey sat carefully in the regulation chair. He glanced around the sterile cabin. There were none of the comforts other captains provided themselves. Screens, charts, built-in cabinets and tables, his desk, everything needed to run his ship, but no photographs and solidos, no paintings and rugs. Just Ramsey and his ship, his wife with the masculine name. He took a glass of whisky from the arm of the chair. It was Scotch and the taste of burnt malt was very strong. Bart tossed it off and replaced it to be refilled. The intercom buzzed.

"Captain here."

"Bridge, sir. Call from Base Commandant Torrin."

"Put him on."

"Aye, aye, sir." The watch midshipman's face vanished and Rap Torrin's broad features filled the screen. The rear admiral looked at the bare cabin, grimaced, then smiled at Ramsey.

"I'm going to pull rank on you, Bart," Torrin said. "Expect that courtesy call in an hour. You can plan on having dinner with me, too."

Ramsey forced a smile. "Very good, sir. My pleasure. In an hour, then."

"Right." The screen went blank and Ramsey cursed. He drank the second whisky and cursed again, this time at himself.

What's wrong with you? he thought. *Rap Torrin is as good a friend as you have in the Navy. Shipmate way back in Ajax under Sergei Lermontov. Now Rap has a star, well, that was expected. And Lermontov is Vice Admiral Commanding, the number two man in the whole CoDominium Space Navy.*

And so what? I could have had stars. As many as I wanted. I'm that good, or I was. And with Martin Grant's influence in the Grand Senate and Martin's brother John in charge of United States security, Senator Martin Grant's son-in-law could have had any post no matter how good . . .

Ramsey took another whisky from the chair and looked at it for a long time. He'd once had his star, polished and waiting, nothing but formalities to go, while Rap and Sergei grinned at his good luck. Sergei Lermontov had just made junior vice admiral then. Five years ago.

Five years. Five years ago Barbara Jean Ramsey and their son Harold were due back from Meiji. Superstitiously, Bart had waited for them before accepting his promotion. When he took it he'd have to leave *Daniel Webster* for something dirtside and wait until a spacing admiral was needed. That wouldn't have been long. The Danube situation was heating up back then. Ramsey could have commanded the first punitive expedition, but it had gone out under an admiral who botched the job. Barbara Jean had never come home from Meiji.

Her ship had taken a new direct route along an Alderson path just discovered. It never came out into normal space. A scoutcraft was sent to search for the liner, and Senator Grant had enough influence to send a frigate after that. Both vanished, and there weren't any more ships to send. Bartholomew Ramsey stayed a captain. He couldn't leave his ship because he couldn't face the empty house in Luna Base compound.

He sighed, then laughed cynically at himself. Time to get dressed. Rap wanted to show off his star, and it would be cruel to keep him waiting.

The reunion was neither more nor less than he'd expected, but Admiral Torrin cut short the time in his office. "Got to get you home, Bart. Surprise for you there. Come along, man, come along."

Bart followed woodenly. *Something really wrong with me*, he thought. *Man doesn't go on like this for five years. I'm all right aboard Old Danny Boy. It's only when I leave my ship, now why should that be?* But a man can marry a ship, even a slim steel whiskey bottle four hundred meters long and sixty across; he wouldn't be the first captain married to a cruiser.

Most of Ceres Base was underground, and Bart was lost in the endless rock corridors. Finally they reached a guarded area. They returned the Marines' salutes and went through to broader hallways lined with carpets. There were battle paintings on the walls. Some reached back to wet navy days and every CD base, insystem or out, had them. There were scenes from all the great navies of the world. Russian, Soviet, U.S., British, Japanese . . . there weren't any of Togo at Tshushima, though. Or Pearl Harbor. Or Bengal Bay.

Rap kept up his hearty chatter until they got inside his apartment. The admiral's quarters were what Bart had visualized before he entered, richly furnished, filled with the gifts and mementos that a successful independent command captain could collect on a dozen worlds after more than twenty years in service. Shells and stuffed exotic fauna, a cabinet made of the delicately veined snakewood of Tanith, a table of priceless Spartan roseteak. There was a house on Luna Base that had been furnished like this . . .

Bart caught sight of the man who entered the room and snapped to attention in surprise. Automatically he saluted.

Vice Admiral Lermontov returned the salute. The admiral was a tall, slim man who wore rimless spectacles which made his gray eyes look large and round as they bored through his subordinates. Men who served under Lermontov either loved him or hated him. Now his thin features distorted in genuine pleasure. "Bartholomew, I am sorry to surprise you like this."

Lermontov inspected Ramsey critically. The smile faded slightly. "You have not taken proper care of yourself, my friend. Not enough exercise."

"I can still beat you. Arm wrestling, anything you name—uh, sir."

Lermontov's smile broadened again. "That is better. But you need not call me 'sir'. You would say 'sir' only to Vice Admiral Lermontov, and it is quite obvious that the Vice Admiral Commanding cannot possibly be on Ceres. So, since you have not seen me . . ."

"I see," Ramsey said.

Lermontov nodded. "It is rather important. You will

know why in a few moments. Rap, can you bring us
something to drink?"

Torrin nodded and fussed with drinks from the snakewood cabinet. The ringing tone of a crystal glass was very
loud in the quiet apartment. Ramsey was vaguely amused
as he took a seat at the roseteak table in the center of the
lush room. A rear admiral waiting on a captain, and no
enlisted spacers to serve the Vice Admiral Commanding,
who, after all, wasn't really there in the first place . . .
the whisky was from Inveraray and was very good.

"You have been in space nearly two years," Lermontov
said. "You have not seen your father-in-law in that time?"

"More like three since Martin and I really talked about
anything," Ramsey said. "We—we remind each other too
much of Barbara Jean and Harold."

The pain in Ramsey's face was reflected as a pale
shadow in Lermontov's eyes. "But you knew he had become chairman of the appropriations committee."

"Yes."

"The Navy's friend, Grand Senator Grant. Without him
these last years would have been disaster for us all. For
the Navy, and for Earth as well if those politicians could
only see it." Lermontov cut himself off with an angry
snap. The big eyes matching his steel gray hair focused on
Bart. "The new appropriations are worse," the admiral
growled. "While you have been away, everything has become worse. Millington, Harmon, Bertram, they all
squeeze President Lipscomb's Unity Party in your country, and Kaslov gains influence every day in mine. I think
it will not be long before one or the other of the CoDominium sponsors withdraws from the treaties, Bart. And after that, war."

"War." Ramsey said it slowly, not believing. After a
hundred and fifty years of uneasy peace between the
United States and the Soviets, war again, and with the
weapons they had . . .

"Any spark might set it off," Lermontov was saying.
"We must be ready to step in. The fleet must be strong,

strong enough to cope with the national forces and do whatever we must do."

Ramsey felt as if the admiral had struck him. War? Fleet intervention? "What about the Commanding Admiral? The Grand Senate?"

Lermontov shrugged. "You know who are the good men, who are not. But so long as the fleet is strong, something perhaps can be done to save Earth from the idiocy of the politicians. Not that the masses are better, screaming for a war they can never understand." Lermontov drank quietly, obviously searching for words, before he turned back to Ramsey. "I have to tell you something painful, my friend. Your father-in-law is missing."

"Missing—where? I told Martin to be careful, that Millington's Liberation Army people . . ."

"No. Not on Earth. Outsystem. Senator Grant went to Meiji to visit relatives there . . ."

"Yes." Ramsey felt the memory like a knife in his vitals. "His nephew, Barbara Jean's cousin, an officer in the Diplomatic Corps on Meiji. Grew up in the senator's home. Barbara Jean was visiting him when . . ."

"Yes." Lermontov leaned closer to Ramsey so that he could touch his shoulder for a moment. Then he took his hand away. "I do not remind you of these things because I am cruel, my friend. I must know—would the senator have tried to find his daughter? After all these years?"

Bart nodded. "She was his only child. As Harold was mine. If I thought there was any chance I'd look myself. You think he tried it?"

"We do." Lermontov signaled Torrin to bring him another drink. "Senator Grant went to Meiji with the visit to his relatives as cover. With the Japanese representation question to come up soon, and the budget after that, Meiji is important. The Navy provided a frigate for transportation. It took the usual route through Colby and around, and was supposed to return the same way. But we have confirmed reports that Senator Grant's ship went instead to the jumpoff point for the direct route."

"What captain in his right mind would let him get away with that?"

"His name was Commander John Grant, Jr. The senator's nephew."

"Oh." Bart nodded again, exaggerating the gesture as he realized the full situation. "Yeah. Johnny would do it if the old man asked. So you came all the way out here for my opinion, Sergei? I can give it quick. Senator Grant was looking for Barbara Jean. So you can write him off and whatever other plans you've got for the goddam Navy you can write off too. Learn to live without him, Sergei. The goddam jinx has another good ship and another good man. Now if you'll excuse me I want to get back to my ship and get drunk."

Captain Ramsey strode angrily toward the door. Before he reached it the vice admiral's voice crackled through the room. "Captain, you are not excused."

"Sir." Ramsey whirled automatically. "Very well, sir. Your orders?"

"My orders are for you to sit down and finish your drink, Captain." There was a long silence as they faced each other. Finally Ramsey sat at the expensive table.

"Do you think so badly of me, Bart, that you believe I would come all the way out here, meet you secretly, for as little as this?"

Bart looked up in surprise. Emotions welled up inside him, emotions he hadn't felt in years, and he fought desperately to force them back. *No, God, don't let me hope again. Not that agony. Not hope* . . . But Lermontov was still speaking.

"I will let Professor Stirner explain it to you, since I am not sure any of us understand him. But he has a theory, Bart. He believes that the senator may be alive, and that there may be a chance to bring him home before the Senate knows he is missing. For years the Navy has preserved the peace, now a strong fleet is needed more than ever. We have no choice, Bart. If there is any chance at all, we must take it.

Professor Hermann Stirner was a short Viennese with thinning red hair, improbable red freckles, and a neat round belly. Ramsey thought him about fifty, but the man's age was indeterminate. It was unlikely that he was younger, but with regeneration therapy he could be half that again. Rap Torrin brought the professor in through a back entrance.

"Dr Stirner is an intelligence adviser to the fleet," Lermontov said. "He is not a physicist."

"No, no physicist," Stirner agreed quickly. "Who would want to live under the restrictions of a licensed physicist? CoDominium intelligence officers watching every move, suppressing most of your discoveries . . ." He spoke intently giving the impression of great emotion no matter what he said. "And most physicists I have met are not seeing beyond the end of their long noses. Me, I worry mostly about politics, Captain. But when the Navy loses ships, I want to know what happened to them. I have a theory about those ships, for years."

Ramsey gripped the arms of his chair until his knuckles were white, but his voice was deadly calm. "Why didn't you bring up your theory before now?"

Stirner eyed him critically. Then he shrugged. "As I said, I am no physicist. Who would listen to me? But now, with the senator gone . . ."

"We need your father-in-law badly," Lermontov interrupted. "I do not really believe Professor Stirner's theories, but the fleet needs Senator Grant so desperately we will try anything. Let Dr. Stirner explain."

"Ja. You are a bright young CoDominium Navy captain, I am going to tell you things you know already, maybe. But I do not myself understand everything I should know, so you let me explain my own way, ja?" Stirner paced briskly for a moment, then sat restlessly at the table. He gave no chance to answer his question, but spoke rapidly, so that he gave the impression of interrupting himself.

"You got five forces in this universe we know about,

ja? Only one of them maybe really isn't in this universe, we do not quibble about that, let the cosmologists worry. Now we look at two of those forces, we can forget the atomics and electromagnetics. Gravity and the Alderson force, these we look at. Now you think about the universe as flat like this table, eh?" He swept a pudgy hand across the roseteak surface. "And wherever you got a star, you got a hill that rises slowly, gets all the time steeper until you get near the star when it's so steep you got a cliff. And you think of your ships like roller coasters. You get up on the hill, aim where you want to go, and pop on the hyperspace drivers. Bang, you are in a universe where the Alderson effect acts like gravity. You are rolling downhill, across the table, and up the side of the next hill, not using up much potential energy, so you are ready to go again somewhere else if you can get lined up right, O.K.?"

Ramsey frowned. "It's not quite what we learned as middies—you've got ships repelled from a star rather than—"

"Ja, ja, plenty of quibble we can make if we want to. Now, Captain, how is it you get out of hyperspace when you want to?"

"We don't," Ramsey said. "When we get close enough to a gravity source, the ship comes out into normal space whether we want it to or not."

Stirner nodded. "Ja. And you use your photon drivers to run around in normal space where the stars is like wells, not hills, at least thinking about gravities. Now, suppose you try to shoot past one star to another, all in one jump?"

"It doesn't work," Ramsey said. "You'd get caught in the gravity field of the in-between star. Besides, the Alderson paths don't cross each other. They're generated by stellar nuclear activities, and you can only travel along lines of equal flux. In practice that means almost line of sight, with range limits, but they aren't really straight lines . . ."

"Ja. O.K. That's what I think is happening to them. I

think there is a star between A-7820 and 82 Eridani, which is the improbable name Meiji's sun is stuck with."

"Now wait a minute," Admiral Torrin protested. "There can't be a star there, Professor. There's no question of missing it, not with our observations. Man, do you think the Navy didn't look for it? A liner and an explorer class frigate vanished on that route. We looked, first thing we thought of."

"Suppose there is a star there but you are not seeing it?"

"How could that be?" Torrin asked.

"A Black Hole, Admiral. Ja," Stirner continued triumphantly. "I think Senator Grant fell into a Black Hole."

Ramsey looked puzzled. "I seem to remember something about Black Holes, but I don't remember what."

"Theoretical concept," Stirner said. "Hundred, hundred and fifty years ago, before the CoDominium Treaty puts a stop to so much scientific research. Lots of people talk about Black Holes then, but nobody ever finds any, so now there's no appropriations for licensed physicists to work on them.

"But way back we have a man named Schwartzchild, Viennese chap, he thinks of them." Stirner puffed with evident pride. "Then another chap, Oppenheimer, and some more, all make the calculations. A Black Hole is like a neutron star that goes all the way. Collapsed down so far, a whole star collapsed to maybe two, three kilometers diameter. Gravity is so tough nothing gets out. Not light; not anything gets out of the gravity well. Infinite red shift. Some ways a Black Hole isn't even theoretically inside this universe."

The others looked incredulous and Stirner laughed. "You think that is strange? There was even talk once about whole galaxies, a hundred billion stars, whole thing collapsed to smaller than the orbit of Venus. They wouldn't be in the universe for real either."

"Then how would Black Holes interact with—oh," Rap Torrin said, "gravity. It still has that."

Stirner's round face bobbed in agreement. "Ja, ja, which is how we know is no black galaxy out there. Would be too much gravity, but there is plenty room for a star. Now one thing I do not understand though, why the survey ship gets through, others do not. Maybe gravity changes for one of those things, ja?"

"No, look, the Alderson path really isn't a line of sight, it can shift slightly—maybe just enough!" Torrin spoke rapidly. "If the geometry were just right, then sometimes the Hole wouldn't be in the way . . ."

"O.K.," Stirner said. "I leave that up to you Navy boys. But you see what happens, the ship is taking sights or whatever you do when you are making a jump, the captain pushes the button, and maybe you come out in normal space near this Black Hole. Nothing to see anywhere around you. *And no way to get back home.*"

"Of course." Ramsey stood, twisted his fingers excitedly. "The Alderson effect is generated by nuclear reactions. And the dark holes—"

"Either got none of those, or the Alderson force stuffs is caught inside the Black Hole like light and everything else. So you are coming home in normal space or you don't come home at all."

"Which is light-years. You'd never make it." Ramsey found himself near the bar. Absently he poured a drink. "But in that case—the ships can sustain themselves a long time on their fuel!"

"Yes." Lermontov said it carefully. "It is at least possible that Senator Grant is alive. If his frigate dropped into normal space at a sufficient distance from the Black Hole so that it did not vanish down."

"Not only Martin," Bart Ramsey said wonderingly. His heart pounded. "Barbara Jean. And Harold. They were on a Norden Lines luxury cruiser, only half the passenger berths taken. There should have been enough supplies and hydrogen to keep them going five years, Sergei. More than enough!"

Vice Admiral Lermontov nodded slowly. "That is why we thought you should go. But you realize that . . ."

"I haven't dared hope. I've wanted to die for five years, Sergei. Found that out about myself, had to be careful. Not fair to my crew to be so reckless. I'll go after Martin and—I'll go. But what does that do for us? If I do find them, I'll be as trapped as they are."

"Maybe. Maybe not." Stirner snorted. "Why you think we came out here, just to shake up a captain and maybe lose the Navy a cruiser? What made me think about this Black Hole business, I am questioning a transportee. Sentence to the labor market on Tanith, the charge is unauthorized scientific research. I look into all those crazies, might be something the Navy can use, ja? This one was fooling around with gravity waves, theories about Black Holes. Hard to see how the Navy could use it. I was for letting them take this one to Tanith when I start to think, we are losing those ships coming from Meiji, and click! So I pulled the prisoner off the colony ship."

"And he says he can get us home from a dark hole in blank space?" Ramsey asked. He tried to suppress the wave of excitement that began in his bowels and crept upward until he could hardly speak. Not hope! Hope was an agony, something to be dreaded. It was much easier to live with resignation . . .

"Ja. Only is not a him. Is a her. Not very attractive her. She *says* she can do this." Stirner paused significantly.

"Miss Ward hates the CoDominium, Bart," Lermontov said carefully. "With what she thinks is good reason. She won't tell us how she plans to get the ship home."

"By God, she'll tell me!" *Why can't anything be simple? To know Barbara Jean is dead, or to know what mountain to climb to save her . . . "If I can't think of something we can borrow a State Security man from the—"*

"No." Lermontov's voice was a flat refusal. "Leave aside the ethics of the situation, we need this girl's creative energies. You can get that with brainscrubs."

"Maybe." *And maybe I'll try it anyway if nothing else works. Barbara Jean, Barbara Jean . . .* "Where is this uncooperative scientist?"

"On Ceres." Vice Admiral Lermontov stretched a long arm toward the bar and poured for everyone. Stirner swished his brandy appreciatively in a crystal snifter. "Understand something, Bart," the Admiral said. "Miss Ward may not know a thing. She may hate us enough to destroy a CD ship even at the cost of her life. You're gambling on a theory we don't know exists and could be wrong even if she has one."

"So I'm gambling. My God, Sergei, do you know what I've been through these last years? It isn't normal for a man to brood like I do, you think I don't know that? That I don't know you whisper about it when I'm not around? Now you say there's a chance but it might cost my life. *You're* gambling a cruiser you can't spare, my ship is worth more to the Navy than I am."

Lermontov ignored Ramsey's evaluation, and Bart wished it had been challenged. But it was probably true, although the old Bart Ramsey was something else again, a man headed for the job Sergei held now . . .

"I am gambling a ship because if we do not get Martin Grant back in time for the appropriations hearings, I will lose more than a ship. We might lose half the fleet."

"Ja, ja," Stirner sighed. He shook his round head sadly, slowly, a big gesture. "It is not usual that one man may be so important, I do not believe in the indispensable-man theory myself. Yet, without Senator Grant I do not see how we are getting the ships in time or even keeping what we have, and without those ships . . . but maybe it is too late anyway, maybe even with the senator we cannot get the ships, or with the ships we can still do nothing when a planet full of people are determined to kill themselves."

"That's as it may be," Lermontov said. "But for now we need Senator Grant. I'll have the prisoner aboard *Daniel Webster* in four hours, Bart. You'll want to fill the tanks. Trim the crew down to minimum also. We must try this, but I do not really give very good odds on your coming home."

"STAND BY FOR JUMPOFF. Jump stations, man your jump stations." The unemotional voice of the officer of the watch monotoned through steel corridors, showing no more excitement than he would have used to announce an off-watch solido show. It took years to train that voice into Navy officers, but it made them easier to understand in battle. "Man your jump stations."

Bart Ramsey looked up from his screens as First Lieutenant Trevor ushered Marie Ward onto the bridge. She was a round, dumpy woman, her skin a faint red color. Shoulder length hair fell almost straight down to frame her face, but dark brown wisps poked out at improbable angles despite combings and hair ribbons. Her hands were big, as powerful as a man's, and the nails, chewed to the quick, were colorless. When he met her Ramsey had estimated her age in the mid-thirties and was surprised to learn she was only twenty-six.

"You may take the assistant helmsman's acceleration chair," Ramsey told her. He forced a smile. "We're about to make the jump to Meiji." In his lonely ship. She'd been stripped down, empty stations all through her.

"Thank you, Captain." Marie sat and allowed Trevor to strap her in. The routine for jumpoff went on. As he listened to the reports, Ramsey realized Marie Ward was humming.

"What is that?" he asked. "Catchy tune . . ."

"Sorry. It's an old nursery thing. 'The bear went over the mountain, the bear went over the mountain, the bear went over the mountain, to see what he could see.' "

"Oh. Well, we haven't seen anything yet."

" 'The other side of the mountain, was all that he could

see.' But it's the third verse that's interesting. 'He fell into a dark hole, and covered himself over with charcoal—' "

"Warning, warning, take your posts for jumpoff."

Ramsey examined his screens. His chair was surrounded by them. "All right, Trevor, make your search."

"Aye, aye, sir."

Lieutenant Trevor would be busy for a while. He had been assigned the job of looking after Marie Ward, but for the moment Ramsey would have to be polite to her. "You haven't told us much about what we're going to see on the other side of that mountain. Why?"

"Captain, if you knew everything I did, you wouldn't need to take me along," she said. "I wish they'd hurry up. I *don't like* starjumps."

"It won't be long now—" Just what do you say to a convict genius? The whole trip out she'd been in everybody's hair, seldom talking about anything but physics. She'd asked the ship's officers about the drive, astrogation, instruments, the guns, nearly everything. Sometimes she was humorous, but more often scathingly sarcastic. And she wouldn't say a word about Black Holes, except to smile knowingly. More and more Ramsey wished he'd borrowed a KGB man from the Soviets . . .

"WARNING, WARNING. Jumpoff in one minute," the watch officer announced. Alarm bells sounded through the ship.

"Lined up, Captain," Trevor said. "For all I can tell, we're going straight through to 81 Eridani. If there's anything out there, I can't see it."

"Humph," Marie Ward snorted. "Why should you?"

"Yes, but if the Alderson path's intact, the Hole won't have any effect on us," Trevor protested. "And to the best we can measure, that path is there."

"No, no," Marie insisted. "You don't measure the Alderson path at all! You only measure the force, Lieutenant. Then your computer deduces the existence of the path from the stellar geometry. I'd have thought they'd teach you that much anyway. And that you could remember it."

"FINAL WARNING. Ten seconds to jump." A series of chimes, descending in pitch. Marie grimaced. Her mannish hands clutched the chair arms as she braced herself. At the tenth tone everything blurred for an instant that stretched to a million years.

There is no way to record the time a jump takes. The best chronological instruments record nothing whatever. Ships vanish into the state of nonbeing conveniently called "hyperspace" and reappear somewhere else. Yet it always *seems* to take forever, and while it happens everything in the universe is wrong, *wrong*, WRONG . . .

Ramsey shook his head. The screens around his command seat remained blurred. "Jump completed. Check ship," he ordered.

Crewmen moved fuzzily to obey despite the protests of tortured nerves. Electronic equipment, computers, nearly everything complex suffers from jump induced transients although there is no known permanent effect.

"Captain, we're nowhere near Meiji!" the astrogator exclaimed. "I don't know *where* we are . . ."

"Stand by to make orbit," Ramsey ordered.

"Around *what?*" Lieutenant Trevor asked. "There's no star out there, Captain. There's nothing!"

"Then we'll orbit nothing." Ramsey turned to Marie Ward. "Well, we've found the damn thing. You got any suggestions about locating it? I'd as soon not fall into it."

"Why not?" she asked. Ramsey was about to smile politely when he realized she was speaking seriously. "According to some theories, a Black Hole is a time/space gate. You could go into it and come out—somewhere else. In another century. Or another universe."

"Is that why the hell you brought us out here? To kill yourself testing some theory about Black Holes and space/time?"

"I am here because the CoDominium Marines put me aboard," she said. Her voice was carefully controlled. "And I have no desire to test any theory. Yet." She turned to Lieutenant Trevor. "Dave, is it really true? There's no star out there at all?"

"It's true enough."

She smiled. A broad, face-cracking smile that, with the thousand meter stare in her eyes, made her look strangely happy. Insanely happy, in fact. "My god, it worked! There really is a Black Hole . . ."

"Which we haven't found yet," Trevor reminded her.

"Oh. Yes. Let's see—it should have started as about five stellar masses in size. That's my favorite theory, anyway. When it began to collapse it would have radiated over eighty percent of its mass away. X rays, mostly. Lots of them. And if it had planets, they might still be here . . . Anyway, it should be about as massive as Sol. There won't be any radiation coming out. X rays, light, nothing can climb out of that gravity well . . . just think of it, infinite red shift! It really happens!"

"Infinite red shift," Ramsey repeated carefully. "Yes, ma'm. Now, just how do we find this source of tired light?"

"It isn't tired light! That's a very obsolete theory. Next I suppose you'll tell me you think photons slow down when they lose energy."

"No, I—"

"Because they don't. They wouldn't *be* photons if they *could* slow down. They just lose energy until they vanish."

"Fine, but *how do we find it?*"

"It can't reach out and grab you, Captain," she said. The grin wasn't as wide as before, but still she smiled softly to herself. It made her look much better, although the mocking tones didn't help Ramsey's appreciation. "It's just a star, Captain. A very small star, very dense, as heavy as most other stars, but it doesn't have any more gravity than Sol. You could get quite close and still pull away—"

"If we knew which direction was away."

"Yes. Hm-m-m. It will bend light rays, but you'd have to be pretty close to see any effect at all from that . . ."

"Astrogation!" Ramsey ordered crisply. "How do we find a star we can't see?"

"We're about dead in space relative to whatever stopped us," the astrogator told him. "We can wait until we accelerate toward it and get a vector from observation of other stars. That will take a while. Or we can see if it's left any planets, but with nothing to illuminate them they'll be hard to find—"

"Yeah. Do the best you can, Mister." Marie Ward was still looking happily at the screens. They showed absolutely nothing. Ramsey punched another button in the arm of his command chair.

"Comm room, sir."

"Eyes, there are ships out there somewhere." *God, I hope there are. Or one ship.* "Find them and get me communications."

"Aye, aye, sir. I'll use the distress frequencies. They might be monitoring those."

"Right. And Eyes, see if your bright electronics and physics boys can think of a way to detect gravity. So far as I can make out that's the only effect that Black Hole has on the real universe."

"On *our* real universe. Imagine a universe in which there are particles with non-zero rest masses able to move faster than light. Where you get rid of energy to go faster. Sentient beings in that universe would think of it as real. It might even be where our ships go when they make an Alderson jump. And the Black Holes could be gates to get you there."

"Yes, Miss Ward," Ramsey said carefully. Two enlisted spacers on the other side of the bridge grinned knowingly at each other and waited for the explosion. They'd been waiting ever since Marie Ward came aboard, and it ought to be pretty interesting. But Ramsey's voice became even softer and more controlled. "Meanwhile, have you any useful suggestions on what we should do now?"

"Find the Hole, of course. Your astrogator seems quite competent. His approach is very reasonable. Yes, quite competent. For a Navy man."

Carefully, his hands moving very slowly, Captain Bartholomew Ramsey unstrapped himself from his command chair and launched himself across the bridge to the exit port. "Take the con, Mr Trevor," he said. And left.

For fifty hours *Daniel Webster* searched for the other ships. Then, with no warning at all, Ramsey was caught in the grip of a giant vise.

For long seconds he felt as if titanic hands were squeezing him. They relaxed, ending the agony for a brief moment. And tried to pull him apart. The screens blurred, and he heard the sound of rending metal as the hands alternately crushed, then pulled.

Somehow the watch officer sounded General Quarters. Klaxons blared through the ship as she struggled with her invisible enemy. Ramsey screamed, as much in rage and frustration as pain, hardly knowing he had made a sound. He had to take control of his ship before she died, but there were no orders to give. This was no attack by an enemy, but what, what?

The battle damage screen flared red. Ramsey was barely able to see as it showed a whole section of the ship's outer corridors evacuated to space. How many men were in there? Most wouldn't be in armor. *My God!* Daniel Webster *too? My wife and now my ship?*

Slowly it faded away. Ramsey pulled himself erect. Around him on the bridge the watch crew slumped at their stations. The klaxons continued, adding their confusion, until Ramsey shut them off.

"What—what was it?" Lieutenant Trevor gasped. His usually handsome features were contorted with remembered pain, and he looked afraid.

"All stations report damage," Ramsey ordered. "I don't know what it was, Lieutenant."

"I do!" Marie Ward gasped excitedly. Her eyes darted

about in wonder. "I know! Gravity waves from the Black Hole! A tensor field! And these were tensor, not scalar—"

"Gravity waves?" Ramsey asked stupidly. "But gravity waves are weak things, only barely detectable."

Marie Ward snorted. "In your experience, Captain. And in mine. But according to one Twentieth Century theory—they had lots of theories then, when intellectuals were free, Captain—according to one theory if a Black Hole is rotating and a mass enters the Schwartzchild Limit, part of the mass will be converted to gravity waves. *They* can escape from the Hole and affect objects outside it. So can Alderson forces, I think. But they didn't know about the Alderson force then . . ."

"But—is that going to happen again?" Ramsey demanded. Battle damage reports appeared on his screens. "We can't live through much of that."

"I really don't know how often it will happen," Marie answered. She chewed nervously on her right thumbnail. "I do know one thing. We have a chance to get home again."

"Home?" Ramsey took a deep breath. That depended on what had been done to Danny Boy. A runner brought him another report. Much of the ship's internal communications were out, but the chief engineer was working with a damage-control party. Another screen came on, and Ramsey heard the bridge speaker squawk.

"Repairable damage to normal space drive in main engine room," the toneless voice said. "Alderson drive appears unaffected."

"Gunnery reports damage to laser lenses in number one battery. No estimate of time to repair."

Big rigid objects had broken. Ramsey later calculated the actual displacement at less than a millimeter/meter; not very much, but enough to damage the ship and kill half a dozen crewmen unable to get into battle armor. Explosive decompression wasn't a pretty death, but it was quick.

With all her damage, *Daniel Webster* was only hurt. She could sail, his ship wasn't dead. Not yet. Ramsey gave orders to the damage control parties. When he was sure they were doing everything they could he turned back to the dumpy girl in the assistant helmsman's seat.

"How do we get home?"

She had been scribbling on a pad of paper, but her pencil got away from her when she tried to set it down without using the clips set into the arm of the seat. Now she stared absently at her notes, a thin smile on her lips. "I'm sorry, Captain. What did you say?"

"I asked, how do we get home?"

"Oh." She tried to look serious but only succeeded in appearing sly. "I was hasty in saying that. I don't know."

"Sure. Don't you want to get home?"

"Of course, Captain. I'd just love to get back on a colony ship. I understand Tanith has such a wonderful climate."

"Come off it. The Navy doesn't forget people who've helped us. You aren't going to Tanith." He took a deep breath. "We have a rescue mission, Miss Ward. Some of those people have been out here for five years." *Five years of that? Nobody could live through five years of that. O God, where is she? Crushed, torn apart, again and again, her body drifting out there in black space without even a star? Rest eternal grant them, O Lord, and let light perpetual shine upon them . . .*

"How do we get home?"

"I told you, I don't know."

But you do. And come to think of it, so do I. "Miss Ward, you implied that if we knew when a mass would enter the Black Hole, we could use the resulting Alderson forces to get us out of here."

"I'll be damned." She looked at Ramsey as if seeing him for the first time. "The man can actually—yes, of course." She smiled faintly. "I *thought* so before we left Ceres. Theory said that would work . . ."

"But we'd have to know the timing rather precisely, wouldn't we?"

"Yes. Depending on the size of the mass. The larger it is, the longer the effect would last. I think. Maybe not, though."

Ramsey nodded to himself. There was only one possible mass whose entry into the Hole they could predict. "Trevor."

"Sir?"

"One way you might amuse yourself is in thinking of ways to make a ship impact a solar mass not much more than two kilometers in diameter; a star you can't see and whose location you can't know precisely."

"Aye, aye, skipper." Dave Trevor frowned. He didn't often do that and it distorted his features. "Impact, Captain? But unless you were making corrections all the way in, you'd probably miss—as it is, the ship would pick up so much velocity that it's more likely to whip right around—"

"Exactly, Lieutenant. But it's the only way home."

One hundred and eight hours after breakout Chief Yeoman Karabian located the other ships. *Daniel Webster*'s call was answered by the first frigate sent out to find the Norton liner:

"DANIEL WEBSTER THIS IS HENRY HUDSON BREAK BREAK WE ARE IN ORBIT ELEVEN ASTRONOMICAL UNITS FROM WHATEVER THAT THING DOWN THERE IS STOP WE WILL SEND A CW SIGNAL TO GIVE YOU A BEARING STOP

"THE NORTON LINER LORELEI AND CDSN CONSTELLATION ARE WITH US STOP YOUR SIGNAL INDICATES THAT YOU ARE LESS THAN ONE AU FROM THE DARK STAR STOP YOU ARE IN EXTREME DANGER REPEAT EXTREME DANGER STOP ADVISE YOU MOVE AWAY FROM DARK STAR IMMEDIATELY STOP THERE ARE STRONG GRAVITY FLUXES NEAR THE DARK STAR STOP THEY CAN TEAR YOU APART STOP ONE SCOUTSHIP AL-

READY DESTROYED BY GRAVITY WAVES STOP REPEAT AD-
VISE YOU MOVE AWAY FROM DARK STAR IMMEDIATELY AND
HOME ON OUR CW SIGNAL STOP.

"REQUEST FOLLOWING INFORMATION COLON WHO IS MAS-
TER ABOARD DANIEL WEBSTER INTERROGATIVE BREAK
BREAK MESSAGE ENDS."

Ramsey read the message on his central display screen,
then punched the intercom buttons. "Chief, get this out:

"HENRY HUDSON THIS IS DANIEL WEBSTER BREAK BREAK
CAPTAIN BARTHOLOMEW RAMSEY COMMANDING STOP WE
WILL HOME ON YOUR BEACON STOP HAVE EXPERIENCED
GRAVITY STORM ALREADY STOP SHIP DAMAGED BUT SPACE-
WORTHY STOP

"IS SENATOR MARTIN GRANT ABOARD CONSTELLATION IN-
TERROGATIVE IS MRS RAMSEY THERE INTERROGATIVE
BREAK MESSAGE ENDS."

The hundred-and-sixty-minute round trip for message
and reply would be a lifetime.

"Trevor, get us moving when you've got that beacon,"
Ramsey ordered. "Pity he couldn't tell us about the gravity waves before we found out the hard way."

"Yes, sir." The acceleration alarm rang through the
ship as Trevor prepared the new course. "We can only
make about a half G, Captain. We're lucky to get that.
We took more damage from that gravity storm than
Danny Boy's ever got from an enemy."

"Yeah." *Pity indeed. But communications did all they
could. Space is just too big for omni signals, and we had
maser damage to boot. Had to send in narrow cones,
lucky we made contact this soon even sweeping messages.
And no ecliptic here either. Or none we know of.*

"Communications here," Ramsey's speaker announced.

"Yes, Eyes."

"We're getting that homing signal. Shouldn't be any problem."

"Good." Ramsey studied the figures that flowed across his screen. "Take the con, Mr Trevor. And call me when there's an answer from *Henry Hudson.* I'll wait in my patrol cabin." *And a damn long wait that's going to be. Barbara Jean, Barbara Jean, are you out there?*

The hundred and sixty minutes went past. Then another hour, and another. It was nearly six hours before there was a message from the derelicts; and it was in code the Navy used for eyes of commanding officers only.

Captain Ramsey sat in his bare room and stared at the message flimsy. In spite of the block letters from the coding printer his eyes wouldn't focus on the words.

"DANIEL WEBSTER THIS IS HENRY HUDSON BREAK FOLLOWING IS PERSONAL MESSAGE FOR CAPTAIN BARTHOLOMEW RAMSEY FROM GRAND SENATOR MARTIN GRANT BREAK BREAK PERSONAL MESSAGE BEGINS

"BART WE ARE HERE AND ALIVE STOP THE SCOUTSHIP WAS LOST TO GRAVITY WAVES STOP THE LINER LORELEI THE FRIGATE HENRY HUDSON AND THE FRIGATE CONSTELLATION ARE DAMAGED STOP LORELEI IN SPACEWORTHY CONDITION WITH MOST OF CREW SURVIVING DUE TO HEROIC EFFORTS OF MASTER OF HENRY HUDSON STOP

"BOTH BARBARA JEAN AND ARNOLD ARE WELL STOP REGRET TO INFORM YOU THAT BARBARA JEAN MARRIED COMMANDER JAMES HARRIMAN OF HENRY HUDSON THREE YEARS AGO STOP BREAK END PERSONAL MESSAGE BREAK BREAK MESSAGE ENDS."

Ramsey automatically reached for a drink, then angrily tossed the glass against the bare steel wall. It wouldn't be fair to the crew. Or to his ship. And *Daniel Webster* was still the only wife he had.

The intercom buzzed. "Bridge, Captain."

"Go ahead, Trevor."

"Two hundred eighty plus hours to rendezvous. Captain. We're on course."

"Thank you." *Damn long hours those are going to be. How could she—but that's simple. For all Barbara Jean could know she and the boy were trapped out here forever. I can bet there were plenty of suicides on those ships. And the boy would be growing up without a father.*

Not that I was so much of one. Half the time I was out on patrol anyway. But I was home when he caught pneumonia from going with us to Ogden Base. Harold just had to play in that snow . . .

He smiled in remembrance. They'd built a snowman together. But Harold wasn't used to Earth gravity, and that more than the cold weakened him. The boy never did put in enough time in the centrifuge on Luna Base. Navy kids grew up on the Moon because the Navy was safe only among its own . . .

Ramsey made a wry face. Hundreds of Navy kids crowding into the big centrifuge . . . they were hard to control, and Barbara Jean like most mothers hated to take her turn minding them. She needed a hairdo. Or had to go shopping. Or something . . .

She should have remarried. Of course she should. He pictured Barbara Jean with another man. *What did she say to him when they made love? Did she use the same words? Like our first time, when we—oh, damn.*

He fought against the black mood. *Harriman. James Harriman. Fleet spatball champ seven years ago. A good man. Tough. Younger than Barbara Jean. Harriman used to be a real comer before he vanished. Never married and the girls at Luna Base forever trying to get—never married until now.*

Stop it! Would you rather she was dead? The thought crept through unwanted. *If you would, you'll godammit not admit it, you swine. Not now and not ever.*

She's alive! Bart Ramsey, you remember that and forget the rest of it. Barbara Jean is alive!

Savagely he punched the intercom buttons.

"Bridge. Aye, aye, Captain."

"We on course, Mister?"

"Yes, sir."

"Damage control parties working?"

"Yes, sir." Trevor's voice was puzzled. He was a good first lieutenant, and it wasn't like Ramsey to ride him . . .

"Excellent." Ramsey slapped the off button, waited a moment, and reached for another whiskey. This time he drank it. And waited.

There was little communication as *Daniel Webster* accelerated, turned over, and slowed again to approach the derelicts. Messages took energy, and they'd need it all. To get out, or to survive if Marie Ward proved wrong with her theories. Someday there'd be a better theory. Lermontov might come up with something, and even now old Stirner would be examining ancient records at Stanford and Harvard. If Ward was wrong, they still had to survive . . .

"Getting them on visual now," the comm officer reported. The unemotional voice broke. "Good God, Captain!"

Ramsey stared at the screens. The derelicts were worse than he could have imagined. *Lorelei* was battered, although she seemed intact, but the other ships seemed *bent*. The frigate *Constellation* was a wreck, with gaping holes in her hull structure. *Henry Hudson* was crumpled, almost unrecognizable. The survivors must all be on the Norton liner.

Ramsey watched in horror as the images grew on the screens. *Five years, with all hope going, gone. Harriman must be one hell of a man to keep anyone alive through that.*

When they were alongside Navy routine carried Ramsey through hours that were lifetimes. Like one long continuous Jump. Everything *wrong*.

Spacers took *Daniel Webster's* cutter across to *Lorelei* and docked. After another eternity she lifted away with passengers. CDSN officers, one of the merchant service survivors from *Lorelei*—and the others. Senator Grant. Johnny Grant. Commander Harriman. Barbara Jean, Harold—and Jeanette Harriman, age three.

"I'll be in my cabin, Trevor."

"Yes, sir."

"And get some spin on the ship as soon as that boat's fast aboard."

"Aye, aye, sir."

Ramsey waited. Who would come? It was his ship, he could send for anyone he liked. Instead he waited. Let Barbara Jean make up her own mind. Would she come? And would Harriman be with her?

Five years. Too long, he's had her for five years. But we had ten years together before that. Damned if I don't feel like a Middie on his first prom.

He was almost able to laugh at that.

The door opened and she came in. There was no one with her, but he heard voices in the corridor outside. She stood nervously at the bulkhead, staring around the bare cabin, at the empty desk and blank steel walls.

Her hair's gone. The lovely black hair that she never cut, whacked off short and tangled—God, you're beautiful. Why can't I say that? Why can't I say anything?

She wore shapeless coveralls, once white, but now grimy, and her hands showed ground-in dirt and grease. They'd had to conserve water, and there was little soap. Five years is a long time to maintain a closed ecology.

"No pictures, Bart? Not even one of me?"

"I—I thought you were dead." He stood, and in the small cabin they were very close. "There wasn't anybody else to keep a picture of."

Her tightly kept smile faded. "I—I would have waited, Bart. But we were dead. I don't even know why we tried to stay alive. Jim drove everybody, he kept us going, and then—he needed help."

Ramsey nodded, it was going to be all right. Wasn't it? He moved closer and put his hands on her shoulders, pulling her to him. She responded woodenly, then broke away. "Give me—give me a little time to get used to it, Bart."

He backed away from her. "Yeah. The rest of you can come in now," he called.

"Bart, I didn't mean—"

"It's all right, Barbara Jean. We'll work it out." Somehow.

The boy came in first. He was very hesitant. Harold didn't look so very different. He still had a round face, a bit too plump. But he was *big*. And he was leading a little girl, a girl with dark hair and big round eyes, her mother's him.

Harold stood for a long moment. "Sir—ah," he began formally, but then he let go of the girl and rushed to his father. "Daddy! I knew you'd come get us, I told them you'd come!" He was tall enough that his head reached Bart's shoulder, and his arms went all the way around him.

Finally he broke away. "Dad, this is my little sister." He said it defiantly, searchingly, watching his father's face. Finally he smiled. "She's a nuisance sometimes, but she grows on you."

"I'm sure she does," Ramsey said. It was very still in the bare cabin. Ramsey wanted to say something else, but he had trouble with his voice.

Daniel Webster's wardroom was crowded. There was barely room at the long steel table for all the surviving astrogation officers to sit with Ramsey, Senator Grant, and Marie Ward. They waited tensely.

The senator was thinner than Ramsey had ever seen him despite the short time he'd been marooned. *Constellation* had been hit hard by a gravity storm—it was easier to think of them that way, although the term was a little silly. Now the senator's hands rested lightly on the wardroom table, the tips of the fingers just interlocked, motionless. Like everyone else Senator Grand watched Commander Harriman.

Harriman paced nervously. He had grown a neatly trimmed beard, brown, with both silver and red hairs woven through it. His uniform had been patched a dozen times, but it was still the uniform of the Service, and Harriman wore it proudly. There was no doubt of who had been in command.

"The only ship spaceworthy is *Lorelei*," Harriman reported. "*Henry Hudson* was gutted to keep *Lorelei* livable, and Johnny Grant's *Constellation* took it hard in the gravity storms before we could get him out far enough from that thing."

Senator Grant sighed loudly. "I hope never to have to live through anything like that again. Even out this far you can feel the gravity waves, although it's not dangerous. But in close, before we knew where to go . . ."

"But *Lorelei* can space?" Ramsey asked. Harriman nodded. "Then *Lorelei* it'll have to be. Miss Ward, explain what it takes to get home again."

"Well, I'm not *sure*, Captain. I think we should wait."

"We can't wait. I realize you want to stay out here and look at the Black Hole until doomsday, but these people want to go home. Not to mention my orders from Lermontov."

Reluctantly she explained her theory, protesting all the while that they really ought to make a better study. "And the timing will have to be perfect," she finished. "The ship must be at the jumpoff point and turn on the drive at just the right time."

"Throw a big mass down the hole," Harriman said. "Well, there's only the one mass to throw. *Lorelei*." He sotpped pacing for a moment and looked thoughtful. "And that means somebody has to ride her in."

"Gentlemen?" Ramsey looked around the table. One by one the astrogation officers nodded mutely. Trevor, seeing his captain's face, paused for a long second before he also nodded agreement.

"There's no way to be sure of a hit if we send her in on automatic," Trevor said. "We can't locate the thing close enough from out here. We can't send *Lorelei* on remote, either. The time lag's too long."

"Couldn't you build some kind of homing device?" Senator Grant asked. His voice was carefully controlled, and it compelled attention. In the Grand Senate, Martin Grant's speeches were worth listening to, although senators usually voted from politics anyway.

"What would you home on?" Marie asked caustically. "There's nothing to detect. In close enough you should see bending light rays, but I'm not sure. I'm just not sure of anything, but I know we couldn't build a homing device."

"Could we wait for a gravity storm and fly out on that?" Trevor asked. "If we were ready for it, we could make the jump . . ."

"Nonsense," Harriman snapped. "Give me credit for a little sense, Lieutenant. We tried that. I didn't know what we were up against, but I figured those were gravity waves after they'd nearly wrecked my ships. Where there's gravity there may be Alderson forces. But you can't predict the damn gravity storms. We get one every thousand hours, sometimes close together, sometimes a long time apart, but about a thousand-hour average. How can you be in a position for a jump when you don't know it's coming? And the damn gravity waves do things to the drives."

"Every thousand hours!" Marie demanded excitedly. "But that's impossible! What could cause that—so much matter! Commander Harriman, have you observed asteroids in this system?"

"Yeah. There's a whole beehive of them, all in close to the dark star. Thousands and thousands of them, it looks like. But they're *really* close, it's a swarm in a thick plane, a ring about ten kilometers thick. It's hard to observe anything, though. They move so fast, and if you get in close the gravity storms kill you. From out here we don't see much."

"A ring—are they large bodies?" Marie asked. Her eyes shone.

Harriman shrugged. "We've bounced radar off them and we deduce they're any where from a few millimeters to maybe a full kilometer in diameter, but it's hard to tell. There's nothing stable about the system, either."

Marie chewed both thumbnails. "There wouldn't be," she said. She began so softly that it was difficult to hear her. "There wouldn't be if chunks keep falling into the Hole. Ha! We won't be able to use the asteroids to give a position on the Black Hole. Even if you had better observations, the Hole is rotating. There must be enormous gravitational anomalies."

Harriman shrugged again, this time helplessly. "You understand, all we ever really observed was some bending light and a fuzzy occultation of stars. We deduced there was a dark star, but there was nothing in our data banks about them. Even if we'd known what a Black Hole was, I don't know how much good it would have done. I burned out the last of the Alderson drives three years ago trying to ride out. We were never in the right position . . . I was going to patch up *Constellation* and have another stab at it."

Just like that, Ramsey thought. *Just go out and patch up that wreck of a ship.* How many people would even try, much less be sure they could . . . so three years ago they'd lost their last hope of getting out of there. And after that, Barbara Jean had . . .

"Did you ever try throwing something down the Hole yourself?" Trevor asked.

"No. Until today we had no idea what we were up against. I still don't, but I'll take your word for it." Harriman drew in a deep breath and stopped pacing. "I'll take *Lorelei* down."

Bart looked past Harriman to a painting on the wardroom bulkhead. Trevor had liked it and hung it there long ago. John Paul Jones strode across the blazing decks of his flagship. Tattered banners blew through sagging rigging, blood ran in the scuppers, but Jones held his old cutlass aloft.

Well, why not? Somebody's got to do it, why not Harriman? But—but what will Barbara Jean think?

"I want to go too." Marie Ward spoke softly, but everyone turned to look at her. "I'll come with you, Commander Harriman."

"Don't be ridiculous," Harriman snapped.

"Ridiculous? What's ridiculous about it? This is an irreplaceable opportunity. We can't leave the only chance we'll ever have to study Black Holes for an amateur. There is certainly nothing ridiculous about a trained observer going." Her voice softened. "Besides, you'll be too busy with the ship to take decent observations."

"Miss Ward," Harriman compelled attention although it was difficult to say exactly why. Even though Ramsey was senior officer present, Harriman seemed to dominate the meeting. "Miss Ward, we practically rebuilt *Lorelei* over the past five years. I doubt if anyone else could handle her, so I've *got* to go. But just why do you want to?"

"Oh—" the arrogant tone left her voice. "Because this is my one chance to do something important. Just what am I? I'm not pretty." She paused, as if she hoped someone would disagree, but there was only silence.

"And no one ever took me seriously as an intellectual. I've no accomplishments at all. No publications. Nothing. But as the only person ever to study a Black Hole, I'll be recognized!"

"You've missed a point." Ramsey spoke quickly before anyone else could jump in. His voice was sympathetic and concerned. "We take you seriously. Admiral Lermontov took you so seriously he sent this cruiser out here. And you're our only expert on Black Holes. If Commander Harriman's attempt fails or for any other reason we don't get out of this system on this try, you'll have to think of something else for us."

"But—"

Harriman clucked his tongue impatiently. "Will *Lorelei* be mass enough, Miss Ward?"

"I don't know." She answered softly, but when they all stared at her she pouted defensively. "Well, I don't! How could I! There should be more than enough energy but I don't *know!*" Her voice rose higher. "If you people hadn't suppressed everything we'd have more information. But I've had to work all by myself, and I—"

Dave Trevor put his hand gently on her arm. "It'll be all right. You haven't been wrong yet."

"Haven't I?"

Senator Grant cleared his throat. "This isn't getting us anywhere at all. We have only one ship capable of sailing down to that Hole and only one theory of how to get away from here. We'll just have to try it."

There was a long silence before Bart spoke. "You sure you want to do this, Commander?" Ramsey cursed himself for the relief he felt, knowing what Harriman's answer would be.

"I'll do it, Captain. Who else could? Let's get started."

Ramsey nodded. *If 'twere done, 'twere best done quickly* . . . what was that from? Shakespeare? "Mr. Trevor, take an engineering crew over to *Lorelei* and start making her ready. Get all the ship's logs too."

"Logs!" Marie smiled excitedly. "Dave, I want to see those as soon as possible."

As Trevor nodded agreement, Ramsey waved dismissal to the officers. "Commander Harriman, if you'd stay just a moment . . ."

The wardroom emptied. There was a burst of chatter as the others left. Their talk was too spirited, betraying their relief. *They* didn't have to take *Lorelei* into a Black Hole. Ramsey and Harriman sat for what seemed like a long time.

"Is there something I can say?" Ramsey asked.

"No. I'd fight you for her if there wasn't a way home. But if there's any chance at all—you'll take care of

Jeanette, of course." Harriman looked at the battered mug on the table, then reached for the coffee pot. After years in space he didn't notice the strange angle the liquid made as it flowed into the cup under spin gravity. "That's fine coffee, Captain. We ran out, must be three, four years ago. You get to miss coffee after a while."

"Yeah." *What the Hell can I say to him? Do I thank him for not making me order him to take that ship in? He really is the only one who could do it, and we both knew that.* Unwanted, the image of Barbara Jean in this man's arms came to him. Ramsey grimaced savagely. "Look, Harriman; there's got to be some way we can—"

"There isn't and we both know it. Sir. Even if there were, what good would it do? We can't both go back with her."

And I'm glad it's me who's going home, Ramsey thought. *Hah. The first time in five years I've cared about staying alive. But will she ever really be mine again?*

Was that all that was wrong with me?

"Your inertial navigation gear working all right?" Harriman asked. "Got an intact telescope?"

"Eh? Yeah, sure."

"You shouldn't have too much trouble finding the Jumpoff point, then."

"I don't expect any." Marie Ward's ridiculous song came back to him. "He fell into a dark hole, and covered himself over with charcoal, he went back over the mountain—" But Harriman wouldn't be going back over the mountain. Or would he? What was a Black Hole, anyway? Could it really be a time tunnel?

Harriman poured more coffee. "I better get over to *Lorelei* myself. Can you spare a pound of coffee?"

"Sure."

Harriman stood. He drained the mug. "Don't see much point in coming back to *Daniel Webster* in that case. Your people can plot me a course and send it aboard *Lorelei*." He flexed his fingers as if seeing them for the first time, then brushed imaginary lint from his patched uniform. "Yeah. I'll go with the cutter. Now."

"Now? But don't you want to—"

"No, I think not. What would I say?" Harriman very carefully put the coffee mug into the table rack. "Tell her I loved her, will you? And be sure to send that coffee over. Funny the things you can get to miss in five years."

"DANIEL WEBSTER THIS IS LORELEI BREAK BREAK TELL TREVOR HIS COURSE WAS FINE STOP I APPEAR TO BE ONE HALF MILLION KILOMETERS FROM THE BLACK HOLE WITH NO OBSERVABLE ORBITAL VELOCITY STOP WILL PROCEED AT POINT 1 G FROM HERE STOP STILL CANNOT SEE THAT BEEHIVE AT ALL WELL STOP NOTHING TO OBSERVE IN BEST CALCULATED POSITION OF BLACK HOLE STOP TELL MARIE WARD SHE IS NOT MISSING A THING STOP BREAK MESSAGE ENDS."

Barbara Jean and her father sat in Captain Ramsey's cabin. Despite the luxury of a shower she didn't feel clean. She read the message flimsy her father handed her.

"I ought to say something to him, hadn't I? Shouldn't I? Dad, I can't just let him die like this."

"Leave him alone, kitten," Senator Grant told her. "He's got enough to do, working that half-dead ship by himself. And he has to work fast. One of those gravity storms while he's this close and—" Grant shuddered involuntarily.

"But—God, I've made a mess of things, haven't I?"

"How? Would you rather it was Bart taking that ship in there?"

"No. No, no, no! But I still—wasn't there any other way, Daddy? Did somebody *really* have to do it?"

"As far as I can tell, Barbara Jean. I was there when Jim volunteered. Bart tried to talk him out of it, you know."

She didn't say anything.

"You're right, of course," Grant sighed. "He didn't try

very hard. There wasn't any point in it anyway. Commander Harriman was the obvious man to do it. You didn't enter the decision at all."

"I wish I could believe that."

"Yes. So does your husband. But it's still true. Are you coming down to the bridge? I don't think it's a good idea but you can."

"No. You go on, though. I have to take care of Jeanette. Bill Hartley has her in the sick bay. Daddy, what am I going to do?"

"You're going to go home with your husband and be an admiral's lady. For a while, anyway. And when there aren't any admirals because there isn't any fleet, God knows what you'll do. Make the best of it like all the rest of us, I guess."

The bridge was a blur of activity as they waited for *Lorelei* to approach the Black Hole. As the minutes ticked off, tension grew. A gravity storm just now would wipe out their only chance.

Finally Ramsey spoke. "You can get the spin off the ship, Mr Trevor. Put the crew to jump stations."

"Aye, aye, sir."

"Can we talk to Harriman still?" Senator Grant asked.

Ramsey's eyes flicked to the screens, past the predicted time of impact to the others, taking in every detail. "No." He continued to look at the data pouring across the screens. Their position had to be right. Everything had to be right, they'd get only the one chance at best . . . "Not to get an answer. You could get a message to *Lorelei* but before we'd hear a reply it'll be all over."

Grant looked relieved. "I guess not, then."

"Damnedest thing." Harriman's voice was loud over the bridge speaker. "Star was occulted by the Hole. Made a bright ring in space. Real bright. Just hanging there, never saw anything like it."

"Nobody else ever will," Marie Ward said quietly. "Or

will they? Can the Navy send more ships out here to study it? Oh, I wish I could *see!*"

They waited forever until Harriman spoke again. "Got a good position fix," they heard. "Looks good, Ramsey, damn good."

"Stand by for jumpoff," Bart ordered. Alarm bells rang through *Daniel Webster.*

"Another bright ring. Must be getting close."

"What's happening to his voice?" Senator Grand demanded.

"Time differential," Marie Ward answered. "His ship is accelerating to a significant fraction of light velocity. Time is slowing down for him relative to us."

"Looks good for jump here, skipper," Trevor announced.

"Right." Bart inspected his screens again. The predicted time to impact ticked off inexorably, but it was only a prediction. Without a more exact location of the Hole it couldn't be perfect. As Ramsey watched, the ship's computers updated the prediction from Harriman's signals.

Ramsey fingered the keys on his console. The Alderson drive generators could be kept on for less than a minute in normal space, but if they weren't on when *Lorelei* hit . . . he pressed the key. *Daniel Webster* shuddered as the ship's fusion engines went to full power, consuming hydrogen and thorium catalyst at a prodigal rate, pouring out energy into the drive where it—vanished.

Into hyperspace, if that was a real place. Or on the other side of the Lepton Barrier. Maybe to where you went when you fell through a Black Hole if there was anything to that theory. Marie Ward had been fascinated by it and had seen nothing to make her give it up.

Wherever the energy went, it left the measurable universe. But not all of it. The efficiency wasn't that good. The drive generators screamed . . .

"There's another bright ring. Quite a sight. Best damn view in the universe." The time distortion was quite noticeable now. Time to impact loomed big on Ramsey's screens, seconds to go.

Marie Ward hummed her nursery rhyme. Unwanted, the words rang through Ramsey's head. "He fell into a dark hole—" The time to impact clicked off to zero. Nothing happened.

"Ramsey, you lucky bastard," the speaker said. "Did you know she kept your damned picture the whole time? The whole bloody time, Ramsey. Tell her—"

The bridge blurred. There was a twisted, intolerable, eternal instant of agony. And confusion. Ramsey shook his head. The screens remained blurred.

"We—we're in the 81 Eridani system, skipper!" Trevor shouted. "We—hot damn, we made it!"

Ramsey cut him off. "Jump completed. Check ship."

"It worked," Marie Ward said. Her voice was low, quiet, almost dazed. "It really worked." She grinned at Dave Trevor, who grinned back. "Dave, it worked! There *are* Black Holes, and they *do* bend light, and they *can* generate Alderson forces, and I'm the first person to ever study one! Oh!" Her face fell.

"What's wrong?" Trevor asked quickly.

"I can't publish." She pouted. That was what had got her in trouble in the first place. The CoDominium couldn't keep people from thinking. *Die Gedanken, Sie sind frei.* But CDI could ruthlessly suppress books and letters and arrest everyone who tried to tell others about their unlicensed speculations.

"I can arrange something," Senator Grant told her. "After all, you're *the* expert on Black Holes. We'll see that you get a chance to study them for the fleet." He sighed and tapped the arm of his acceleration chair, then whacked it hard with his open palm. "I don't know. Maybe the CoDominium Treaty wasn't such a good idea. We got peace, but—you know, all we ever wanted to do was keep national forces from getting new weapons. Just suppress *military* technology. But that turned out to be nearly everything. And did we really get peace?"

"We'll need a course, Mr Trevor," Ramsey growled. "This is still a Navy ship. I want the fastest route home."

Home. Sol System, and the house in Luna Base compound. It's still there. And I'll leave you, Daniel Webster, but I'll miss you, old girl, old boy, whatever you are. I'll miss you, but I can leave you.

Or can I? Barbara Jean, are you mine now? Some of you will always belong to Jim Harriman. Five goddam years that man kept his crew and passengers alive, five years when there wasn't a shred of hope they'd get home again. She'll never forget him.

And that's unworthy, Bart Ramsey. Neither one of us ought to forget him.

"But I still wonder," Marie Ward said. Her voice was very low and quiet, plaintive in tone. "I don't suppose I'll ever know."

"Know what?" Ramsey asked. It wasn't hard to be polite to her now.

"It's the song." She hummed her nursery rhyme. "What did he really see on the other side of the mountain?"

THE HOLE MAN

Larry Niven

After "Dark Hole" was published, I received a call from Dr Robert Forward of Hughes Research Laboratories. Bob Forward is their genius in charge of far-out research and development. He had already invented a mass detector and was at work on other marvels.

His call was to say that he'd read "Dark Hole" and would like to meet the author. Forward had been about to publish an article suggesting that if you got too close to a large source of gravity waves they might do terrible damage; and I had beat him into print. It isn't often that science fiction writers can pull such a coup.

The result of the phone calls was a visit to Forward's laboratories, where we saw marvels indeed. Naturally I took along my partner, Larry Niven. We were at the time engaged in a book, and unfortunately it was my turn to do some of the major work on it; thus Larry had time to write this story just after our visit. Naturally it won him a Hugo.

One day Mars will be gone.

Andrew Lear says that it will start with violent quakes, and end hours or days later, very suddenly. He ought to know. It's all his fault.

Lear also says that it won't happen for from years to centuries. So we stay, Lear and the rest of us. We study the alien base for what it can tell us, while the center of the world we stand on is slowly eaten away. It's enough to give a man nightmares.

It was Lear who found the alien base.

We had reached Mars: fourteen of us, in the cramped bulbous life-support system of the *Percival Lowell*. We were circling in orbit, taking our time, correcting our maps and looking for anything that thirty years of Mariner probes might have missed.

We were mapping mascons, among other things. Those mass concentrations under the lunar maria were almost certainly left by good-sized asteroids, mountains of rock falling silently out of the sky until they struck with the energies of thousands of fusion bombs. Mars has been cruising through the asteroid belt for four billion years. Mars would show bigger and better mascons. They would affect our orbits.

So Andrew Lear was hard at work, watching pens twitch on graph paper as we circled Mars. A bit of machinery fell alongside the *Percival Lowell*, rotating. Within its thin shell was a weighted double lever system, deceptively simple: a Forward Mass Detector. The pens mapped its twitchings.

Over Sirbonis Palus, they began mapping strange curves.

Another man might have cursed and tried to fix it. Andrew Lear thought it out, then sent the signal that would stop the free-falling widget from rotating.

It had to be rotating to map a stationary mass.

But now it was mapping simple sine waves.

Lear went running to Captain Childrey.

Running? It was more like trapeze artistry. Lear pulled himself along by handholds, kicked off from walls, braked with a hard push of hands or feet. Moving in free fall is hard work when you're in a hurry, and Lear was a forty-year-old astrophysicist, not an athlete. He was blowing hard when he reached the control bubble.

Childrey—who *was* an athlete—waited with a patient, slightly contemptuous smile while Lear caught his breath.

He already thought Lear was crazy. Lear's words only confirmed it. "Gravity for sending signals? Dr Lear, will you please quit bothering me with your weird ideas. I'm busy. We all are."

This is not entirely unfair. Some of Lear's enthusiasms were peculiar. Gravity generators. Black holes. He thought we should be searching for Dyson spheres: stars completely enclosed by an artificial shell. He believed that mass and inertia were two separate things: that it should be possible to suck the inertia out of a spacecraft, say, so that it could accelerate to near lightspeed in a few minutes. He was a wide-eyed dreamer, and when he was flustered he tended to wander from the point.

"You don't understand," he told Childrey. "Gravity radiation is harder to block than electromagnetic waves. Patterned gravity waves would be easy to detect. The advanced civilizations in the galaxy may all be communicating by gravity. Some of them may even be modulating pulsars—rotating neutron stars. That's where Project Ozma went wrong: they were only looking for signals in the electromagnetic spectrum."

Childrey laughed. "Sure. Your little friends are using

neutron stars to send you messages. What's that got to do with us?"

"Well, look!" Lear held up the strip of flimsy, nearly weightless paper he'd torn from the machine. "I got this over Sirbonis Palus. I think we ought to land there."

"We're landing in Mare Cimmerium, as you perfectly well know. The lander is already deployed and ready to board. Dr Lear, we've spent four days mapping this area. It's flat. It's in a green-brown area. When spring comes next month, we'll find out whether there's life there! And everybody wants it that way except you!"

Lear was still holding the graph paper before him like a shield. "Please. Take one more circuit over Sirbonis Palus."

Childrey opted for the extra orbit. Maybe the sine waves convinced him. Maybe not. He would have liked inconveniencing the rest of us in Lear's name, to show him for a fool.

But the next pass showed a tiny circular feature in Sirbonis Palus. And Lear's mass indicator was making sine waves again. The aliens had gone. During our first few months we always expected them back any minute. The machinery in the base was running smoothly and perfectly, as if the owners had only just stepped out.

The base was an inverted pie plate two stories high, and windowless. The air inside was breathable, like Earth's air three miles up, but with a bit more oxygen. Mars's air is far thinner, and poisonous. Clearly they were not of Mars.

The walls were thick and deeply eroded. They leaned inward against the internal pressure. The roof was somewhat thinner, just heavy enough for the pressure to support it. Both walls and roof were of fused Martian dust.

The heating system still worked—and it was also the lighting system: grids in the ceiling glowing brick red. The base was always ten degrees too warm. We didn't find the off switches for almost a week: they were behind locked panels. The air system blew gusty winds through the base until we fiddled with the fans.

We could guess a lot about them from what they'd left behind. They must have come from a world smaller than Earth, circling a red dwarf star in close orbit. To be close enough to be warm enough, the planet would have to be locked in by tides, turning one face always to its star. The aliens must have evolved on the lighted side, in a permanent red day, with winds constantly howling over the border from the night side.

And they had no sense of privacy. The only doorways that had doors in them were airlocks. The second floor was a hexagonal metal gridwork. It would not block you off from your friends on the floor below. The bunk room was an impressive expanse of mercury-filled waterbed, wall to wall. The rooms were too small and cluttered, the furniture and machinery too close to the doorways, so that at first we were constantly bumping elbows and knees. The ceilings were an inch short of six feet high on both floors, so that we tended to walk stooped even if we were short enough to stand upright. Habit. But Lear was just tall enough to knock his head if he stood up fast, anywhere in the base.

We thought they must have been smaller than human. But their padded benches seemed human-designed in size and shape. Maybe it was their minds that were different: they didn't need psychic elbow room.

The ship had been bad enough. Now this. Within the base was instant claustrophobia. It put all of our tempers on hair triggers.

Two of us couldn't take it.

Lear and Childrey did not belong on the same planet.

With Childrey, neatness was a compulsion. He had enough for all of us. During those long months aboard *Percival Lowell,* it was Childrey who led us in calisthenics. He flatly would not let anyone skip an exercise period. We eventually gave up trying.

Well and good. The exercise kept us alive. We weren't getting the helathy daily exercise anyone gets walking around the living room in a one-gravity field.

But after a month on Mars, Childrey was the only man who still appeared fully dressed in the heat of the alien base. Some of us took it as a reproof, and maybe it was, because Lear had been the first to doff his shirt for keeps. In the mess Childrey would inspect his silverware for water spots, then line it up perfectly parallel.

On Earth, Andrew Lear's habits would have been no more than a character trait. In a hurry, he might choose mismatched socks. He might put off using the dishwasher for a day or two if he were involved in something interesting. He would prefer a house that looked "lived in". God help the maid who tried to clean up his study. He'd never be able to find anything afterward.

He was a brilliant but one-sided man. Backpacking or skin diving might have changed his habits—in such pursuits you learn not to forget any least trivial thing—but they would never have tempted him. An expedition to Mars was something he simply could not turn down. A pity, because neatness is worth your life in space.

You don't leave your fly open in a pressure suit.

A month after the landing, Childrey caught Lear doing just that.

The "fly" on a pressure suit is a soft rubber tube over your male member. It leads to a bladder, and there's a spring clamp on it. You open the clamp to use it. Then you close the clamp and open an outside spigot to evacuate the bladder into vacuum.

Similar designs for women involve a catheter, which is hideously uncomfortable. I presume the designers will keep trying. It seems wrong to bar half the human race from our ultimate destiny.

Lear was addicted to long walks. He loved the Martian desert scene: the hard violet sky and the soft blur of whirling orange dust, the sharp close horizon, the endless emptiness. More: he needed the room. He was spending all his working time on the alien communicator, with the ceiling too close over his head and everything else too close to his bony elbows.

He was coming back from a walk, and he met Childrey coming out. Childrey noticed that the waste spigot on Lear's suit was open, the spring broken. Lear had been out for hours. If he'd had to go, he might have bled to death through flesh ruptured by vacuum.

We never learned all that Childrey said to him out there. But Lear came in very red about the ears, muttering under his breath. He wouldn't talk to anyone.

The NASA psychologists should not have put them both on that small a planet. Hindsight is wonderful, right? But Lear and Childrey were each the best choice for competence coupled to the kind of health they would need to survive the trip. There were astrophysicists as competent and as famous as Lear, but they were decades older. And Childrey had a thousand spaceflight hours to his credit. He had been one of the last men on the moon.

Individually, each of us was the best possible man. It was a damn shame.

The aliens had left the communicator going, like everything else in the base. It must have been hellishly massive, to judge by the thick support pillars slating outward beneath it. It was a bulky tank of a thing, big enough that the roof had to bulge slightly to give it room. That gave Lear about a square meter of the only head room in the base.

Even Lear had no idea why they'd put it on the second floor. It would send through the first floor, or through the bulk of a planet. Lear learned that by trying it, once he knew enough. He beamed a dot-dash message through Mars itself to the Forward Mass Detector aboard *Lowell*.

Lear had set up a Mass Detector next to the communicator, on an extremely complex platform designed to protect it from vibration. The Detector produced waves so sharply pointed that some of us thought they could *feel* the gravity radiation coming from the communicator.

Lear was in love with the thing.

He skipped meals. When he ate he ate like a starved wolf. "There's a heavy point-mass in there," he told us, talking around a mouthful of food, two months after the landing. "The machine uses electromagnetic fields to vibrate it at high speed. Look—" He picked up a toothpaste tube of tuna spread and held it in front of him. He vibrated it rapidly. Heads turned to watch him around the zigzagged communal table in the alien mess. "I'm make gravity waves now. But they're too mushy because the tube's too big, and their amplitude is virtually zero. There's something very dense and massive in that machine, and it takes a hell of a lot of field strength to keep it there."

"What is it?" someone asked. "Neutronium? Like the heart of a neutron star?"

Lear shook his head and took another mouthful. "That size, neutronium wouldn't be stable. I think it's a quantum black hole. I don't know how to measure its mass yet."

I said, "A *quantum* black hole?"

Lear nodded happily. "Luck for me. You know, I was against the Mars expedition. We could get a lot more for our money by exploring the asteroids. Among other things, we might have found if there are really quantum black holes out there. But this one's already captured!" He stood up, being careful of his head. He turned in his tray and went back to work.

I remember we stared at each other along the zigzag mess table. Then we drew lots . . . and I lost.

The day Lear left his waste spigot open, Childrey had put a restriction on him. Lear was not to leave the base without an escort.

Lear had treasured the aloneness of those walks. But it was worse than that. Childrey had given him a list of possible escorts: half a dozen men Childrey could trust to see to it that Lear did nothing dangerous to himself or others. Inevitably they were the men most thoroughly trained in space survival routines, most addicted to Childrey's own compulsive neatness, least likely to sympathize with Lear's way of living. Lear was as likely to ask Childrey himself to go walking with him.

He almost never went out any more. I knew exactly where to find him.

I stood beneath him, looking up through the gridwork floor.

He'd almost finished dismantling the protective panels around the gravity communicator. What showed inside looked like parts of a computer in one spot, electromagnetic coils in most places, and a square array of pushbuttons that might have been the aliens' idea of a typewriter. Lear was using a magnetic induction sensor to try to trace wiring without actually tearing off the insulation.

I called, "How you making out?"

"No good," he said. "The insulation seems to be one hundred per cent perfect. Now I'm afraid to open it up. No telling how much power is running through there, if it needs shielding that good." He smiled down at me. "Let me show you something."

"What?"

He flipped a toggle above a dull gray circular plate. "This thing is a microphone. It took me a while to find it. I am Andrew Lear, speaking to whoever may be listening." He switched it off, then ripped paper from the Mass Indicator and showed me squiggles interrupting smooth sine waves. "There. The sound of my voice in gravity radiation. It won't disappear until it's reached the edges of the universe."

"Lear, you mentioned quantum black holes there. What's a quantum black hole?"

"Um. You know what a black hole is."

"I ought to." Lear had educated us on the subject, at length, during the months aboard *Lowell.*

When a not too massive star has used up its nuclear fuel, it collapses into a white dwarf. A heavier star—say, 1.44 times the mass of the sun and larger—can burn out its fuel, then collapse into itself until it is ten kilometers across and composed solely of neutrons packed edge to edge: the densest matter in this universe.

But a big star goes further than that. When a really massive star runs its course . . . when the radiation pressure within is no longer strong enough to hold the outer layers against the star's own ferocious gravity . . . then it can fall into itself entirely, until gravity is stronger than any other force, until it is compressed past the Schwartzchild radius and effectively leaves the universe. What happens to it then is problematical. The Schwartzchild radius is the boundary beyond which nothing can climb out of the gravity, not even light.

The star is gone then, but the mass remains: a lightless hole in space, perhaps a hole into another universe.

"A collapsing star can leave a black hole," said Lear. "There may be bigger black holes, whole galaxies that have fallen into themselves. But there's no other way a black hole can form, *now*."

"So?"

"There was a time when black holes of all sizes could form. That was during the Big Bang, the explosion that started the expanding universe. The forces in that blast could have compressed little local vortices of matter past the Schwartzchild radius. What that left behind—the smallest ones, anyway—we call quantum black holes."

I heard a distinctive laugh behind me as Captain Childrey walked into view. The bulk of the communicator would have hidden him from Lear, and I hadn't heard him come up. He called, "Just how big a thing are you talking about? Could I pick one up and throw it at you?"

"You'd disappear into one that size," Lear said seriously. "A black hole the mass of the Earth would only be a centimeter across. No, I'm talking about things from ten-to-the-minus-fifth grams on up. There could be one at the center of the sun—"

"Eek!"

Lear was trying. He didn't like being kidded, but he didn't know how to stop it. Keeping it serious wasn't the way, but he didn't know that either. "Say ten-to-the-seventeenth grams in mass and ten-to-the-minus-eleven centimeters across. It would be swallowing a few atoms a day."

"Well, at least you know where to find it," said Childrey. "Now all you have to do is go after it."

Lear nodded, still serious. "There could be quantum black holes in asteroids. A small asteroid could capture a quantum black hole easily enough, especially if it was charged; a black hole can hold a charge, you know—"

"Ri-ight."

"All we'd have to do is check out a small asteroid with the Mass Detector. If it masses more than it should, we push it aside and see if it leaves a black hole behind."

"You'd need little teeny eyes to see something that small. Anyway, what would you do with it?"

"You put a charge on it, if it hasn't got one already, and electromagnetic fields. You can vibrate it to make gravity; then you manipulate it with radiation. I think I've got one in here," he said, patting the alien communicator.

"Ri-ight," said Childrey, and we went away laughing.

Within a week the whole base was referring to Lear as the Hole Man, the man with the black hole between his ears.

It hadn't sounded funny when Lear was telling me about it. The rich variety of the universe . . . But when Childrey talked about the black hole in Lear's Anything Box, it sounded hilarious.

Please note: Childrey did not misunderstand anything Lear had said. Childrey wasn't stupid. He merely thought Lear was crazy. He could not have gotten away with making fun of Lear, not among educated men, without knowing exactly what he was doing.

Meanwhile the work went on.

There were pools of Marsdust, fascinating stuff, fine enough to behave like viscous oil, and knee-deep. Wading through it wasn't dangerous, but it was very hard work, and we avoided it. One day Brace waded out into the nearest of the pools and started feeling around under the dust. Hunch, he said. He came up with some eroded plastic-like containers. The aliens had used the pool as a garbage dump.

We were having little luck with chemical analysis of the base materials. They were virtually indestructible. We learned more about the chemistry of the alien visitors themselves. They had left traces of themselves on the benches and on the communal waterbed. The traces had most of the chemical components of protoplasm, but Arsvey found no sign of DNA. Not surprising, he said. There must be other giant organic molecules suitable for gene coding.

The aliens had left volumes of notes behind. The script was a mystery, of course, but we studied the photographs and diagrams. A lot of them were notes on anthropology!

The aliens had been studying Earth during the first Ice Age.

None of us were anthropologists, and that was a damn shame. We never learned if we'd found anything new. All we could do was photograph the stuff and beam it up to *Lowell*. One thing was sure: the aliens had left very long ago, and they had left the lighting and air systems running and the communicator sending a carrier wave.

For us? Who else?

The alternative was that the base had been switched off for some six hundred thousand years, then come back on when something detected *Lowell* approaching Mars. Lear didn't believe it. "If the power had been off in the communicator," he said, "the mass wouldn't be in there any more. The fields have to be going to hold it in place. It's smaller than an atom; it'd fall through anything solid."

So the base power system had been running for all that

time. What the hell could it be? And where? We traced some cables and found that it was under the base, under several yards of Marsdust fused to lava. We didn't try to dig through that.

The source was probably geophysical: a hole deep into the core of the planet. The aliens might have wanted to dig such a hole to take core samples. Afterward they would have set up a generator to use the temperature difference between the core and the surface.

Meanwhile, Lear spent some time tracing down the power sources in the communicator. He found a way to shut off the carrier wave. Now the mass, if there was a mass, was at rest in there. It was strange to see the Forward Mass Detector pouring out straight lines instead of drastically peaked sine waves.

We were ill-equipped to take advantage of these riches. We had been fitted out to explore Mars, not a bit of civilization from another star. Lear was the exception. He was in his element, with but one thing to mar his happiness.

I don't know what the final argument was about. I was engaged on another project.

The Mars lander still had fuel in it. NASA had given us plenty of fuel to hover while we looked for a landing spot. After some heated discussion, we had agreed to take the vehicle up and hover it next to the nearby dust pool on low thrust.

It worked fine. The dust rose up in a great soft cloud and went away toward the horizon, leaving the pond bottom covered with otherworldly junk. And more! Arsvey started screaming at Brace to back off. Fortunately Brace kept his head. He tilted us over to one side and took us away on a gentle curve. The backblast never touched the skeletons.

We worked out there for hours, being very finicky indeed. Here was another skill none of us would own to, but we'd read about how careful an archaeologist has to be, and we did our best. Traces of water had had time to turn some of the dust to natural cement, so that some of the skeletons were fixed to the rock. But we got a couple free. We put them on stretchers and brought them back. One crumbled the instant the air came hissing into the lock. We left the other outside.

The aliens had not had the habit of taking baths. We'd set up a bathtub with very tall sides, in a room the aliens had reserved for some incomprehensible ritual. I had stripped off my pressure suit and was heading for the bathtub, very tired, hoping that nobody would be in it.

I heard voices before I saw them.

Lear was shouting.

Childrey wasn't, but his voice was a carrying one. It carried mockery. He was standing between the supporting pillars. His hands were on his hips, his teeth gleamed white, his head was thrown back to look up at Lear.

He finished talking. For a time neither of them moved. Then Lear made a sound of disgust. He turned away and pushed one of the buttons on what might have been an alien typewriter keyboard.

Childrey looked startled. He slapped at his right thigh and brought the hand away bloody. He stared at it, then looked up at Lear. He started to ask a question.

He crumpled slowly in the low gravity. I got to him before he hit the ground. I cut his pants open and tied a handkerchief over the blood spot. It was a small puncture, but the flesh was puckered above it on a line with his groin.

Childrey tried to speak. His eyes were wide. He coughed, and there was blood on his mouth.

I guess I froze. How could I help if I couldn't tell what had happened? I saw a blood spot on his right shoulder, and I tore the shirt open and found another tiny puncture wound.

The doctor arrived.

It took Childrey an hour to die, but the doctor had given up much earlier. Between the wound in his shoulder and the wound in his thigh, Childrey's flesh had been ruptured in a narrow line that ran through one lung and his stomach and part of his intestinal tract. The autopsy showed a tiny, very neat hole drilled through the hip-bones.

We looked for, and found, a hole in the floor beneath the communicator. It was the size of a pencil lead, and packed with dust.

"I made a mistake," Lear told the rest of us at the inquest. "I should never have touched that particular button. It must have switched off the fields that held the mass in place. It just dropped. Captain Childrey was underneath."

And it had gone straight through him, eating the mass of him as it went.

"No, not quite," said Lear. "I'd guessed it massed about ten-to-the-fourteenth grams. That only makes it ten-to-the-minus-sixth Angstrom across, much smaller than an atom. It wouldn't have absorbed much. The damage was done to Childrey by tidal effects as it passed through him. You saw how it pulverized the material of the floor."

Not surprisingly, the subject of murder did come up.

Lear shrugged it off. "Murder with what? Childrey didn't believe there was a black hole in there at all. Neither did many of you." He smiled suddenly. "Can you imagine what the trial would be like? Imagine the prosecuting attorney trying to tell a jury what he thinks happened. First he's got to tell them what a black hole is. Then a quantum black hole. Then he's got to explain why he doesn't have the murder weapon, and where he left it, freely falling through Mars! And if he gets that far without being laughed out of court, he's still got to explain how a thing smaller than an atom could hurt anyone!"

But didn't Dr Lear know the thing was dangerous? Could he not have guessed its enormous mass from the way it behaved?

Lear spread his hands. "Gentlemen, we're dealing with more variables than just mass. Field strength, for instance. I might have guessed its mass from the force it took to keep it there, but did any of us expect the aliens to calibrate their dials in the metric system?"

Surely there must have been safeties to keep the fields from being shut off accidentally. Lear must have bypassed them.

"Yes, I probably did, accidentally. I did quite a lot of fiddling to find out how things worked."

It got dropped there. Obviously there would be no trial. No ordinary judge or jury could be expected to understand what the attorneys would be talking about. A couple of things never did get mentioned.

For instance: Childrey's last words. I might or might not have repeated them if I'd been asked to. They were: "All right, show me! Show it to me or admit it isn't there!"

As the court was breaking up I spoke to Lear with my voice lowered. "That was probably the most unique murder weapon in history."

He whispered, "If you said that in company I could sue for slander."

"Yeah? Really? Are *you* going to explain to a jury what you think I implied happened?"

"No, I'll let you get away with it this time."

"Hell, you didn't get away scot-free yourself. What are you going to study now? The only known black hole in the universe, and you let it drop through your fingers."

Lear frowned. "You're right. Partly right, anyway. But I knew as much about it as I was going to, the way I was going. Now . . . I stopped it vibrating in there, then took the mass of the entire setup with the Forward Mass Sensor. Now the black hole isn't in there any more. I can get the mass of the black hole by taking the mass of the communicator alone."

"Oh."

"And I can cut the machine open, see what's inside. How they controlled it. Damn it, I wish I were six years old."

"What? Why?"

"Well . . . I don't have the times straightened out. The math is chancy. Either a few years from now, or a few centuries, there's going to be a black hole between Earth and Jupiter. It'll be big enough to study. I think about forty years."

When I realized what he was implying, I didn't know whether to laugh or scream. "Lear, you can't think that something that small could absorb Mars!"

"Well, remember that it absorbs everything it comes near. A nucleus here, an electron there . . . and it's not just waiting for atoms to fall into it. Its gravity is ferocious, and it's falling back and forth through the center of the planet, sweeping up matter. The more it eats, the bigger it gets, with its volume going up as the cube of the mass. Sooner or later, yes, it'll absorb Mars. By then it'll be just less than a millimeter across—big enough to see."

"Could it happen within thirteen months?"

"Before we leave? Hmm." Lear's eyes took on a faraway look. "I don't think so. I'll have to work it out. The math is chancy . . ."

FUZZY BLACK HOLES HAVE NO HAIR

Jerry Pournelle

After our visit to Bob Forward's laboratories Larry wrote his prize-winning story, while I got to work on our then-current collaboration (Inferno).

It didn't seem very fair. Larry got a Hugo, and I got a couple of columns. Still, things have a habit of balancing. At least it turned out that way—although I expect I'd rather have the Hugo, instead of the satisfaction of this:

Black holes have no hair, but they're fuzzy. Because they're fuzzy, they're not really black.

This column is a bit of a scoop. At the moment there's no mention anywhere in the scientific journals of why black holes aren't black, and I expect this to be published before there will be any. [*It was. JEP*]

To review, if a chunk of matter gets squeezed small enough, it becomes a black hole. For our Sun, "small enough" means about three kilometers in radius. The equation for the radius of a black hole is,

$$r = 2GM/c^2$$

for mass M in grams, G the universal constant of gravitation, and c the velocity of light.

We call the region that satisfies this equation the Schwartzchild radius. Inside it gravity has become so strong that nothing, including light, can escape, and outsiders can know nothing of what's going on in there. Also inside there lurks a singularity which does strange things to time and causality.

If you watched a star collapse you'd never see it get quite so small as that. Instead it would appear that the collapse kept slowing down and everything was now hovering just outside the Schwartzchild radius. The light would get redder and redder, and also dimmer and dimmer, and in milliseconds it would go out.

Since nothing can come out of the hole, we can't see in. We call the region from which nothing can escape the "event horizon", and we'll never know what happens inside because of the law of cosmic censorship. If you want to know more about *that,* read the introduction to this book.

Classical black hole theory dictates several laws of black hole dynamics. Some aren't too interesting, but the Second Law says the area of the event horizon can never decrease, and increases as matter and energy are pumped into the hole. This means that black holes never get smaller. Feed them matter and/or energy and they grow.

That lets us deduce one thing instantly. What happens if a normal matter and an anti-matter black hole collide?

Well, nothing that wouldn't happen if two normal matter holes, or two anti-matter holes, collided, of course. The holes eat each other to form one larger than either, but we'll never know which ones contain normal or anti-matter. In fact, the question is meaningless.

You see, black holes have no hair.

This is a convenient way to say that everything we'll ever know about a black hole can be deduced from three parameters. Once you specify the mass M, the angular momentum J, and the electric charge Q, you've said it all. Nothing remains but location, which isn't important for the physics of the hole, but may be for the physicist who wants to study it.

Mass we understand. It doesn't really matter whether that mass is in the form of energy or matter; Einstein's $e = Mc^2$ takes care of that, and down in the hole it's irrelevant whether the rest mass is e or M.

Angular momentum comes from rotation of the object before it collapsed. Naturally it's conserved, so that if the star were rotating, the thing inside the hole rotates as well. It also rotates *fast,* just as a skater speeds up in a spin when she pulls her arms in.

The last parameter, charge, is just what it says, and it gives us a way to move a black hole around. If it isn't charged, feed it charged particles until it is, then use magnets to tow it.

The laws of black hole dynamics say that you can never recover the rest mass energy (that's the Mc^2 energy, of course) of the original body. It's lost forever. Even shoving anti-matter down the hole gains you nothing.

However, you can get energy out of a spinning black hole. Up to 29% of the rotational energy is available, and in the case of a star that's a *lot.* To get it you throw something down the hole, and one of the things that comes out is gravity waves.

In our experience gravity waves are puny things, but we're a long way from their source. Up close is another matter entirely. You could be torn apart by them, as the characters in my story, *He Fell Into a Dark Hole,* very nearly were.

Most of what we know about black holes comes from Stephen Hawking of the University of Cambridge. Many physicists think Hawking is to Einstein what Einstein was to Newton, and he's still a young man. This year Hawking has added quantum mechanics to classical black-hole theory, and he's ruined a lot of good science fiction stories.

Somewhat over a year ago Larry Niven and I went out to Hughes Research Laboratories in Malibu. The laser was invented at Hughes, so of course they do a lot of laser research there. They're also among the top people in ion drive engines, and they've done a lot with advanced communications concepts.

All that was fascinating, but we went to talk with Dr Robert Forward, who's known as one of *the* experts on gravitation. I'd met him because he liked my previously mentioned black hole story (nominated for a Hugo last year, but alas . . .) and had been kind enough to call and tell me so.

Bob Forward is the inventor of the Forward Mass Detector, a widget that can track a tank miles away by mass alone. It can't distinguish between a tank at a mile and a fly on the end of the instrument, but if you use two and triangulate you're safe enough. His detector can also be lowered into oil wells, or towed behind an airplane to map mass concentrations below.

After lunch we talked about black holes. Dr Forward was particularly interested in Stephen Hawking's then-new notion that tiny black holes might have been formed during the Big Bang of Creation. Since the Second Law predicts that they never get smaller, there should be holes of all sizes left. Some might be in our solar system.

They would come to rest in the interior of large masses. There might be quite a large one inside the Sun, for example—and in the Earth and Moon as well. A hole of very large mass, say 10^8 kilograms, would still be tiny: about 10^{-19} centimeters radius. An atomic radius is around 10^9 cm., very large compared to such a hole, so that the hole couldn't be expected to eat more than a few atoms a day, and wouldn't grow very fast.

(Readers who don't understand powers-of-ten notation should find a highschool—new highschool, since they didn't teach that in my day—text and learn, because you can't deal with very large or very small numbers without it. The number 10^8 means a one with eight zeroes, or 100,000,000 while 10^{-9} is one divided by 1,000,000,000 or one billionth. Thus 10^{-19} is one divided by a one followed by 19 zeroes, or .0000000000000000001, a rather small number.)

Anyway, black holes inside the Earth or Sun aren't too useful because they're hard to get at. Bob Forward wanted to go to the asteroids. You search for a rock that weighs far too much for its size. Push the rock aside and there in the orbit where the asteroid used to be you'll find a little black hole.

You could do a lot with such a hole. For example, you could wiggle it with magnetic fields to produce gravity waves at precise frequencies. There might be a lot of holes of many sizes, even down to a kilogram or two.

It sounded marvelous. Larry and I figured there were a dozen stories there. I'd already written my black hole story, and Larry hadn't, so he beat me into print with a thing called *The Hole Man*. All I got from the trip was a couple articles and columns.

Well, Larry's story has just been reprinted in this new collection, while the columns I did about little black holes have been forgotten—I hope!

I'm glad I have nothing in print about tiny black holes, because Hawking has just proved they can't exist. Oh, they can be formed all right, but they won't be around very long. It seems that black holes aren't really black. They radiate, and left to themselves they get smaller all the time. The Second Law needs modifying.

Stephen Hawking's new paper hasn't been widely published yet because he submitted it to this year's Gravity Research Foundation prize essay contest. The GRF was founded by Edison's friend, stock market analyst Roger Babson. It's been around for many years, and received scornful treatment in Martin Gardiner's *Fads and Fallacies in the Name of Science*. It may or may not have deserved that in the 50's, but for a number of years the leading people in gravitational theory have been entering the competition.

Hawking won first prize from GRF in 1971 with his paper on cosmic censorship and black hole dynamics. This year he took only third prize, first going to a Cal Berkeley astronomer. Even third prize was enough to tear Larry's *The Hole Man* to shreds. (Not that Hawking ever mentioned science fiction; but then the Pioneer probes weren't intended to wreck all our stories about Jupiter, either.)

Hawking points out that Einstein's general relativity, which produces most of the primary equations for black holes, is a classical theory. It doesn't take quantum effects into account.

Hawking corrects this. In quantum theory a length, L, is not fixed. It has an uncertainty or fluctuation on the order of L_0/L, where L_0 is the Planck length 10^{-33} cm.

Since there is uncertainty in the length scale, it follows that the event horizon of the black hole isn't actually fixed. It fluctuates through the uncertainty region.

In fact, the black hole is FUZZY, and energy and radiation can tunnel out of the hole to escape forever. It's the same kind of effect as observed in tunnel diodes, where particles appear on the other side of a potential barrier.

Since black holes have no hair, although they do have fuzz, the quantum radiation temperature—that is, the rate at which they radiate—must depend entirely on mass, angular momentum, and charge.

It does, but I'm not going to prove it for you. Hawking uses math that I *can* tool up to follow, but I'm not really keen on Hermetian scalar fields, and I doubt many *Galaxy* readers are either. If you want this proof, send a dollar to Gravity Research Foundation, 58 Middle Street, Gloucester, Mass 01930 and request a copy of Hawking's paper *Black Holes Aren't Black*.

TABLE ONE
MASS, RADIUS, AND LIFETIMES OF BLACK HOLES

Description	Mass (grams)	Radius (cm)	Lifetime (seconds)	Lifetime (years)
Kilogram	1000	1.48×10^{-25}	10^{-19}	—
Billion gm.	10^9	1.48×10^{-19}	.1	—
2365 tons	2.15×10^9	3.19×10^{-19}	1	
—	6.7×10^{11}	9.9×10^{-17}	31.5 million	1
	6.7×10^{13}	9.9×10^{-15}		million
	1.5×10^{18}	2.18×10^{13}		10^{10}
Ceres	8×10^{23}	1.2×10^{-4}		10^{36}
Earth	6×10^{27}	9×10^{-1}		Eternal
Sun	1.99×10^{33}	3 kilometers		
Galaxy	10^{11} suns	$3 \times 10^{16} = .03$ lightyear		
Universe	10^{23} suns	$2.95 \times 10^{27} = 3$ billion lightyears		

Hawking shows that the temperature of a black hole is,
$$T = 10^{26} M°K$$
where M is mass in grams, and the lifetime of a black hole in seconds is
$$t_L = 10^{-28} M^3$$
Using my new Texas Instruments SR-50 that handles scientific notation and takes powers and roots in milliseconds, it wasn't hard to work up Table One from these equations.*

There are more numbers than we need, of course. It's a consequence of the pocket computer. Not long ago I'd have had to use logs and sliderule, and I'd have done no more than I needed. Now look.

The first thing to see is that small holes have uninter-

* My SR-50 has long since been replaced with first an SR-51, then SR-52, now a TI 58. Progress.

esting lifetimes. In order for one to be around long enough to use it, the hole must be massive.

Any black holes formed in the Big Bang would be 10^{10} old now; so if they weren't larger than a small asteroid they're gone already. Worse, than exponential decay rate defeats us even if we find a hole just decayed to an interesting size. It will still vanish too fast to use.

So there went Larry's *Hole Man,* and two stories I had plotted but hadn't written, and I suspect a lot of other science fiction as well. Sometimes I feel a bit like Alice when she protested, "Things *flow* here so!"

But it's what we get for living in interesting times, and it ought to teach my friend Larry not to rush into print ahead of me . . .

KYRIE

Poul Anderson

This was one of the first stories ever published about black holes. It's also one of the best. It isn't surprising that Poul Anderson, known for his hard science stories, would be among the first to get into print with a story using the new concept.

To the best physical knowledge, the time effects Anderson describes are real. You may rely on his other physics as well. Anderson is a craftsman.

On a high peak in the Lunar Carpathians stands a convent of St Martha of Bethany. The walls are native rock;

they lift dark and cragged as the mountainside itself, into a sky that is always black. As you approach from North-pole along Route Plato, you see the cross which sur-mounts the tower, stark athwart Earth's blue disc. No bells resound from there—not in airlessness.

You may hear them inside at the canonical hours, and throughout the crypts below where machines toil to maintain a semblance of terrestrial environment. If you linger a while you will also hear them calling to requiem mass. For it has become a tradition that prayers be of-fered at St Martha's for those who have perished in space; and they are more with every passing year.

This is not the work of the sisters. They minister to the sick, the needy, the crippled, the insane, all whom space has broken and cast back. Luna is full of such, exiles be-cause they can no longer endure Earth's pull or because it is feared they may be incubating a plague from some un-known planet or because men are so busy with their fron-tiers that they have no time to spare for the failures. The sisters wear space suits as often as habits, are as likely to hold a medikit as a rosary.

But they are granted some time for contemplation. At night, when for half a month the sun's glare has departed, the chapel is unshuttered and stars look down through the glazedome to the candles. They do not wink and their light is winter cold. One of the nuns in particular is there as often as may be, praying for her own dead. And the abbess sees to it that she can be present when the yearly mass, that she endowed before she took her vows, is sung.

Requiem aeternam dona eis, Domine, et lux
perpetua luceat eis.
Kyrie eleison, Christe eleison, Kyrie eleison.

The Supernova Sagittarii expedition comprised fifty hu-man beings and a flame. It went the long way around from Earth orbit, stopping at Epsilom Lyrae to pick up its last member. Thence it approached its destination by stages.

This is the paradox: time and space are aspects of each other. The explosion was more than a hundred years past when noted by men on Lasthope. They were part of a generations-long effort to fathom the civilization of creatures altogether unlike us; but one night they looked up and saw a light so brilliant it cast shadows.

That wave front would reach Earth several centuries hence. By then it would be so tenuous that nothing but another bright point would appear in the sky. Meanwhile, though, a ship overleaping the space through which light must creep could track the great star's death across time.

Suitably far off, instruments recorded what had been before the outburst, incandescence collapsing upon itself after the last nuclear fuel was burned out. A jump, and they saw what happened a century ago, convulsion, storm of quanta and neutrinos, radiation equal to the massed hundred billion suns of this galaxy.

It faded, leaving an emptiness in heaven, and the *Raven* moved closer. Fifty light-years—fifty years—inward, she studied a shrinking fieriness in the midst of a fog which shone like lightning.

Twenty-five years later the central globe had dwindled more, the nebula had expanded and dimmed. But because the distance was now so much less, everything seemed larger and brighter. The naked eye saw a dazzle too fierce to look straight at, making the constellations pale by contrast. Telescopes showed a blue-white spark in the heart of an opalescent cloud delicately filamented at the edges.

The *Raven* made ready for her final jump, to the immediate neighborhood of the supernova.

Captain Teodor Szili went on a last-minute inspection tour. The ship murmured around him, running at one gravity of acceleration to reach the desired intrinsic velocity. Power droned, regulators whickered, ventilation systems rustled. He felt the energies quiver in his bones. But metal surrounded him, blank and comfortless. Viewports gave on a dragon's hoard of stars, the ghostly arch of the Milky Way: on vacuum, cosmic rays, cold not far above absolute zero, distance beyond imagination to the nearest human hearthfire. He was about to take his people where none had ever been before, into conditions none was sure about, and that was a heavy burden on him.

He found Eloise Waggoner at her post, a cubbyhole with intercom connections directly to the command bridge. Music drew him, a triumphant serenity he did not recognize. Stopping in the doorway, he saw her seated with a small tape machine on the desk.

"What's this?" he demanded.

"Oh!" The woman (he could not think of her as a girl, though she was barely out of her teens) started. "I . . . I was waiting for the jump."

"You were to wait at the alert."

"What have I to do?" she answered less timidly than was her wont. "I mean, I'm not a crewman or a scientist."

"You are in the crew. Special communications technician."

"With Lucifer. And he likes the music. He says we come closer to oneness with it than in anything else he knows about us."

Szili arched his brows. "Oneness?"

A blush went up Eloise's thin cheeks. She stared at the deck and her hands twisted together. "Maybe that isn't the right word. Peace, harmony, unity . . . God? . . . I sense what he means, but we haven't any word that fits."

"Hm. Well, you are supposed to keep him happy." The skipper regarded her with a return of the distaste he had tried to suppress. She was a decent enough sort, he supposed, in her gauche and inhibited way; but her looks! Scrawny, big-footed, big-nosed, pop eyes, and stringy dust-colored hair—and, to be sure, telepaths always made him uncomfortable. She said she could only read Lucifer's mind, but was that true?

No. Don't think such things. Loneliness and otherness

can come near breaking you out here, without adding suspicion of your fellows.

If Eloise Waggoner was really human. She must be some kind of mutant at the very least. Whoever could communicate thought to thought with a living vortex had to be.

"What are you playing, anyhow?" Szili asked.

"Bach. The Third Brandenburg Concerto. He, Lucifer, he doesn't care for the modern stuff. I don't either."

You wouldn't, Szili decided. Aloud: "Listen, we jump in half an hour. No telling what we'll emerge in. This is the first time anyone's been close to a recent supernova. We can only be certain of so much hard radiation that we'll be dead if the screenfields give way. Otherwise we've nothing to go on except theory. And a collapsing stellar core is so unlike anything anywhere else in the universe that I'm skeptical about how good the theory is. We can't sit daydreaming. We have to prepare."

"Yes, sir." Whispering, her voice lost its usual harshness.

He stared past her, past the ophidian eyes of meters and controls, as if he could penetrate the steel beyond and look straight into space. There, he knew, floated Lucifer.

The image grew in him: a fireball twenty meters across, shimmering white, red, gold, royal blue, flames dancing like Medusa locks, cometary tail burning for a hundred meters behind, a shiningness, a glory, a piece of hell. Not the least of what troubled him was the thought of that which paced his ship.

He hugged scientific explanations to his breast, though they were little better than guesses. In the multiple star system of Epsilon Aurigae, in the gas and energy pervading the space around, things took place which no laboratory could imitate. Ball lightning on a planet was perhaps analogous, as the formation of simple organic compounds in a primordial ocean is analogous to the life which finally evolves. In Epsilon Aurigae, magnetohydrodynamics had done what chemistry did on Earth. Stable plasma vortices had appeared, had grown, had added complexity, until after millions of years they became something you must needs call an organism. It was a form of ions, nuclei, and force-fields. It metabolized electrons, nucleons, X rays; it maintained its configuration for a long lifetime; it reproduced; it thought.

But what did it think? The few telepaths who could communicate with the Aurigeans, who had first made humankind aware that the Aurigeans existed, never explained clearly. They were a queer lot themselves.

Wherefore Captain Szili said, "I want you to pass this on to him."

"Yes, sir." Eloise turned down the volume on her taper. Her eyes unfocused. Through her ears went words, and her brain (how efficient a transducer was it?) passed the meanings on out to him who loped alongside *Raven* on his own reaction drive.

"Listen, Lucifer. You have heard this often before, I know, but I want to be positive you understand in full. Your psychology must be very foreign to ours. Why did you agree to come with us? I don't know. Technician Waggoner said you were curious and adventurous. Is that the whole truth?

"No matter. In half an hour we jump. We'll come within five hundred million kilometers of the supernova. That's where your work begins. You can go where we dare not, observe what we can't, tell us more than our instruments would ever hint at. But first we have to verify we can stay in orbit around the star. This concerns you too. Dead men can't transport you home again.

"So. In order to enclose you within the jumpfield, without disrupting your body, we have to switch off the shield screens. We'll emerge in a lethal radiation zone. You must promptly retreat from the ship, because we'll start the screen generator up sixty seconds after transit. Then you must investigate the vicinity. The hazards to look for—" Szili listed them. "Those are only what we can foresee. Perhaps we'll hit other garbage we haven't predicted. If anything seems like a menace, return at once, warn us, and prepare for a jump back to here. Do you have that? Repeat."

Words jerked from Eloise. They were a correct recital; but how much was she leaving out?

"Very good." Szili hesitated. "Proceed with your concert if you like. But break it off at zero minus ten minutes and stand by."

"Yes, sir." She didn't look at him. She didn't appear to be looking anywhere in particular.

His footsteps clacked down the corridor and were lost.

—Why did he say the same things over? asked Lucifer.

"He is afraid," Eloise said.

—?—.

"I guess you don't know about fear," she said.

—Can you show me? . . . No, do not. I sense it is hurtful. You must not be hurt.

"I can't be afraid anyway, when your mind is holding mine."

(Warmth filled her. Merriment was there, playing like little flames over the surface of Father-leading-her-by-the-hand-when-she-was-just-a-child-and-they-went-out-one-summer's-day-to-pick-wildflowers; over strength and gentleness and Bach and God.) Lucifer swept around the hull in an exuberant curve. Sparks danced in his wake.

—Think flowers again. Please.

She tried.

—They are like (image, as nearly as a human brain could grasp, of fountains blossoming with gamma-ray colors in the middle of light, everywhere light). But so tiny. So brief a sweetness.

"I don't understand how you can understand," she whispered.

—You understand for me. I did not have that kind of thing to love, before you came.

"But you have so much else. I try to share it, but I'm not made to realize what a star is."

—Nor I for planets. Yet ourselves may touch.

Her cheeks burned anew. The thought rolled on, interweaving its counterpoint to the marching music.—That is why I came, do you know? For you. I am fire and air. I had not tasted the coolness of water, the patience of earth, until you showed me. You are moonlight on an ocean.

"No, don't," she said. "Please."

Puzzlement:—Why not? Does joy hurt? Are you not used to it?

"I, I guess that's right." She flung her head back. "No! Be damned if I'll feel sorry for myself!"

—Why should you? Have we not all reality to be in, and is it not full of suns and songs?

"Yes. To you. Teach me."

—If you in turn will teach me—The thought broke off. A contact remained, unspeaking, such as she imagined must often prevail among lovers.

She glowered at Motilal Mazundar's chocolate face, where the physicist stood in the doorway. "What do you want?"

He was surprised. "Only to see if everything is well with you, Miss Waggoner."

She bit her lip. He had tried harder than most aboard to be kind to her. "I'm sorry," she said. "I didn't mean to bark at you. Nerves."

"We are everyone on edge." He smiled. "Exciting though this venture is, it will be good to come home, correct?"

Home, she thought: four walls of an apartment above a banging city street. Books and television. She might present a paper at the next scientific meeting, but no one would invite her to the parties afterward.

Am I that horrible? she wondered. I know I'm not anything to look at, but I try to be nice and interesting. Maybe I try too hard.

—You do not with me, Lucifer said.

"You're different," she told him.

Mazundar blinked. "Beg pardon?"

"Nothing," she said in haste.

"I have wondered about an item," Mazundar said in an effort at conversation. "Presumably Lucifer will go quite near the supernova. Can you still maintain contact with him? The time dilation effect, will that not change the frequency of his thoughts too much?"

"What time dilation?" She forced a chuckle. "I'm no physicist. Only a little librarian who turned out to have a wild talent."

"You were not told? Why, I assumed everybody was. An intense gravitational field affects time just as a high velocity does. Roughly speaking, processes take place more slowly than they do in clear space. That is why light from a massive star is somewhat reddened. And our supernova core retains almost three solar masses. Furthermore, it has acquired such a density that its attraction at the surface is, ah, incredibly high. Thus by our clocks it will take infinite time to shrink to the Schwartzchild radius; but an observer on the star itself would experience this whole shrinkage in a fairly short period."

"Schwartzchild radius? Be so good as to explain." Eloise realized that Lucifer had spoken through her.

"If I can without mathematics. You see, this mass we are to study is so great and so concentrated that no force exceeds the gravitational. Nothing can counterbalance. Therefore, the process will continue until no energy can escape. The star will have vanished out of the universe. In fact, theoretically the contraction will proceed to zero volume. Of course, as I said, that will take forever as far as we are concerned. And the theory neglects quantum-mechanical considerations which come into play toward the end. Those are still not very well understood. I hope, from this expedition, to acquire more knowledge." Mazundar shrugged. "At any rate, Miss Waggoner, I was wondering if the frequency shift involved would not prevent our friend from communicating with us when he is near the star."

"I doubt that." Still Lucifer spoke, she was his instrument and never had she known how good it was to be used by one who cared. "Telepathy is not a wave phenomenon. Since it transmits instantaneously, it cannot be. Nor does it appear limited by distance. Rather, it is a resonance. Being attuned, we two may well be able to continue thus across the entire breadth of the cosmos; and I am not aware of any material phenomenon which could interfere."

"I see." Mazundar gave her a long look. "Thank you," he said uncomfortably. "Ah . . . I must get to my own station. Good luck." He bustled off without stopping for an answer.

Eloise didn't notice. Her mind was become a torch and a song. "Lucifer!" she cried aloud. "Is that true?"

—I believe so. My entire people are telepaths, hence we have more knowledge of such matters than yours do. Our experience leads us to think there is no limit.

"You can always be with me? You always will?"

—If you so wish, I am gladdened.

The comet body curvetted and danced, the brain of fire laughed low.—Yes, Eloise, I would like very much to remain with you. No one else has ever—Joy. Joy. Joy.

They named you better than they knew, Lucifer, she wanted to say, and perhaps she did. They thought it was a joke; they thought by calling you after the devil they could make you safely small like themselves. But Lucifer isn't the devil's real name. It means only Light Bearer. One Latin prayer even addresses Christ as Lucifer. Forgive me, God, I can't help remembering that. Do you mind? He isn't Christian, but I think he doesn't need to be, I think he must never have felt sin, Lucifer, Lucifer.

She sent the music soaring for as long as she was permitted.

The ship jumped. In one shift of world line parameters she crossed twenty-five light-years to destruction.

Each knew it in his own way, save for Eloise who also lived it with Lucifer.

She felt the shock and heard the outraged metal scream, she smelled the ozone and scorch and tumbled through the infinite that is weightlessness. Dazed, she fumbled at the intercom. Words crackled through: ". . . unit blown . . . back EMF surge . . . how should I know how long to fix the blasted thing? . . . stand by, stand by . . ." Over all hooted the emergency siren.

Terror rose in her, until she gripped the crucifix around her neck and the mind of Lucifer. Then she laughed in the pride of his might.

He had whipped clear of the ship immediately on arrival. Now he floated in the same orbit. Everywhere around, the nebula filled space with unrestful rainbows. To him, *Raven* was not the metal cylinder which human eyes would have seen, but a lambence, the shield screen reflecting a whole spectrum. Ahead lay the supernova core, tiny at this remove but alight, alight.

—Have no fears (he caressed her). I comprehend. Turbulence is extensive, so soon after the detonation. We emerged in a region where the plasma is especially dense. Unprotected for the moment before the guardian field was reestablished, your main generator outside the hull was short-circuited. But you are safe. You can make repairs. And I, I am in an ocean of energy. Never was I so alive. Come, swim these tides with me.

Captain Szili's voice yanked her back. "Waggoner! Tell that Aurigean to get busy. We've spotted a radiation source on an intercept orbit, and it may be too much for our screen." He specified coordinates. "What *is* it?"

For the first time, Eloise felt alarm in Lucifer. He curved about and streaked from the ship.

Presently his thought came to her, no less vivid. She lacked words for the terrible splendor she viewed with him: a million-kilometer ball of ionized gas where luminance blazed and electric discharges leaped, booming through the haze around the star's exposed heart. The thing could not have made any sound, for space here was still almost a vacuum by Earth's parochial standards; but she heard it thunder, and felt the fury that spat from it.

She said for him: "A mass of expelled material. It must have lost radial velocity to friction and static gradients, been drawn into a cometary orbit, held together for a while by internal potentials. As if this sun were trying yet to bring planets to birth—"

"It'll strike us before we're in shape to accelerate," Szili said, "and overload our shield. If you know any prayers, use them."

"Lucifer!" she called; for she did not want to die, when he must remain.

—I think I can deflect it enough, he told her with a grimness she had not hitherto met in him.—My own fields, to mesh with its; and free energy to drink; and an unstable configuration; yes, perhaps I can help you. But help me, Eloise. Fight by my side.

His brightness moved toward the juggernaut shape.

She felt how its chaotic electromagnetism clawed at his. She felt him tossed and torn. The pain was hers. He battled to keep his own cohesion, and the combat was hers. They locked together, Aurigean and gas cloud. The forces that shaped him grappled as arms might; he poured power from his core, hauling that vast tenuous mass with him down the magnetic torrent which streamed from the sun; he gulped atoms and thrust them backward until the jet splashed across heaven.

She sat in her cubicle, lending him what will to live and prevail she could, and beat her fists bloody on the desk.

The hours brawled past.

In the end, she could scarcely catch the message that flickered out of his exhaustion:—Victory.

"Yours," she wept.

—Ours.

Through instruments, men saw the luminous death pass them by. A cheer lifted.

"Come back," Eloise begged.

—I cannot. I am too spent. We are merged, the cloud and I, and are tumbling in toward the star. (Like a hurt hand reaching forth to comfort her:) Do not be afraid for me. As we get closer, I will draw fresh strength from its glow, fresh substance from the nebula. I will need a while to spiral out against that pull. But how can I fail to come back to you, Eloise? Wait for me. Rest. Sleep.

Her shipmates led her to sickbay. Lucifer sent her dreams of fire flowers and mirth and the suns that were his home.

But she woke at last, screaming. The medic had to put her under heavy sedation.

He had not really understood what it would mean to confront something so violent that space and time themselves were twisted thereby.

His speed increased appallingly. That was in his own measure; from *Raven* they saw him fall through several days. The properties of matter were changed. He could not push hard enough or fast enough to escape.

Radiation, stripped nuclei, particles born and destroyed and born again, sleeted and shouted through him. His substance was peeled away, layer by layer. The supernova core was a white delirium before him. It shrank as he approached, ever smaller, denser, so brilliant that brilliance ceased to have meaning. Finally the gravitational forces laid their full grip upon him.

—Eloise! he shrieked in the agony of his disintegration.—Oh, Eloise, help me!

The star swallowed him up. He was stretched infinitely long, compressed infinitely thin, and vanished with it from existence.

The ship prowled the farther reaches. Much might yet be learned.

Captain Szili visited Eloise in sickbay. Physically she was recovering.

"I'd call him a man," he declared through the machine mumble, "except that's not praise enough. We weren't even his kin, and he died to save us."

She regarded him from eyes more dry than seemed natural. He could just make out her answer. "He is a man. Doesn't he have an immortal soul too?"

"Well, uh, yes, if you believe in souls, yes, I'd agree."

She shook her head. "But why can't he go to his rest?"

He glanced about for the medic and found they were alone in the narrow metal room. "What do you mean?" He made himself pat her hand. "I know, he was a good friend of yours. Still, his must have been a merciful death. Quick, clean; I wouldn't mind going out like that."

"For him . . . yes, I suppose so. It has to be. But—" She could not continue. Suddenly she covered her ears. "Stop! Please!"

Szili made soothing noises and left. In the corridor he encountered Mazundar. "How is she?" the physicist asked.

The captain scowled. "Not good. I hope she doesn't crack entirely before we can get her to a psychiatrist."

"Why, what is wrong?"

"She thinks she can hear him."

Mazundar smote fist into palm. "I hoped otherwise," he breathed.

Szili braced himself and waited.

"She does," Mazundar said. "Obviously she does."

"But that's impossible! He's dead!"

"Remember the time dilation," Mazundar replied. "He fell from the sky and perished swiftly, yes. But in supernova time. Not the same as ours. To us, the final stellar collapse takes an infinite number of years. And telepathy has no distance limits." The physicist started walking fast, away from that cabin. "He will always be with her."

KILLING VECTOR

Charles Sheffield

An Englishman by birth, Charles Sheffield is one of the newest science fiction writers. By trade he is an engineer and physicist working in satellite communications, and he seems to be familiar with everything going on in his sciences. Like Anderson he is a craftsman, and you can rely on his work.

He can also tell stories.

Everyone on the Control Stage found a reason to be working aft when Yifter came on board. There was maximum security, of course, so no one could get really close without a good reason. Even so, we all took the best look we could manage—after all, you don't often have a chance to see a man who has killed a billion people.

Bryson, from the Planetary Coordinators' office, was at Yifter's elbow. The two men weren't shackled together, or anything melodramatic like that. Past a certain level of notoriety, criminals are treated with some deference and even respect. Bryson and Yifter were talking together in a friendly way, although they were in the middle of a group of toprank security men, all heavily armed and watchful. They were taking safety to extremes. When I stepped forward to greet Bryson and his prisoner, two guards carefully frisked me before I could get within hand-kill range, and they stood close behind me when the introductions were made. I haven't been on Earth for a long time, and they must have known that I have no close relatives there; but they were taking no chances. Yifter was a prime target for personal revenge. A billion people leave a lot of friends and relatives.

From a distance of one meter, Yifter's appearance did not match his reputation. He was of medium height, slightly built, with bushy, prematurely white hair and mild, sad eyes. He smiled at me in a tired, tolerant way as Bryson introduced us.

"I am sorry, Captain Roker," he said. "Your ship will be filled with strangers on this trip. I'll do my best to keep out of your way and let you do your job."

I hoped he could live up to his words. Since I took over the runs to Titan, I've carried most things in the connected set of cargo spheres that make up the Assembly. Apart from the kernels, and we carry a few of those on the outbound leg of every trip, we've had livestock, mega-crystals, the gravity simulator, and the circus. That's right, the circus. They must have had a terrible agent, that's all I can say. I took them both ways, to Titan and back to L-5. Even with all that, Yifter was still a novelty item. After he had been caught and the rest of the

Lucies had gone underground, nobody had known quite what to do with him. He was Earth's hottest property, the natural target for a billion guns and knives. Until they decided how and when he would come to trial, they wanted him a long way from Earth. It was my job to deliver him to the Titan penal colony, and return him when they got themselves sorted out on Earth.

"I'll arrange for you and your guards to travel in a separate part of the Assembly," I said. "I assume that you will prefer privacy."

Yifter nodded agreeably, but Bryson wasn't having any.

"Captain Roker," he said. "Let me remind you that Mr Yifter has not been found guilty on any charge. On this journey, and until his trial, he will be treated with proper courtesy. I expect you to house both of us here in the Control Stage, and I expect that you will invite us to take our meals here with you."

In principle, I could have told him to go and take a walk outside. As captain, I said who would travel in the Control Stage, and who would eat with me—and innocent people were not usually sent to the Titan penal colony, even before their trial. On the other hand. Bryson was from the Planetary Coordinators' office, and even off-Earth that carried weight.

I suppressed my first reaction and said quietly, "What about the guards?"

"They can travel in the Second Section, right behind the Control Stage," replied Bryson.

I shrugged. If he wanted to make nonsense of Earth's security efforts, that was his choice. Nothing had ever happened on any of my two-month runs from Earth to Titan, and Bryson was probably quite right; nothing would happen this time. On the other hand, it seemed like a damned silly charade, to ship twenty-five guards to keep an eye on Yifter, then house them in a separate part of the Assembly.

Yifter, with an uncanny empathy, had read through my shrug. "Don't worry about security, Captain Roker," he said. He smiled again, that tired, soothing smile that began deep in his sad, brown eyes. "You have my assurance, I will be a model prisoner."

He and Bryson walked on past me, into the main quarters. Was that really Yifter, the bogey-man, the notorious head of the Hallucinogenic Freedom League? It seemed hard to believe. Three months earlier, the Lucies—under Yifter's messianic direction—had planted hallucinogenic drugs in the water supply lines of most of Earth's major cities. An eighth of the world had died in the resulting chaos. Starvation, epidemic, exposure and mindless combat had re-visited the Earth and exacted their age-old tribute. The monster who had conceived, planned and directed that horror was difficult to match with Yifter, the seemingly mild and placid man.

My thoughts were quickly diverted to more immediate practical matters. We had the final masses of all the cargo, and it was time for the final balancing of the whole Assembly. One might assume that means just balancing the kernels correctly, since they out-mass everything else by a factor of a million. But each Section containing a kernel has an independent drive unit, powered by the kernel itself. We leave those on Titan, and travel back light, but on the trip out the dynamic balancing is quite tricky.

I reviewed the final configuration, then looked around for McAndrew. I wanted him to look over the balance calculations. It's my responsibility, but he was the kernel expert. I realized that he hadn't been present when Yifter came aboard. Presumably he was over on one of the other Sections, crooning over his beloved power sources.

I found him in Section Seven. The Assembly is made up of a variable number of Sections, and there would be twelve on this trip, plus the Control Stage. Until we accelerate away from the Libration Colony station, all the Sections are physically connected—with actual cables—to each other and to the Control Stage. In flight, the coupling is done electromagnetically, and the drives for the powered Sections are all controlled by a computer on the

Control Stage. The Assembly looks like a small bunch of grapes, but the stalks are non-functional—there are no cables in the System that could take the strains, even at lowest acceleration. Moving among the spherical Sections when we're in flight isn't easy. It means we have to cut the drives, and turn off the coupling between the Sections. That's why I thought the idea of having Yifter's guards in a different Section was so dumb—from there, they couldn't even reach the Control Stage when the drives were on.

I wanted McAndrew to check the configuration that we would hold in flight, to see if he agreed that the stresses were decently balanced among the different Sections. We never run near the limit on any of them, but there's a certain pride of workmanship in getting them all approximately equal, and the stresses as low as possible.

He was standing on the ten-meter shield that surrounded the Section Seven kernel, peering through a long boresight pointed in towards the center. He was aware of my presence but did not move or speak until the observation was complete. Finally he nodded in satisfaction, closed the boresight cap, and turned to me.

"Just checking the optical scalars," he said. "Spun up nicely, this one. So, what can I do for you, Captain?"

I led him outside the second shield before I handed him the trim calculations. I know a kernel shield has never failed, but I'm still not comfortable when I get too close to one. I once asked McAndrew how he felt about working within ten meters of Hell, where you could actually feel the gravity gradient and the inertial dragging. He looked at me with his little, introspective smile, and made a sort of throat-clearing noise—the only trace of his ancestry that I could ever find in him.

"Och," he said. "The shields are triply protected. They won't fail."

That would have reassured me, but then he had rubbed his high, balding forehead and added, "And if they do, it won't make any difference if you are ten meters away, or five hundred. That kernel would radiate at about two gigawatts, most of it high-energy gammas."

The trouble was, he always had the facts right. When I first met McAndrew, seven years earlier, we were taking the first shipment of kernels out to Titan. He had showed up with them, and I assumed that he was just another engineer—a good one, maybe, but I expected that. Five minutes of conversation with him told me that he had probably forgotten more about Kerr-Newman black holes —kernels—than I was ever likely to learn. I have degrees in Electrical Engineering and Gravitational Engineering, in my job I have to, but I'm really no gravity specialist. I felt like an idiot after our first talk. I made a few inquiries, and found that McAndrew was a full professor at the Penrose Institute, and probably the System's leading expert on space-time structure.

When we got to know each other better, I asked him why he would give up his job for four months of the year, to ride herd on a bunch of kernels being shipped around the Solar System. It was a milk-run, with lots of time and very little to do. Most people would be bored silly.

"I need it," he said simply. "It's very nice to work with colleagues, but in my line of business the real stuff is mostly worked out alone. And I can do experiments here that wouldn't be allowed back home."

After that, I accepted his way of working, and took vicarious pride in the stream of papers that appeared from McAndrew at the end of each Titan run. He was no trouble on the trips. He spent most of his time in the Sections carrying the kernels, only appearing in the Control Stage for his meals—and frequently missing them. He was a tinkerer as well as a theorist. Isaac Newton was his idol. His work had paid off in higher shielding efficiencies, better energy extraction methods, and more sensitive manipulation of the charged kernels. Each trip, we had something new.

I left the trim calculations with him, and he promised to check them over and give me his comments in an hour or two. I had to move along and check the rest of the cargo.

"By the way," I said, elaborately casual as I turned to go. "We'll be having company for dinner on this trip. Bryson insists that Yifter should eat with us."

He stood quietly for a moment, head slightly bowed. Then he nodded and ran his hand over his sandy, receding hair-line.

"That sounds like Bryson," he said. "Well, I doubt if Yifter will eat any of us for breakfast. I'm not sure he'll be any worse than the rest of you. I'll be there."

I breathed a small sigh of relief, and left him. McAndrew, as I knew from experience, was the Compleat Pacifist. I had wanted to be sure that he could stand the idea of meals with Yifter.

Four hours later, all our checks were complete. I switched on the fields. The dull grey exterior of each Section turned to silver, shattering the sunlight and turning the Assembly to a cluster of brilliants. The cables linking the Sections were still in position, but now they were hanging loose. All stresses had been picked up by the balancing fields. In the Control Stage, I gradually turned on the propulsion units of each powered Section. Plasma was fed through the ergosphere of each kernel, picked up energy, and streamed aft. The relative positions of the Sections, Mössbauer-controlled to within fractions of a micrometer, held steady. We accelerated slowly away from L-5, and began the long spiral of a continuous-impulse orbit to Titan.

My work was just about finished until crossover time. The computers monitored the drive feeds, the accelerations, and all the balance of the Sections. On this trip, we had three units without operating drive units: Section Two, where Yifter's guards were housed, just behind the Control Stage; Section Seven, where McAndrew had taken the kernel out of commission for his usual endless and mysterious experiments; and of course, the Control Stage itself. I had made the mistake of asking McAndrew what experiments he was planning for this trip. He looked at me with his innocent blue eyes and scribbled an answer full of twistor diagrams and spinor notation—knowing damn well that I wouldn't be able to follow it. He didn't like to talk about his work "half-cooked", as he put it.

I had been more worried than I wanted to admit about dinner on that first ship-evening. I knew we would all be itching to ask Yifter about the Lucies, but there was no easy way to introduce the subject into the conversation. How could we do it? "By the way, I hear that you killed a billion people a few months ago. I wonder if you would like to say a few words on the subject? It would liven up the table-talk at dinner." I could foresee that our conversation might be a little strained.

As it turned out, my worries were unnecessary. The first impression that I'd had of Yifter, of a mild and amiable man, strengthened on longer exposure. It was Bryson, during dinner, who caused the first tricky moment.

"Most of Earth's problems are caused by the United Space Federation's influence," he said as the robo-server, always on best form at the beginning of the trip, rolled in the courses. "If it weren't for the USF, there wouldn't be as much discontent and rioting on Earth. It's all relative, living space and living standards, and the USF sets a bad example. We can't compete."

According to Bryson, three million people were causing all the problems for seven billion—eight, before Yifter's handiwork. It was sheer nonsense, and as a USF citizen, I should have been the one to bridle; but it was McAndrew who made a growling noise of disapproval, down in his throat; and it was Yifter, of all people, who sensed the atmosphere quickest, and deftly steered the conversation to another subject.

"I think Earth's worst problems are caused by the power shortage," he said. "That affects everything else. Why doesn't Earth use the kernels for power, the way that the USF does?"

"Too afraid of an accident," replied McAndrew. His irritation evaporated immediately at the mention of his specialty. "If the shields ever failed, you would have a Kerr-Newman black hole sitting there, pumping out a thousand megawatts—mostly as high-energy radiation and fast particles. Worse than that, it would pull in free charge and become electrically neutral. As soon as that happened, there'd be no way to hold it electromagnetically. It would sink down and orbit inside the Earth. We couldn't afford to have that happen."

"But couldn't we use smaller kernels on Earth?" asked Yifter. "They would be less dangerous."

McAndrew shook his head. "It doesn't work that way. The smaller the black hole, the higher the effective temperature and the faster it radiates. You'd be better off with a much more massive black hole. But then you've got the problem of supporting it against Earth's gravity. Even with the best electromagnetic control, anything that massive would sink down into the Earth."

"I suppose it wouldn't help to use a non-rotating, uncharged hole, either," said Yifter. "That might be easier to work with."

"A Schwartzchild hole?" McAndrew looked at him in disgust. "Now, Mr Yifter, you know better than that." He grew eloquent. "A Schwartzchild hole gives you no control at all. You can't get a hold of it electromagnetically. It just sits there, spewing out energy all over the spectrum, and there's nothing you can do to change it—unless you want to charge it and spin it up, and make it into a kernel. With the kernels, now, you have control."

I tried to interrupt, but McAndrew was just getting warmed up. "A Schwartzchild hole is like a naked flame," he went on. "A caveman's device. A kernel is *refined,* it's controllable. You can spin it up and store energy, or you can use the ergosphere to pull energy out and spin it down. You can use the charge on it to move it about as you want. It's a real working instrument—not a bit of crudity from the Dark Ages."

I shook my head, and sighed in simulated despair. "McAndrew, you have an unconsummated love affair with those blasted kernels." I turned to Yifter and Bryson, who had watched McAndrew's outburst with some surprise. "He spends all his waking hours spinning those things up and down. All the last trip, he was working the kernels in gravitational focusing experiments. You know, using the fact that a gravity field bends light rays. He insists that one day we won't use lenses for optics—we'll focus light using arrays of kernels."

I made the old joke. "We hardly saw him on that trip. We were convinced that one day he'd get careless with the shields, fall into one of the kernels, and really make a spectacle of himself."

They didn't get it. Yifter and Bryson looked at me blankly, while McAndrew, who'd heard it all ten times before, chuckled. We have the same sense of humor—a bad joke is always funny, even if it's the hundredth time you've heard it told.

It's a strange thing, but after the first half-hour I had stopped thinking of Yifter as our prisoner. I could understand now why Bryson had objected to the idea of surrounding Yifter with armed guards. I'd have objected myself. He seemed the most civilized man in the group, with a warm personality and a very dry and subtle sense of humor.

When Bryson left the table, pleading a long day and a lack of familiarity with a space environment, Yifter, McAndrew and I stayed on, chatting about the previous trips I had made to Titan. I mentioned the time I had taken the circus.

"Do you know, I'd never seen most of those animals before," I said. "They were all on the list of endangered species. I don't think you could find them on Earth any more, except in a circus or a zoo."

There was a moment of silence, then Yifter spoke. His eyes were mild and smiling, and his voice sounded dreamy and distant.

"Endangered species," he said. "That's the heart of it. Earth has no room for failures. The weaker species, like weaker specimens of a species, must be eliminated. Only the strong—the mentally strong—may survive. The weak must be culled, for our own sake; whether that means one tenth, one half, or nine tenths of the total."

There was a chilling pause. I looked at Yifter, whose expression had not changed, then at McAndrew, whose face reflected the horror that I was feeling. Yet behind all that, I could feel the unique power of the man. My mind was rejecting him, but I still had a sense of well-being, of warmth in the pit of my stomach, as he was speaking.

"We have made a beginning," went on Yifter quietly. "Just a beginning. Last time we were less successful than I had hoped. We had a breakdown in the distribution system for the drugs. I managed to eliminate the responsible individuals, but it was too late to correct the problem. Next time, God willing, it will be different."

He rose to his feet, white hair shining like silver, face beatific. "Good night, Captain. Good night, Professor McAndrew. Sleep well."

After he had left, McAndrew and I sat and looked at each other for a long time. Finally, he broke the spell.

"Now we know, Captain. We should have guessed it from the beginning. Mad as a hatter. The man's a raving lunatic. Completely psychotic."

That said most of it. McAndrew had used up all the good phrases. I nodded.

"But did you feel the strength in him?" went on McAndrew. "Like a big magnet."

I was glad that the penal colony was so far from Earth, and the avenues of communication so well-guarded. "Next time . . . it will be different." Our two-month trip suddenly seemed to have doubled in length.

After that single, chilling moment, there were no more shocks for some time. Our regular meal-time conversations continued, and on several occasions McAndrew voiced views on pacifism and the protection of human life. Each time, I waited for Yifter's reply, expecting the worst. He never actually agreed with Mac—but he did not come out with any statement that resembled his comments of the first ship-evening.

We soon settled into the ship-board routine. McAndrew spent less and less time in the Control Stage, and more in Section Seven. On this trip, he brought a new set of equipment for his experiments, and I was very curious to know what he was up to. He wouldn't tell. I had only one clue. Section Seven was drawing enormous energy from the other kernels, in the rest of the Assembly. That energy could only be going to one place—into the kernel in Section Seven. I suspected that McAndrew must be spinning it up—making it closer to an "extreme" kernel, a Kerr-Newman black hole where the rotation energy matches the mass energy. I knew that couldn't be the whole story. McAndrew had spun up the kernels before, and he had told me that there was no direct way of getting a really extreme kernel—that would take an infinite amount of energy. This time, he was doing something different. He insisted that Section Seven had to be off-limits to everybody.

I couldn't get him to talk about it. There would be a couple of seconds of silence from him, then he would stand there, cracking his finger joints as though he was snapping out a coded message to me. He could be a real sphinx when he chose.

Two weeks from Earth, we were drawing clear of the main Asteroid Belt. I had just about concluded that my worries for the trip were over, when the radar reported another ship, closing slowly with us from astern. Its spectral signature identified it as the *Lesotho,* a cruise liner that usually ran trajectories in the Inner System. It was braodcasting a Mayday, and flying free under zero drive power.

I thought about it for a moment, then posted Emergency Stations throughout the Assembly. The computed trajectory showed that we would match velocities at a separation of three kilometers. That was incredibly close, far too close to be accidental. After closest approach, we would pull away again—we were still under power, accelerating outward, and would leave the *Lesotho* behind.

I was still watching the displays, trying to decide whether or not to take the next step—shutting off the drives—when Bryson appeared, with Yifter just behind him.

"Captain Roker," he said, in his usual imperious manner. "That's an Earth ship there, giving you a distress signal. Why aren't you doing anything about it?"

"If we waited just a few minutes," I said. "We'll be within spitting distance of her. I see no point in rushing in, until we've had a good look at her. I can't think what an Inner System ship would be doing, free-falling out here beyond the Belt."

That didn't cool him. "Can't you recognize an emergency when you see one?" he said. "If you won't do something productive with your people, I'll do something with mine."

I wondered what he wanted me to do, but he walked away from me without saying anything more, down the stairs that led to the rear communication area of the Control Stage. I turned back to the displays. The *Lesotho* was closing on us steadily, and now I could see that her locks were open. I cut our propulsion to zero and switched off all the drives. The other ship was tumbling slowly, drive lifeless and aft nacelles crumpled. Even from this distance, I could see that she would need extensive repairs before she could function again.

I was beginning to think that I had been over-cautious when two things happened. Yifter's guards, who had been housed behind the Control Stage in Section Two, began to float into view on the viewing screen that pointed towards the *Lesotho*. They were all in space armor and heavily weaponed. At the same time two suited figures appeared in the open forward lock of the other vessel. I cut in the suit frequencies on our main board.

"—shield failure," said the receiver. "Twenty-seven survivors, and bad injuries. We must have pain-killers, medical help, water, food, oxygen and power-packs."

With that, one group of our guards outside began to move towards the two suited figures in the *Lesotho*'s lock, while the remainder stayed close to the Assembly, looking across at the other ship. Subconsciously, I noted the number of our guards in each party, then gave them my full attention and did a rapid re-count. Twenty-five. All our guards. I swore and cut in the transmitter.

"Sergeant, get half of those men back inside the Assembly shields. This is Captain Roker. I'm over-riding any other orders you may have received. Get the nearer party—"

I was interrupted. The display screen flashed blue-white, then over-loaded. The whole Control Stage rang like a great bell, as something slapped hard on the outer shield. I knew what it was: a huge pulse of hard radiation and highly energetic particles, smashing into us in a fraction of a microsecond.

Yifter had been floating within a couple of meters of me, watching the screens. He put his hand to the wall to orient himself as the Control Stage vibrated violently. "What was that?"

"Thermonuclear explosion," I said shortly. "Hundred megaton plus. On the *Lesotho*."

All the screens on that side were dead. I activated the standby system. The *Lesotho* had vanished. The guards had vanished with it, vaporized instantly. All the cables linking the parts of the Assembly, all the scanners and sensors that were not protected behind the shields, were gone. The Sections themselves were intact, but their coupling fields would have to be completely recalibrated. We wouldn't be arriving at Titan on schedule.

I looked again at Yifter. His face was now calm and thoughtful. He seemed to be waiting, listening expectantly. For what? If the *Lesotho* had been a suicide mission, manned by volunteers who sought revenge on Yifter, they hadn't had a chance. They couldn't destroy the Assembly, or get at Yifter. If revenge were not the purpose, what *was* the purpose?

I ran through in my mind the events of the past hour. With the drives switched off in the Assembly, we had an unprotected blind spot, dead astern. We had been putting all our attention on the *Lesotho*. Now, with the guards all dead, the Control Stage was undefended.

It was quicker to go aft and take a look, than to call Bryson or McAndrew and ask them what they could see from the rear viewing screens of the Control Stage. Leaving Yifter, I dived head-first down the stairway—a risky maneuver if there were any chance that the drive might come back on, but I was sure it couldn't.

It took me about thirty seconds to travel the length of the Control Stage. By the time that I was half-way, I knew I had been thinking much too slowly. I heard the clang of a lock, a shout, and the sputtering crackle of a hand laser against solid metal. When I got to the rear compartment, it was all finished. Bryson, pale and open-mouthed, was floating against one wall. He seemed unhurt. McAndrew had fared less well. He was ten meters further along, curled into a fetal ball. Floating near him I saw a family of four stubby pink worms with red-brown heads, still unclenching with muscle spasm. I could also see the deep burn on his side and chest, and his right hand, from which a laser had neatly clipped the fingers and cauterized the wound instantly as it did so. At the far end of the room, braced against the wall, were five suited figures, all well-armed.

Heroics would serve no purpose. I spread my arms wide to show that I was not carrying a weapon, and one of the newcomers pushed off from the wall and floated past me, heading towards the front of the Control Stage. I moved over to McAndrew and inspected his wounds. They looked bad, but not fatal. Fortunately, laser wounds are very clean. I could see that we would have problems with his lung unless we treated him quickly. A lobe had been penetrated, and his breathing was slowly breaking the seal of crisped tissue that the laser had made. Blood was beginning to well through and stain his clothing.

McAndrew's forehead was beaded with sweat. As the shock of his wound wore off, the pain was beginning. I pointed to the medical belt of one of the invaders, who nodded and tossed an ampoule across to me. I injected McAndrew intravenously at the big vein inside his right elbow.

The figure who had pushed past me was returning, followed by Yifter. The face plate of the suit was now open, revealing a dark-haired woman in her early thirties. She looked casually at the scene, nodded at last, and turned back to Yifter.

"Everything's under control here," she said. "But we'll have to take a Section from the Assembly. The ship we were following in caught some of the blast from the *Lesotho*, and it's no good for powered flight now."

Yifter shook his head reprovingly. "Impatient as usual, Akhtar. I'll bet you were just too eager to get here. You must learn patience if you are to be of maximum value to us, my dear. Where did you leave the main group?"

"A few hours drive inward from here. We have waited for your rescue, before making any plans for the next phase."

Yifter, calm as ever, nodded approvingly. "The right decision. We can take a Section without difficulty. Most of them contain their own drives, but some are less effective than others."

He turned to me, smiling gently. "Captain Roker, which Section is the best equipped to carry us away from the Assembly? As you see, it is time for us to leave you and rejoin our colleagues."

His calm was worse than any number of threats. I floated next to McAndrew, trying to think of some way that we could delay or impede the Lucies' escape. It might take days for a rescue party to reach us. In that time, Yifter and his followers could be anywhere.

I hesitated. Yifter waited. "Come now," he said at last. "I'm sure you are as eager as I am to avoid any further annoyance"—he moved his hand, just a little, to indicate McAndrew and Bryson—"for your friends."

I shrugged. All the Sections contained emergency life-support systems, more than enough for a trip of a few hours. Section Two, where the guards had been housed, lacked a full, independent drive unit, but it was still capable of propulsion. I thought it might slow their escape enough for us somehow to track it.

"Section Two should be adequate," I said. "It housed your guards in comfort. Those poor devils certainly have no need for it now."

I paused. Beside me, McAndrew was painfully straightening from his contorted position. The drugs were beginning to work. He coughed, and red globules floated away across the room. That lung needed attention.

"No," he said faintly. "Not Two, Yifter. Seven. Section Seven."

He paused and coughed again, while I looked at him in surprise.

"Seven," he said at last. He looked at me. "No killing, Captain. No—Killing vector."

The woman was listening closely. She regarded both of us suspiciously. "What was all that about?"

My mouth was gaping open as wide as Bryson's. I had caught an idea of what McAndrew was trying to tell me, but I didn't want to say it. Fortunately, I was helped out by Yifter himself.

"No killing," he said. "My dear, you have to understand that Professor McAndrew is a devoted pacifist—and carrying his principles through admirably. He doesn't want to see any further killing. I think I can agree with that—for the present."

He looked at me and shook his head. "I won't inquire what dangers and drawbacks Section Two might contain,

Captain—though I do seem to recall that it lacks a decent drive unit. I think we'll follow the Professor's advice and take Section Seven. Akhtar is a very competent engineer, and I'm sure she'll have no trouble coupling the drive to the kernel."

He looked at us with a strange expression. If it didn't sound so peculiar, I'd describe it as wistful. "I shall miss our conversations," he said. "But I must say goodbye now. I hope that Professor McAndrew will recover. He is one of the strong—unless he allows himself to be killed by his unfortunate pacifist fancies. We may not meet again, but I am sure that you will be hearing about us in the next few months."

They left. McAndrew, Bryson and I watched the screens in silence, as the Lucies made their way over to Section Seven and entered it. Once they were inside, I went over to McAndrew and took him by the left arm.

"Come on," I said. "We have to get a patch on that lung."

He shook his head weakly. "Not yet. It can wait a few minutes. After that, it might not be necessary."

His forehead was beading with sweat again—and this time it was not from pain. I felt my own tension mounting steadily. We stayed by the display screen, and as the seconds ticked away my own forehead began to film with perspiration. We did not speak. I had one question, but I was terribly afraid of the answer I might get. I think that Bryson spoke to both of us several times. I have no idea what he said.

Finally, a pale nimbus grew at the rear of the Section Seven drive unit.

"Now," said McAndrew. "He's going to tap the kernel."

I stopped breathing. There was a pause of a few seconds, stretching to infinity, then the image on the screen rippled slightly. Suddenly, we could see stars shining through that area. Section Seven was gone, vanished, with no sign that it had ever existed.

McAndrew took in a long, pained breath, wincing as his injured lung expanded. Somehow, he managed a little smile.

"Well now," he said. "That answers a theoretical question that I've had on my mind for some time."

I could breathe again, too. "I didn't know what was going to happen there," I said. "I was afraid all the energy might come out of that kernel in one go."

McAndrew nodded. "To be honest, that thought was in my head, too. At this range, the shields would have been useless. We'd have gone like last year's lovers."

Bryson had been watching the whole thing in confusion. We had been ignoring him completely. At last, pale and irritable, he spoke to us again.

"What are you two talking about? And what's happened to the Section with Yifter in it? I was watching on the screen, then it just seemed to disappear."

"McAndrew tried to tell us earlier," I said. "But he didn't want the Lucies to know what he was getting at. He'd been fiddling with the kernel in that Section. You heard what he said—no Killing vector. I don't know what he did, but he fixed it so that the kernel in Section Seven had no Killing vector."

"I'm sure he did," said Bryson tartly. "Now perhaps you'll tell me what a Killing vector is."

"Well, Mac could tell you a lot better than I can. But a Killing vector is a standard sort of thing in relativity—I guess you never had any training in that. You get a Killing vector when a region of space-time has some sort of symmetry—say, about an axis of spin. And *every* sort of black hole, every sort of kernel we've ever encountered before, has at least one symmetry of that type. So if McAndrew had changed the kernel and made it into something with no Killing vector, it's like no kernel we've ever seen. Right, Mac?"

He looked dreamy. The drugs had taken hold. "I took it past the extreme Kerr-Newman form," he said. "Put it into a different form, metastable equilibrium. Event horizon had disappeared, all the Killing vectors had disappeared."

"Christ!" I hadn't expected that. "No event horizon? Doesn't that mean that you get——?"

McAndrew was still nodding, eye pupils dilated. "——a naked singularity. That's right, Captain. I had a naked singularity, sitting there in equilibrium in Section Seven. You don't get there by spinning-up—needs different method." His speech was slurring, as though his tongue was swollen. "Didn't know what would happen if somebody tried to tap it, to use for a drive. Either the signature of space-time there would change, from three space dimensions and one time, to two space and two time. Or we might see the System's biggest explosion. All the mass coming out as radiation, in one flash."

It was slowly dawning on Bryson what we were saying. "But just where is Yifter now?" he asked.

"Gone a long way," I said. "Right out of this universe."

"And he can't be brought back?" asked Bryson.

"I hope not." I'd seen more than enough of Yifter.

"But I'm supposed to deliver him safely to Titan," said Bryson. "I'm responsible for his safe passage. What am I going to tell the Planetary Coordinators?"

I didn't have too much sympathy. I was too busy looking at McAndrew's wounds. The fingers could be re-generated using the bio-feedback equipment on Titan, but the lung would need watching. It was still bleeding a little.

"Tell them you had a very singular experience," I said. McAndrew grunted as I probed the deep cut in his side. "Sorry, Mac. Have to do it. You know, you've ruined your reputation forever as far as I'm concerned. I thought you were a pacifist? All that preaching at us, then you send Yifter and his lot all the way to Hell—and good riddance to them."

McAndrew was drifting far away on his big dose of painkillers. He half-winked at me and made his curious throat-clearing noise.

"Och, I'm a pacifist all right. We pacifists have to look after each other. How could we ever hope for peace with people like Yifter around to stir up trouble? There's a bunch more of them, a few hours travel behind us. Fix me up quick. I should be tinkering with the other kernels a bit, just in case the other Lucies decide to pay us a visit, later . . ."

THE BORDERLAND OF SOL

Larry Niven

Niven, that rascal, wasn't satisfied to parlay our visit to Forward's labs into one Hugo-winner. No indeed, he had to write another—and this one beat one of my own stories.

I don't even have the satisfaction of showing that he's got the science wrong. If he did I couldn't admit it. He had me read this one before he sent it off.

I suppose I have to say it deserved its award.

Three months on Jinx, marooned.

I played tourist for the first couple of months. I never saw the high-pressure regions around the ocean because the only way down would have been with a safari of hunting tanks. But I traveled the habitable lands on either side of the sea, the East Band civilized, the West Band a developing frontier. I wandered the East End in a vacuum suit, toured the distilleries and other vacuum industries, and stared up into the orange vastness of Primary, Jinx's big twin brother.

I spent most of the second month between the Institute of Knowledge and the Camelot Hotel. Tourism had palled.

For me, that's unusual. I'm a born tourist. But—

Jinx's one point seven eight gravities put an unreasonable restriction on elegance and ingenuity in architectural design. The buildings in the habitable bands all look alike: squat and massive.

The East and West Ends, the vacuum regions, aren't that different from any industrialized moon. I never developed much of an interest in touring factories.

As for the ocean shorelines, the only vehicles that go there go to hunt Bandersnatchi. The Bandersnatchi are freaks: enormous, intelligent white slugs the size of mountains. They hunt the tanks. There are rigid restrictions to the equipment the tanks can carry, covenants established between men and Bandersnatchi, so that the Bandersnatchi win about forty percent of the duels. I wanted no part of that.

And all my touring had to be done in three times the gravity of my home world.

I spent the third month in Sirius Mater, and most of that in the Camelot Hotel, which has gravity generators in most of the rooms. When I went out I rode a floating contour couch. I passed like an invalid among the Jinxians, who were amused. Or was that my imagination?

I was in a hall of the Institute of Knowledge when I came on Carlos Wu running his fingertips over a Kdatlyno touch-sculpture.

A dark, slender man with narrow shoulders and

straight black hair, Carlos was lithe as a monkey in any normal gravity; but on Jinx he used a travel couch exactly like mine. He studied the busts with his head tilted to one side. And I studied the familiar back, sure it couldn't be him.

"Carlos, aren't you supposed to be on Earth?"

He jumped. But when the couch spun around he was grinning. "Bey! I might say the same for you."

I admitted it. "I was headed for Earth, but when all those ships started disappearing around Sol system the captain changed his mind and steered for Sirius. Nothing any of the passengers could do about it. What about you? How are Sharrol and the kids?"

"Sharrol's fine, the kids are fine, and they're all waiting for you to come home." His fingers were still trailing over the Lloobee touch-sculpture called *HEROES*, feeling the warm, fleshy textures. *HEROES* was a most unusual touch-sculpture; there were visual as well as textural effects. Carlos studied the two human busts, then said, "That's *your* face, isn't it?"

"Yah."

"Not that you ever looked that good in your life. How did a Kdatlyno come to pick Beowulf Shaeffer as a classic hero? Was it your name? And who's the other guy?"

"I'll tell you about it sometime. Carlos, what are you doing *here*?"

"I . . . I left Earth a couple of weeks after Louis was born." He was embarrassed. Why? "I haven't been off Earth in ten years. I needed the break."

But he'd left just before I was supposed to get home. And . . . hadn't someone once said that Carlos Wu had a touch of the flatland phobia? I began to understand what was wrong. "Carlos, you did Sharrol and me a valuable favor."

He laughed without looking at me. "Men have killed other men for such favors. I thought it was . . . tactful . . . to be gone when you came home."

Now I knew. Carlos was here because the Fertility

Board on Earth would not favor me with a parenthood license.

You can't really blame the Board for using any excuse at all to reduce the number of producing parents. I am an albino. Sharrol and I wanted each other; but we both wanted children, and Sharrol can't leave Earth. She has the flatland phobia, the fear of strange air and altered days and changed gravity and black sky beneath her feet.

The only solution we'd found had been to ask a good friend to help.

Carlos Wu is a registered genius with an incredible resistance to disease and injury. He carries an unlimited parenthood license, one of sixty-odd among Earth's eighteen billion people. He gets similar offers every week . . . but he is a good friend, and he'd agreed. In the last two years Sharrol and Carlos had had two children, who were now waiting on Earth for me to become their father.

I felt only gratitude for what he'd done for us. "I forgive you your odd ideas on tact," I said magnanimously. "Now. As long as we're stuck on Jinx, may I show you around? I've met some interesting people."

"You always do." He hesitated, then, "I'm not actually stuck on Jinx. I've been offered a ride home. I may be able to get you in on it."

"Oh, really? I didn't think there were any ships going to Sol system these days. Or leaving."

"This ship belongs to a government man. Ever heard of a Sigmund Ausfaller?"

"That sounds vaguely . . . Wait! Stop! The last time I saw Sigmund Ausfaller, he had just put a bomb aboard my ship.

Carlos blinked at me. "You're kidding."

"I'm not."

"Sigmund Ausfaller is in the Bureau of Alien Affairs. Bombing spacecraft isn't one of his functions."

"Maybe he was off duty," I said viciously.

"Well, it doesn't really sound like you'd want to share a spacecraft cabin with him. Maybe—"

But now I'd thought of something else, and now there just wasn't any way out of it. "No, let's meet him. Where do we find him?"

"The bar of the Camelot," said Carlos.

Reclining luxuriously on our travel couches, we slid on air cushions through Sirius Mater. The orange trees that lined the walks were foreshortened by gravity; their trunks were thick cones, and the oranges on the branches were not much bigger than ping pong balls.

Their world had altered them, even as our worlds have altered you and me. An underground civilization and point six gravities have made of me a pale stick-figure of a man, tall and attenuated. The Jinxians we passed were short and wide, designed like bricks, men and women both. Among them the occasional offworlder seemed as shockingly different as a Kdatlyno or a Pierson's puppeteer.

And so we came to the Camelot.

The Camelot is a low, two-story structure that sprawls like a cubistic octopus across several acres of downtown Sirius Mater. Most offworlders stay here, for the gravity control in the rooms and corridors and for access to the Institute of Knowledge, the finest museum and research complex in human space.

The Camelot Bar carries one Earth gravity throughout. We left our travel couches in the vestibule and walked in like men. Jinxians were walking in like bouncing rubber bricks, with big happy grins on their wide faces. Jinxians love low gravity. A good many migrate to other worlds.

We spotted Ausfaller easily: a rounded, moon-faced flatlander with thick, dark, wavy hair and a thin black mustache. He stood as we approached. "Beowulf Shaeffer!" he beamed. "How good to see you again! I believe it has been eight years or thereabouts. How have you been?"

"I lived," I told him.

Carlos rubbed his hands together briskly. "Sigmund! Why did you bomb Bey's ship?"

Ausfaller blinked in surprise. "Did he tell you it was his ship? It wasn't. He was thinking of stealing it. I reasoned that he would not steal a ship with a hidden time bomb aboard."

"But how did you come into it?" Carlos slid into the booth beside him. "You're not police. You're in the Extremely Foreign Relations Bureau."

"The ship belonged to General Products Corporation, which is owned by Pierson's puppeteers, not human beings."

Carlos turned on me. "Bey! Shame on you."

"Dammit! They were trying to blackmail me into a suicide mission! And Ausfaller let them get away with it! And that's the least convincing exhibition of tact I've ever seen!"

"Good thing they soundproof these booths," said Carlos. "Let's order."

Soundproofing field or not, people were staring. I sat down. When our drinks came I drank deep. Why had I mentioned the bomb at all?

Ausfaller was saying, "Well, Carlos, have you changed your mind about coming with me?"

"Yes, if I can take a friend."

Ausfaller frowned, looked at me. "You wish to reach Earth too?"

I'd made up my mind. "I don't think so. In fact, I'd like to talk you out of taking Carlos."

Carlos said, "Hey!"

I overrode him. "Ausfaller, do you know who Carlos *is*? He had an unlimited parenthood license at the age of eighteen. Eighteen! I don't mind you risking your own life, in fact I love the idea. But his?"

"It's not that big a risk!" Carlos snapped.

"Yah? What has Ausfaller got that eight other ships didn't have?"

"Two things," Ausfaller said patiently. "One is that we

will be incoming. Six of the eight ships that vanished were *leaving* Sol system. If there are pirates around Sol, they must find it much easier to locate an outgoing ship."

"They caught two incoming. Two ships, fifty crew members and passengers, gone. Poof!"

"They would not take me so easily," Ausfaller boasted. "The *Hobo Kelly* is deceptive. It seems to be a cargo and passenger ship, but it is a warship, armed and capable of thirty gees acceleration. In normal space we can run from anything we can't fight. We are assuming pirates, are we not? Pirates would insist on robbing a ship before they destroy it."

I was intrigued. "Why? Why a disguised warship? Are you *hoping* you'll be attacked?"

"If there are actually pirates, yes, I hope to be attacked. But not when entering Sol system. We plan a substitution. A quite ordinary cargo craft will land on Earth, take on cargo of some value, and depart for Wunderland on a straight-line course. My ship will replace it before it has passed through the asteroids. So you see, there is no risk of losing Mr. Wu's precious genes."

Palms flat to the table, arms straight, Carlos stood looming over us. "Diffidently I raise the point that they are my futzy genes and I'll do what I futzy please with them! Bey, I've already had my share of children, and yours too!"

"Peace, Carlos. I didn't mean to step on any of your inalienable rights." I turned to Ausfaller. "I still don't see why these disappearing ships should interest the Extremely Foreign Relations Bureau."

"There were alien passengers aboard some of the ships."

"Oh."

"And we have wondered if the pirates themselves are aliens. Certainly they have a technique not known to humanity. Of six outgoing ships, five vanished after reporting that they were about to enter hyperdrive."

I whistled. "They can precipitate a ship out of hyper-drive? That's impossible. Isn't it? Carlos?"

Carlos' mouth twisted. "Not if it's being done. But I don't understand the principle. If the ships were just disappearing, that'd be different. Any ship does that if it goes too deep into a gravity well on hyperdrive."

"Then . . . maybe it isn't pirates at all. Carlos, could there be living beings in hyperspace, actually eating the ships?"

"For all of me, there could. I don't know everything, Bey, contrary to popular opinion." But after a minute he shook his head. "I don't buy it. I might buy an uncharted mass on the fringes of Sol system. Ships that came too near in hyperdrive would disappear.

"No," said Ausfaller. "No single mass could have caused all of the disappearances. Charted or not, a planet is bounded by gravity and inertia. We ran computer simulations. It would have taken at least three large masses, all unknown, all moving into heavy trade routes, simultaneously."

"How large? Mars size or better?"

"So you have been thinking about this too."

Carlos smiled. "Yeah. It may sound impossible, but it isn't. It's only improbable. There are unbelievable amounts of garbage out there beyond Neptune. Four known planets and endless chunks of ice and stone and nickel-iron."

"Still, it is most improbable."

Carlos nodded. A silence fell.

I was still thinking about monsters in hyperspace. The lovely thing about that hypothesis was that you couldn't even estimate a probability. We knew too little.

Humanity has been using hyperdrive for almost four hundred years now. Few ships have disappeared in that time, except during wars. Now, eight ships in ten months, all around Sol system.

Suppose one hyperspace beast had discovered ships in this region, say during one of the Man-Kzin Wars? He'd gone to get his friends. Now they were preying around Sol system. The flow of ships around Sol is greater than that around any three colony stars. But if more monsters came, they'd surely have to move on to the other colonies.

I couldn't imagine a defense against such things. We might have to give up interstellar travel.

Ausfeller said, "I would be glad if you would change your mind and come with us, Mr Shaeffer."

"Um? Are you sure you want me on the same ship with you?"

"Oh, emphatically! How else may I be sure that you have not hidden a bomb aboard?" Ausfaller laughed. "Also, we can use a qualified pilot. Finally, I would like the chance to pick your brain, Beowulf Shaeffer. You have an odd facility for doing my job for me."

"What do you mean by that?"

"General Products used blackmail in persuading you to do a close orbit around a neutron star. You learned something about their home world—we still do not know what it was—and blackmailed them back. We know that blackmail contracts are a normal part of Puppeteer business practice. You earned their respect. You have dealt with them since. You have dealt also with Outsiders, without friction. But it was your handling of the Lloobee kidnapping that I found impressive."

Carlos was sitting at attention. I hadn't had a chance to tell him about that one yet. I grinned and said, "I'm proud of that myself."

"Well you should be. You did more than retrieve known space's top Kdatlyno touch-sculptor: you did it with honor, killing one of their number and leaving Lloobee free to pursue the others with publicity. Otherwise the Kdatlyno would have been annoyed."

Helping Sigmund Ausfaller had been the farthest thing from my thoughts for these past eight years; yet suddenly I felt damn good. Maybe it was the way Carlos was listening. It takes a lot to impress Carlos Wu.

Carlos said, "If you thought it was pirates, you'd come

along, wouldn't you, Bey? After all, they probably can't *find* incoming ships."

"Sure."

"And you don't really believe in hyperspace monsters."

I hedged. "Not if I hear a better explanation. The thing is, I'm not sure I believe in supertechnological pirates either. What about those wandering masses?"

Carlos pursed his lips, said, "All right. The solar system has a good number of planets—at least a dozen so far discovered, four of them outside the major singularity around Sol."

"And not including Pluto?"

"No, we think of Pluto as a loose moon of Neptune. It runs *Neptune, Persephone, Caïna, Antenora, Ptolemea*, in order of distance from the sun. And the orbits aren't flat to the plane of the system. Persephone is tilted at a hundred and twenty degrees to the system, and retrograde. If they find another planet out there they'll call it *Judecca*."

"Why?"

"Hell. The four innermost divisions of Dante's Hell. They form a great ice plain with sinners frozen into it."

"Stick to the point," said Ausfaller.

"Start with the cometary halo," Carlos told me. "It's very thin: about one comet per spherical volume of the Earth's orbit. Mass is denser going inward: a few planets, some inner comets, some chunks of ice and rock, all in skewed orbits and still spread pretty thin. Inside Neptune there are lots of planets and asteroids and more flattening of orbits to conform with Sol's rotation. Outside Neptune space is vast and empty. There *could* be uncharted planets. Singularities to swallow ships."

Ausfaller was indignant. "But for three to move into main trade lanes simultaneously?"

"It's not impossible, Sigmund."

"The probability—"

"Infinitesimal, right. Bey, it's damn near impossible. Any sane man would assume pirates."

It had been a long time since I had seen Sharrol. I was sore tempted. "Ausfaller, have you traced the sale of any of the loot? Have you gotten any ransom notes?" *Convince me!*

Ausfaller threw back his head and laughed.

"What's funny?"

"We have hundreds of ransom notes. Any mental deficient can write a ransom note, and these disappearances have had a good deal of publicity. The demands were all fakes. I wish one or another had been genuine. A son of the Patriarch of Kzin was aboard *Wayfarer* when she disappeared. As for loot—hmm. There has been a fall in the black market prices of boosterspice and gem woods. Otherwise—" He shrugged. "There has been no sign of the Barr originals or the Midas Rock or any of the more conspicuous treasures aboard the missing ships."

"Then you don't know one way or another."

"No. Will you go with us?"

"I haven't decided yet. When are you leaving?"

They'd be taking off tomorrow morning from the East End. That gave me time to make up my mind.

After dinner I went back to my room, feeling depressed. Carlos was going, that was clear enough. Hardly my fault . . . but he was here on Jinx because he'd done me and Sharrol a large favor. If he was killed going home . . .

A tape from Sharrol was waiting in my room. There were pictures of the children, Tanya and Louis, and shots of the apartment she'd found us in the Twin Peaks arcology, and much more.

I ran through it three times. Then I called Ausfaller's room. It had been just too futzy long.

I circled Jinx once on the way out. I've always done that, even back when I was flying for Nakamura Lines; and no passenger has ever objected.

Jinx is the close moon of a gas giant planet more massive than Jupiter, and smaller than Jupiter because its core has been compressed to degenerate matter. A billion years ago Jinx and Primary were even closer, before tidal drag moved them apart. This same tidal force had earlier locked Jinx's rotation to Primary and forced the moon into an egg shape, a prolate spheroid. When the moon moved outward its shape became more nearly spherical; but the cold rock surface resisted change.

That is why the ocean of Jinx rings its waist, beneath an atmosphere too compressed and too hot to breathe; whereas the points nearest to and furthest from Primary, the East and West Ends, actually rise out of the atmosphere.

From space Jinx looks like God's Own Easter Egg: the Ends bone white tinged with yellow; then the brighter glare from rings of glittering ice fields at the limits of the atmosphere; then the varying blues of an Earthlike world, increasingly overlaid with the white frosting of cloud as the eyes move inward, until the waist of the planet/moon is girdled with pure white. The ocean never shows at all.

I took us once around, and out.

Sirius has its own share of floating miscellaneous matter cluttering the path to instellar space. I stayed at the controls for most of five days, for that reason and because I wanted to get the feel of an unfamiliar ship.

Hobo Kelly was a belly-landing job, three hundred feet long, of triangular cross section. Beneath an up-tilted, forward-thrusting nose were big clamshell doors for cargo. She had adequate belly jets and a much larger fusion motor at the tail, and a line of windows indicating cabins. Certainly she looked harmless enough; and certainly there was deception involved. The cabin should have held forty or fifty, but there was room only for four. The rest of what should have been cabin space was only windows with holograph projections in them.

The drive ran sure and smooth up to a maximum at ten gravities: not a lot for a ship designed to haul massive cargo. The cabin gravity held without putting out more than a fraction of its power. When Jinx and Primary were invisible against the stars, when Sirius was so distant I could look directly at it, I turned to the hidden control panel Ausfaller had unlocked for me. Ausfaller woke up, found me doing that, and began showing me which did what.

He had a big X-ray laser and some smaller laser cannon set for different frequencies. He had four self-guided fusion bombs. He had a telescope so good that the ostensible ship's telescope was only a finder for it. He had deep-radar.

And none of it showed beyond the discolored hull.

Ausfaller was armed for Bandersnatchi. I felt mixed emotions. It seemed we could fight anything, and run from it too. But what kind of enemy was he expecting?

All through those four weeks in hyperdrive, while we drove through the Blind Spot at three days to the lightyear, the topic of the ship eaters reared its disturbing head.

Oh, we spoke of other things: of music and art, and of the latest techniques in animation, the computer programs that let you make your own holo flicks almost for lunch money. We told stories. I told Carlos why the Kdatlyno Lloobee had made busts of me and Emil Horne. I spoke of the only time the Pierson's Puppeteers had ever paid off the guarantee on a General Products hull, after the supposedly indestructible hull had been destroyed by antimatter. Ausfaller had some good ones . . . a lot more stories than he was allowed to tell, I gathered, from the way he had to search his memory every time.

But we kept coming back to the ship eaters.

"It boils down to three possibilities," I decided. "Kzinti, puppeteers, and human."

Carlos guffawed. "Puppeteers? Puppeteers wouldn't have the guts!"

"I threw them in because they might have some interest in manipulating the interstellar stock market. Look: our hypothetical pirates have set up an embargo, cutting Sol system off from the outside world. The Puppeteers have the capital to take advantage of what that does to the market. And they need money. For their migration."

"The Puppeteers are philosophical cowards."

"That's right. They wouldn't risk robbing the ships, or coming anywhere near them. Suppose they can make them disappear from a distance?"

Carlos wasn't laughing now. "That's easier than dropping them out of hyperspace to rob them. It wouldn't take more than a great big gravity generator . . . and we've never known the limits of Puppeteer technology."

Ausfaller asked, "You think this is possible?"

"Just barely. The same goes for the Kzinti. The Kzinti are ferocious enough. Trouble is, if we ever learned they were preying on our ships we'd raise pluperfect hell. The Kzinti know that, and they know we can beat them. Took them long enough, but they learned."

"So you think it's Humans," said Carlos.

"Yah. If it's pirates."

The piracy theory still looked shaky. Spectrum telescopes had not even found concentrations of ship's metals in the space where they must have vanished. Would pirates steal the whole ship? If the hyperdrive motor were still intact after the attack, the rifled ship could be launched into infinity; but could pirates count on that happening eight times out of eight?

And none of the missing ships had called for help via hyperwave.

I'd never believed pirates. Space pirates have existed, but they died without successors. Intercepting a spacecraft was too difficult. They couldn't make it pay.

Ships fly themselves in hyperdrive. All a pilot need do is watch for radial green lines in the mass sensor. But he has to do that frequently, because the mass sensor is a psionic device; it must be watched by a mind, not another machine.

As the narrow green line that marked Sol grew longer, I became abnormally conscious of the debris around Sol system. I spent the last twelve hours of the flight at the controls, chain-smoking with my feet. I should add that I do that normally, when I want both hands free; but now I did it to annoy Ausfaller. I'd seen the way his eyes bugged the first time he saw me take a drag from a cigarette between my toes. Flatlanders are less than limber.

Carlos and Ausfaller shared the control room with me as we penetrated Sol's cometary halo. They were relieved to be nearing the end of a long trip. I was nervous. "Carlos, just how large a mass would it take to make us disappear?"

"Planet size, Mars and up. Beyond that it depends on how close you get and how dense it is. If it's dense enough it can be less massive and still flip you out of the universe. But you'd see it in the mass sensor."

"Only for an instant . . . and not then, if it's turned off. What if someone turned on a giant gravity generator as we went past?"—

"For what? They couldn't rob the ship. Where's their profit?"

"Stocks."

But Ausfaller was shaking his head. "The expense of such an operation would be enormous. No group of pirates would have enough additional capital on hand to make it worthwhile. Of the Puppeteers I might believe it."

Hell, he was right. No human that wealthy would need to turn pirate.

The long green line marking Sol was almost touching the surface of the mass sensor. I said, "Breakout in ten minutes."

And the ship lurched savagely.

"Strap down!" I yelled, and glanced at the hyperdrive monitors. The motor was drawing no power, and the rest of the dials were going bananas.

I activated the windows. I'd kept them turned off in hyperspace, lest my flatlander passengers go mad watching the Blind Spot. The screens came on and I saw stars. We were in normal space.

"Futz! They got us anyway." Carlos sounded neither frightened nor angry, but awed.

As I raised the hidden panel Ausfaller cried, "Wait!" I ignored him. I threw the red switch, and *Hobo Kelly* lurched again as her belly blew off.

Ausfaller began cursing in some dead flatlander language.

Now two-thirds of *Hobo Kelly* receded, slowly turning. What was left must show as what she was: a Number Two General Products hull, Puppeteer-built, a slender transparent spear three hundred feet long and twenty feet wide, with instruments of war clustered along what was now her belly. Screens that had been blank came to life. And I lit the main drive and ran it up to full power.

Ausfaller spoke in rage and venom. "Shaeffer, you idiot, you coward! We run without knowing what we run from. Now they know exactly what we are. What chance that they will follow us now? This ship was built for a specific purpose, and you have ruined it!"

"I've freed your special instruments," I pointed out. "Why don't you see what you can find?" Meanwhile I could get us futz out of here.

Ausfaller became very busy. I watched what he was getting on screens at my side of the control panel. Was anything chasing us? They'd find us hard to catch and harder to digest. They could hardly have been expecting a General Products hull. Since the Puppeteers stopped making them the price of used GP hulls has gone out of sight.

There *were* ships out there. Ausfaller got a closeup of them: three space tugs of the Belter type, shaped like thick saucers, equipped with oversized drives and powerful electromagnetic generators. Belters use them to tug nickel-iron asteroids to where somebody wants the ore. With those heavy drives they could probably catch us; but would they have adequate cabin gravity?

They weren't trying. They seemed to be neither following nor fleeing. And they looked harmless enough.

But Ausfaller was doing a job on them with his other

instruments. I approved. *Hobo Kelly* had looked peaceful enough a moment ago. Now her belly bristled with weaponry. The tugs could be equally deceptive.

From behind me Carlos asked, "Bey? What happened?"

"How the futz would I know?"

"What do the instruments show?"

He must mean the hyperdrive complex. A couple of the indicators had gone wild; five more were dead. I said so. "And the drive's drawing no power at all. I've never heard of anything like this, Carlos, it's *still* theoretically impossible."

"I'm . . . not so sure of that. I want to look at the drive."

"The access tubes don't have cabin gravity."

Ausfaller had abandoned the receding tugs. He'd found what looked to be a large comet, a ball of frozen gasses a good distance to the side. I watched as he ran the deep-radar over it. No fleet of robber ships lurked behind it.

I asked, "Did you deep-radar the tugs?"

"Of course. We can examine the tapes in detail later. I saw nothing. And nothing has attacked us since we left hyperspace."

I'd been driving us in a random direction. Now I turned us toward Sol, the brightest star in the heavens. Those lost ten minutes in hyperspace would add about three days to our voyage.

"If there was an enemy, you frightened him away. Shaeffer, this mission and this ship have cost my department an enormous sum, and we have learned nothing at all."

"Not quite nothing," said Carlos. "I still want to see the hyperdrive motor. Bey, would you run us down to one gee?"

"Yah. But . . . miracles make me nervous, Carlos."

"Join the club."

We crawled along an access tube just a little bigger

than a big man's shoulders, between the hyperdrive motor housing and the surrounding fuel tankage. Carlos reached an inspection window, He looked in. He started to laugh.

I inquired as to what was so futzy funny.

Still chortling, Carlos moved on. I crawled after him and looked in.

There was no hyperdrive motor in the hyperdrive motor housing.

I went in through a repair hatch and stood in the cylindrical housing, looking about me. Nothing. Not even an exit hole. The superconducting cables and the mounts for the motor had been sheared so cleanly that the cut ends looked like little mirrors.

Ausfaller insisted on seeing for himself. Carlos and I waited in the control room. For a while Carlos kept bursting into fits of giggles. Then he got a dreamy, faraway look that was even more annoying.

I wondered what was going on in his head, and reached the uncomfortable conclusion that I could never know. Some years ago I took IQ tests, hoping to get a parenthood license that way. I am not a genius.

I knew only that Carlos had thought of something I hadn't, and he wasn't telling, and I was too proud to ask.

Ausfaller had no pride. He came back looking like he'd seen a ghost. "Gone! Where could it go? How could it happen?"

"That I can answer," Carlos said happily. "It takes an extremely high gravity gradient. The motor hit that, wrapped space around itself and took off at some higher level of hyperdrive, one we can't reach. By now it could be well on its way to the edge of the universe."

I said, "You're sure, huh? An hour ago there wasn't a theory to cover any of this."

"Well, I'm sure our motor's gone. Beyond that it gets a little hazy. But this is one well-established model of what happens when a ship hits a singularity. At a lower gravity gradient the motor would take the whole ship with it, then strew atoms of the ship along its path till there was nothing left but the hyperdrive field itself."

"Ugh."

Now Carlos burned with the love of an idea. "Sigmund, I want to use your hyperwave. I could still be wrong, but there are things we can check."

"If we are still within the singularity of some mass, the hyperwave will destroy itself."

"Yah. I think it's worth the risk."

We'd dropped out, or been knocked out, ten minutes short of the singularity around Sol. That added up to sixteen light-hours of normal space, plus almost five light-hours from the edge of the singularity inward to Earth. Fortunately hyperwave is instantaneous, and every civilized system keeps a hyperwave relay station just outside the singularity. Southworth Station would relay our message inward by laser, get the return message the same way and pass it on to us ten hours later.

We turned on the hyperwave and nothing exploded.

Ausfaller made his own call first, to Ceres, to get the registry of the tugs we'd spotted. Afterward Carlos called Elephant's computer setup in New York, using a code number Elephant doesn't give to many people. "I'll pay him back later. Maybe with a story to go with it," he gloated.

I listened as Carlos outlined his needs. He wanted full records on a meteorite that had touched down in Tunguska, Siberia, USSR, Earth, in 1908 AD. He wanted a reprise on three models of the origin of the universe or lack of same: the Big Bang, the Cyclic Universe, the Steady State Universe. He wanted data on collapsars. He wanted names, career outlines, and addresses for the best known students of gravitational phenomena in Sol system. He was smiling when he clicked off.

I said, "You got me. I haven't the remotest idea what you're after."

Still smiling, Carlos got up and went to his cabin to catch some sleep.

I turned off the main thrust motor entirely. When we were deep in Sol system we could decelerate at thirty gravities. Meanwhile we were carrying a hefty velocity picked up on our way out of Sirius system.

Ausfaller stayed in the control room. Maybe his motive was the same as mine. No police ships out here. We could still be attacked.

He spent the time going through his pictures of the three mining tugs. We didn't talk, but I watched.

The tugs seemed ordinary enough. Telescopic photos showed no suspicious breaks in the hulls, no hatches for guns. In the deep-radar scan they showed like ghosts: we could pick out the massive force-field rings, the hollow, equally massive drive tubes, the lesser densities of fuel tank and lifesupport system. There were no gaps or shadows that shouldn't have been there.

By and by Ausfaller said, "Do you know what *Hobo Kelly* was worth?"

I said I could make a close estimate.

"It was worth my career. I thought to destroy a pirate fleet with *Hobo Kelly*. But my pilot fled. Fled! What have I now, to show for my expensive Trojan Horse?"

I suppressed the obvious answer, along with the plea that my first responsibility was Carlos' life. Ausfaller wouldn't buy that. Instead, "Carlos has something. I know him. He knows how it happened."

"Can you get it out of him?"

"I don't know." I could put it to Carlos that we'd be safer if we knew what was out to get us. But Carlos was a flatlander. It would color his attitudes.

"So," said Ausfaller. "We have only the unavailable knowledge in Carlos' skull."

A weapon beyond human technology had knocked me out of hyperspace. I'd run. Of *course* I'd run. Staying in the neighborhood would have been insane, said I to myself, said I. But, unreasonably, I still felt bad about it.

To Ausfaller I said, "What about the mining tugs? I can't understand what they're doing out here. In the Belt they use them to move nickel-iron asteroids to industrial sites."

"It is the same here. Most of what they find is useless: stony masses or balls of ice; but what little metal there is, is valuable. They must have it for building."

"For building what? What kind of people would live here? You might as well set up shop in interstellar space!"

"Precisely. There are no tourists, but there are research groups, here where space is flat and empty and temperatures are near absolute zero. I know that the Quicksilver Group was established here to study hyperspace phenomena. We do not understand hyperspace, even yet. Remember that we did not invent the hyperdrive; we bought it from an alien race. Then there is a gene-tailoring laboratory trying to develop a kind of tree that will grow on comets."

"You're kidding."

"But they are serious. A photosynthetic plant to use the chemicals present in all comets . . . it would be very valuable. The whole cometary halo could be seeded with oxygen-producing plants—" Ausfaller stopped abruptly, then, "Never mind. But all these groups need building materials. It is cheaper to build out here than to ship everything from Earth or the Belt. The presence of tugs is not suspicious."

"But there was nothing else around us. Nothing at all."

Ausfaller nodded.

When Carlos came to join us many hours later, blinking sleep out of his eyes, I asked him. "Carlos, could the tugs have had anything to do with your theory?"

"I don't see how. I've got half an idea, and half an hour from now I could look like a halfwit. The theory I want isn't even in fashion any more. Now that we know what the quasars are, everyone seems to like the Steady State Hypothesis. You know how that works: the tension in completely empty space produces more hydrogen atoms, forever. The universe has no beginning and no end." He looked stubborn. "But if I'm right, then I know where the ships went to after being robbed. That's more than anyone else knows."

Ausfaller jumped on him. "Where are they? Are the passengers alive?"

"I'm sorry, Sigmund. They're all dead. There won't even be bodies to bury."

"What is it? What are we fighting?"

"A gravitational effect. A sharp warping of space. A planet wouldn't do that, and a battery of cabin gravity generators wouldn't do it; they couldn't produce that sharply bounded a field."

"A collapsar," Ausfaller suggested.

Carlos grinned at him. "That would do it, but there are other problems. A collapsar can't even form at less than around five solar masses. You'd think someone would have noticed something that big, this close to Sol."

"Then *what*?"

Carlos shook his head. We would wait.

The relay from Southworth Station gave us registrations for three space tugs, used and of varying ages, all three purchased two years ago from IntraBelt Mining by the Sixth Congregational Church of Rodney.

"Rodney?"

But Carlos and Ausfaller were both chortling. "Belters do that sometimes," Carlos told me. "It's a way of saying it's nobody's business who's buying the ships."

"That's pretty funny, all right, but we still don't know who owns them."

"They may be honest Belters. They may not."

Hard on the heels of the first call came the data Carlos had asked for, playing directly into the shipboard computer. Carlos called up a list of names and phone numbers: Sol system's preeminent students of gravity and its effects, listed in alphabetical order.

An address caught my attention:
Julian Forward, #1192326 Southworth Station.

A hyperwave relay tag. He was out *here*, somewhere in

the enormous gap between Neptune's orbit and the cometary belt, out here where the hyperwave relay could function. I looked for more Southworth Station numbers. They were there:

Launcelot Starkey, #1844719 Southworth Station.

Jill Luciano, #1844719 Southworth Station.

Mariana Wilton, #1844719 Southworth Station.

"These people," said Ausfaller. "You wish to discuss your theory with one of them?"

"That's right. Sigmund, isn't 1844719 the tag for the Quicksilver Group?"

"I think so. I also think that they are not within our reach, now that our hyperdrive is gone. The Quicksilver Group was established in distant orbit around Antenora, which is now on the other side of the sun. Carlos, has it occurred to you that one of these people may have built the ship-eating device?"

"What? . . . You're right. It would take someone who knew something about gravity. But I'd say the Quicksilver Group was beyond suspicion. With upwards of ten thousand people at work, how could anyone hide anything?"

"What about this Julian Forward?"

"Forward. Yah. I've always wanted to meet him."

"You know of him? Who is he?"

"He used to be with the Institute of Knowledge on Jinx. I haven't heard of him in years. He did some work on the gravity waves from the galactic core . . . work that turned out to be wrong. Sigmund, let's give him a call."

"And ask him what?"

"Why . . . ?" Then Carlos remembered the situation. "Oh. You think he might—Yah."

"How well do you know this man?"

"I know him by reputation. He's quite famous. I don't see how such a man could go in for mass murder."

"Earlier you said that we were looking for a man skilled in the study of gravitational phenomena."

"Granted."

Ausfaller sucked at his lower lip. Then, "Perhaps we

can do no more than talk to him. He could be on the other side of the sun and still head a pirate fleet—"

"No. That he could not."

"Think again," said Ausfaller. "We are outside the singularity of Sol. A pirate fleet would surely include hyperdrive ships."

"If Julian Forward is the ship eater, he'll have to be nearby. The, uh, device won't move in hyperspace."

I said, "Carlos, what we don't know can kill us. Will you quit playing games—" But he was smiling, shaking his head. Futz. "All right, we can still check on Forward. Call him up and ask where he is! Is he likely to know you by reputation?"

"Sure. I'm famous too."

"Okay. If he's close enough, we might even beg him for a ride home. The way things stand we'll be at the mercy of any hyperdrive ship for as long as we're out here."

"I hope we are attacked," said Ausfaller. "We can outfight—"

"But we can't outrun. They can dodge, we can't."

"Peace, you two. First things first." Carlos sat down at the hyperwave controls and tapped out a number.

Suddenly Ausfaller said, "Can you contrive to keep my name out of this exchange? If necessary you can be the ship's owner."

Carlos looked around in surprise. Before he could answer, the screen lit. I saw ash-blond hair cut in a Belter crest, over a lean white face and an impersonal smile.

"Forward Station. Good evening."

"Good evening. This is Carlos Wu of Earth calling long distance. May I speak to Dr Julian Forward, please?"

"I'll see if he's available." The screen went on HOLD.

In the interval Carlos burst out: "What kind of game are *you* playing now? How can I explain owning an armed, disguised warship?"

But I began to see what Ausfaller was getting at. I said, "You'd want to avoid explaining that, whatever the truth was. Maybe he won't ask. I—" I shut up, because we were facing Forward.

Julian Forward was a Jinxian, short and wide, with arms as thick as legs and legs as thick as pillars. His skin was almost as black as his hair: a Sirius suntan, probably maintained by sunlights. He perched on the edge of a massage chair. "Carlos Wu!" he said with flattering enthusiasm. "Are you the same Carlos Wu who solved the Sealeyham Limits Problem?"

Carlos said he was. They went into a discussion of mathematics—a possible application of Carlos' solution to another limits problem, I gathered. I glanced at Ausfaller—not obtrusively, because for Forward he wasn't supposed to exist—and saw him pensively studying his side view of Forward.

"Well," Forward said, "what can I do for you?"

"Julian Forward, meet Beowulf Shaeffer," said Carlos. I bowed. "Bey was giving me a lift home when our hyperdrive motor disappeared."

"Disappeared?"

I butted in, for verisimilitude. "Disappeared, futzy right. The hyperdrive motor casing is empty. The motor supports are sheared off. We're stuck out here with no hyperdrive and no idea how it happened."

"Almost true," Carlos said happily. "Dr Forward, I do have some ideas as to what happened here. I'd like to discuss them with you."

"Where are you now?"

I pulled our position and velocity from the computer and flashed them to Forward Station. I wasn't sure it was a good idea; but Ausfaller had time to stop me, and he didn't.

"Fine," said Forward's image. "It looks like you can get here a lot faster than you can get to Earth. Forward Station is ahead of you, within twenty a.u. of your position. You can wait here for the next ferry. Better than going on in a crippled ship."

"Good! We'll work out a course and let you know when to expect us."

"I welcome the chance to meet Carlos Wu." Forward gave us his own coordinates and rang off.

Carlos turned. "All right, Bey. Now *you* own an armed and disguised warship. *You* figure out where you got it."

"We've got worse problems than that. Forward Station is exactly where the ship eater ought to be."

He nodded. But he was amused.

"So what's our next move? We can't run from hyperdrive ships. Not now. Is Forward likely to try to kill us?"

"If we don't reach Forward Station on schedule, he might send ships after us. We know too much. We've told him so," said Carlos. "The hyperdrive motor disappeared completely. I know half a dozen people who could figure out how it happened, knowing just that." He smiled suddenly. "That's assuming Forward's the ship eater. We don't know that. I think we have a splendid chance to find out, one way or the other."

"How? Just walk in?"

Ausfaller was nodding approvingly. "Dr Forward expects you and Carlos to enter his web unsuspecting, leaving an empty ship. I think we can prepare a few surprises for him. For example, he may not have guessed that this is a General Products hull. And I will be aboard to fight."

True. Only antimatter could harm a GP hull . . . though things could go through it, like light and gravity and shock waves. "So you'll be in the indestructible hull," I said, "and we'll be helpless in the base. Very clever. I'd rather run for it, myself. But then, you have your career to consider."

"I will not deny it. But there are ways in which I can prepare you."

Behind Ausfaller's cabin, behind what looked like an unbroken wall, was a room the size of a walk-in closet. Ausfaller seemed quite proud of it. He didn't show us everything in there, but I saw enough to cost me what re-

mained of my first impression of Ausfaller. This man did
not have the soul of a pudgy bureaucrat.

Behind a glass panel he kept a couple of dozen
special-purpose weapons. A row of four clamps held three
identical hand weapons, disposable rocket launchers for a
fat slug that Ausfaller billed as a tiny atomic bomb. The
fourth clamp was empty. There were laser rifles and pis-
tols; a shotgun of peculiar design, with four inches of
recoil shock absorber; throwing knives; an Olympic target
pistol with a sculpted grip and room for just one .22 bullet.

I wondered what he was doing with a hobbyist's touch-
sculpting setup. Maybe he could make sculptures to drive
a human or an alien mad. Maybe something less subtle:
maybe they'd explode at the touch of the right finger-
prints.

He had a compact automated tailor's shop. "I'm going
to make you some new suits," he said. When Carlos asked
why, he said, "You can keep secrets? So can I."

He asked us for our preference in styles. I played it
straight, asking for a falling jumper in green and silver,
with lots of pockets. It wasn't the best I've ever owned,
but it fitted.

"I didn't ask for buttons," I told him.

"I hope you don't mind. Carlos, you will have buttons
too."

Carlos chose a fiery red tunic with a green-and-gold
dragon coiling across the back. The buttons carried his
family monogram. Ausfaller stood before us, examining
us in our new finery, with approval.

"Now, watch," he said. "Here I stand before you, unarmed—"

"Right."

"*Sure* you are."

Ausfaller grinned. He took the top and bottom buttons
between his fingers and tugged hard. They came off. The
material between them ripped open as if a thread had
been strung between them.

Holding the buttons as if to keep an invisible thread taut, he moved them on either side of a crudely done plastic touch-sculpture. The sculpture fell apart.

"Sinclair molecule chain. It will cut through any normal matter, if you pull hard enough. You must be very careful. It will cut your fingers so easily that you will hardly notice they are gone. Notice that the buttons are large, to give an easy grip." He laid the buttons carefully on a table and set a heavy weight between them. "This third button down is a sonic grenade. Ten feet away it will kill. Thirty feet away it will stun."

I said, "Don't demonstrate."

"You may want to practice throwing dummy buttons at a target. This second button is Power Pill, the commercial stimulant. Break the button and take half when you need it. The entire dose may stop your heart."

"I never heard of Power Pill. How does it work on crashlanders?"

He was taken aback. "I don't know. Perhaps you had better restrict yourself to a quarter dose."

"Or avoid it entirely," I said.

"There is one more thing I will not demonstrate. Feel the material of your garments. You feel three layers of material? The middle layer is a nearly perfect mirror. It will reflect even X-rays. Now you can repel a laser blast, for at least the first second. The collar unrolls to a hood."

Carlos was nodding in satisfaction.

I guess it's true: all flatlanders think that way.

For a billion and a half years, humanity's ancestors had evolved to the conditions of one world: Earth. A flatlander grows up in an environment peculiarly suited to him. Instinctively he sees the whole universe the same way.

We know better, we who were born on other worlds. On We Made It there are the hellish winds of summer and winter. On Jinx, the gravity. On Plateau, the all-encircling cliff edge, and a drop of forty miles into unbearable heat and pressure. On Down, the red sunlight, and plants that will not grow without help from ultraviolet lamps.

But flatlanders think the universe was made for their benefit. To them, danger is unreal.

"Earplugs," said Ausfaller, holding up a handful of soft plastic cylinders.

We inserted them. Ausfaller said, "Can you hear me?"

"Sure." "Yah." They didn't block our hearing at all.

"Transmitter and hearing aid, with sonic padding between. If you are blasted with sound, as by an explosion or a sonic stunner, the hearing aid will stop transmitting. If you go suddenly deaf you will know you are under attack."

To me, Ausfaller's elaborate precautions only spoke of what we might be walking into. I said nothing. If we ran for it our chances were even worse.

Back to the control room, where Ausfaller set up a relay to the Alien Affairs Bureau on Earth. He gave them a condensed version of what had happened to us, plus some cautious speculation. He invited Carlos to read his theories into the record.

Carlos declined. "I could still be wrong. Give me a chance to do some studying."

Ausfaller went grumpily to his bunk. He had been up too long, and it showed.

Carlos shook his head as Ausfaller disappeared into his cabin. "Paranoia. In his job I guess he has to be paranoid."

"You could use some of that yourself."

He didn't hear me. "Imagine suspecting an interstellar celebrity of being a space pirate!"

"He's in the right place at the right time."

"Hey, Bey, forget what I said. The, uh, ship-eating device has to be in the right place, but the pirates don't. They can just leave it loose and use hyperdrive ships to commute to their base."

That was something to keep in mind. Compared to the

inner system this volume within the cometary halo was enormous; but to hyperdrive ships it was all one neighborhood. I said, "Then why are we visiting Forward?"

"I still want to check my ideas with him. More than that: he probably knows the Head Ship Eater, without knowing it's him. Probably we both know him. It took something of a cosmologist to find the device and recognize it. Whoever it is, he has to have made something of a name for himself."

"Find?"

Carlos grinned at me. "Never mind. Have you thought of anyone you'd like to use that magic wire on?"

"I've been making a list. You're at the top."

"Well, watch it. Sigmund knows you've got it, even if nobody else does."

"He's second."

"How long till we reach Forward Station?"

I'd been rechecking our course. We were decelerating at thirty gravities and veering to one side. "Twenty hours and a few minutes," I said.

"Good. I'll get a chance to do some studying." He began calling up data from the computer.

I asked permission to read over his shoulder. He gave it.

Bastard. He reads twice as fast as I do. I tried to skim, to get some idea of what he was after.

Collapsars: three known. The nearest was one component of a double in Cygnus, more than a hundred light years away. Expeditions had gone there to drop probes.

The theory of the black hole wasn't new to me, though the math was over my head. If a star is massive enough, then after it has burned its nuclear fuel and started to cool, no possible internal force can hold it from collapsing inward past its now Schwartzchild radius. At that point the escape velocity from the star becomes greater than lightspeed; and beyond that deponent sayeth not, because nothing can leave the star, not information, not matter, not radiation. Nothing—except gravity.

Such a collapsed star can be expected to weigh five solar masses or more; otherwise its collapse would stop at the neutron star stage. Afterward it can only grow bigger and more massive.

There wasn't the slightest chance of finding anything that massive out here at the edge of the solar system. If such a thing were anywhere near, the sun would have been in orbit around it.

The Siberia meteorite must have been weird enough, to be remembered for nine hundred years. It had knocked down trees over thousands of square miles; yet trees near the touchdown point were left standing. No part of the meteorite itself had ever been found. Nobody had seen it hit. In 1908, Tunguska, Siberia must have been as sparsely settled as the Earth's moon today.

"Carlos, what does all this have to do with anything?"

"Does Holmes tell Watson?"

I had real trouble following the cosmology. Physics verged on philosophy here, or vice versa. Basically the Big Bang Theory—which pictures the universe as exploding from a single point-mass, like a titanic bomb—was in competition with the Steady State Universe, which has been going on forever and will continue to do so. The Cyclic Universe is a succession of Big Bangs followed by contractions. There are variants on all of them.

When the quasars were first discovered, they seemed to date from an earlier stage in the evolution of the universe . . . which, by the Steady State hypothesis, would not be evolving at all. The Steady State went out of fashion. Then, a century ago, Hilbury had solved the mystery of the quasars. Meanwhile one of the implications of the Big Bang had not panned out. That was where the math got beyond me.

There was some discussion of whether the universe was open or closed in four-space, but Carlos turned it off. "Okay," he said, with satisfaction.

"What?"

"I could be right. Insufficient data. I'll have to see what Forward thinks."

"I hope you both choke. I'm going to sleep."

Out here in the broad borderland between Sol system and interstellar space, Julian Forward had found a stony mass the size of a middling asteroid. From a distance it seemed untouched by technology: a lopsided spheroid, rough-surfaced and dirty white. Closer in, flecks of metal and bright paint showed like randomly placed jewels. Airlocks, windows, projecting antennae, and things less identifiable. A lighted disk with something projecting from the center: a long metal arm with half a dozen ball joints in it and a cup on the end. I studied that one, trying to guess what it might be . . . and gave up.

I brought *Hobo Kelly* to rest a fair distance away. To Ausfaller I said, "You'll stay aboard?"

"Of course. I will do nothing to disabuse Dr Forward of the notion that the ship is empty."

We crossed to Forward Station on an open taxi: two seats, a fuel tank and a rocket motor. Once I turned to ask Carlos something, and asked instead, "Carlos? Are you all right?"

His face was white and strained. "I'll make it."

"Did you try closing your eyes?"

"It was worse. Futz, I made it this far on hypnosis. Bey, it's so *empty*."

"Hang on. We're almost there."

The blond Belter was outside one of the airlocks in a skin-tight suit and a bubble helmet. He used a flashlight to flag us down. We moored our taxi to a spur of rock—the gravity was almost nil—and went inside.

"I'm Harry Moskowitz," the Belter said. "They call me Angel. Dr Forward is waiting in the laboratory."

The interior of the asteroid was a network of straight cylindrical corridors, laser-drilled, pressurized and lined with cool blue light strips. We weighed a few pounds near the surface, less in the deep interior. Angel moved in a fashion new to me: a flat jump from the floor that took him far down the corridor to brush the ceiling; push back to the floor and jump again. Three jumps and he'd wait, not hiding his amusement at our attempts to catch up.

"Doctor Forward asked me to give you a tour," he told us.

I said, "You seem to have a lot more corridor than you need. Why didn't you cluster all the rooms together?"

"This rock was a mine, once upon a time. The miners drilled these passages. They left big hollows wherever they found air-bearing rock or ice pockets. All we had to do was wall them off."

That explained why there was so much corridor between the doors, and why the chambers we saw were so big. Some rooms were storage areas, Angel said; not worth opening. Others were tool rooms, life-support systems, a garden, a fair-sized computer, a sizeable fusion plant. A mess room built to hold thirty actually held about ten, all men, who looked at us curiously before they went back to eating. A hangar, bigger than need be and open to the sky, housed taxis and powered suits with specialized tools, and three identical circular cradles, all empty.

I gambled. Carefully casual, I asked, "You use mining tugs?"

Angel didn't hesitate. "Sure. We can ship water and metals up from the inner system, but it's cheaper to hunt them down ourselves. In an emergency the tugs could probably get us back to the inner system."

We moved back into the tunnels. Angel said, "Speaking of ships, I don't think I've ever seen one like yours. Were those *bombs* lined up along the ventral surface?"

"Some of them," I said.

Carlos laughed. "Bey won't tell me how he got it."

"Pick, pick, pick. All right, I *stole* it. I don't think anyone is going to complain."

Angel, frankly curious before, was frankly fascinated as I told the story of how I had been hired to fly a cargo ship in the Wunderland system. "I didn't much like the looks of the guy who hired me, but what do I know about Wunderlanders? Besides, I needed the money." I told of my surprise at the proportions of the ship: the solid wall behind the cabin, the passenger section that was only holographs in blind portholes. By then I was already afraid that if I tried to back out I'd be made to disappear.

But when I learned my destination I got really worried. "It was in the Serpent Stream—you know, the crescent of asteroids in Wunderland system? It's common knowledge that the Free Wunderland Conspiracy is *all through* those rocks. When they gave me my course I just took off and aimed for Sirius."

"Strange they left you with a working hyperdrive."

"Man, they *didn't*. They'd ripped out the relays. I had to fix them myself. It's lucky I looked, because they had the relays wired to a little bomb under the control chair." I stopped, then, "Maybe I fixed it wrong. You heard what happened? My hyperdrive motor just plain vanished. It must have set off some explosive bolts, because the belly of the ship blew off. It was a dummy. What's left looks to be a pocket bomber."

"That's what I thought."

"I guess I'll have to turn it in to the goldskin cops when we reach the inner system. Pity."

Carlos was smiling and shaking his head. He covered by saying, "It only goes to prove that you *can* run away from your problems."

The next tunnel ended in a great hemispherical chamber, lidded by a bulging transparent dome. A man-thick pillar rose through the rock floor to a seal in the center of the dome. Above the seal, gleaming against night and stars, a multi-jointed metal arm reached out blindly into space. The arm ended in what might have been a tremendous iron puppy dish.

Forward was in a horseshoe-shaped control console near the pillar. I hardly noticed him. I'd seen this arm-

and-bucket thing before, coming in from space, but I hadn't grasped its *size*.

Forward caught me gaping. "The Grabber," he said.

He approached us in a bouncing walk, comical but effective. "Pleased to meet you, Carlos Wu. Beowulf Shaeffer." His handshake was not crippling, because he was being careful. He had a wide, engaging smile. "The Grabber is our main exhibit here. After the Grabber there's nothing to see."

I asked, "What does it do?"

Carlos laughed. "It's beautiful! Why does it have to do anything?"

Forward acknowledged the compliment. "I've been thinking of entering it in a junk-sculpture show. What is does is manipulate large, dense masses. The cradle at the end of the arm is a complex of electromagnets. I can actually vibrate masses in there to produce polarized gravity waves."

Six massive arcs of girder divided the dome into pie sections. Now I noticed that they and the seal at their center gleamed like mirrors. They were reinforced by stasis fields. More bracing for the Grabber? I tried to imagine forces that would require such strength.

"What do you vibrate in there? A megaton of lead?"

"Lead sheathed in soft iron was our test mass. But that was three years ago. I haven't worked with the Grabber lately, but we had some satisfactory runs with a sphere of neutronium enclosed in a stasis field. Ten billion metric tons."

I said, "What's the point?"

From Carlos I got a dirty look. Forward seemed to think it was a wholly reasonable question. "Communication, for one thing. There must be intelligent species all through the galaxy, most of them too far away for our ships. Gravity waves are probably the best way to reach them."

"Gravity waves travel at lightspeed, don't they? Wouldn't hyperwave be better?"

"We can't count on their having it. Who but the Outsiders would think to do their experimenting this far from a sun? If we want to reach beings who haven't dealt with the Outsiders, we'll have to use gravity waves . . . once we know how."

Angel offered us chairs and refreshments. By the time we were settled I was already out of it; Forward and Carlos were talking plasma physics, metaphysics, and what are our old friends doing? I gathered that they had large numbers of mutual acquaintances. And Carlos was probing for the whereabouts of cosmologists specializing in gravity physics.

A few were in the Quicksilver Group. Others were among the colony worlds . . . especially on Jinx, trying to get the Institute of Knowledge to finance various projects, such as more expeditions to the collapsar in Cygnus.

"Are you still with the Institute, Doctor?"

Forward shook his head. "They stopped backing me. Not enough results. But I can continue to use this station, which is Institute property. One day they'll sell it and we'll have to move."

"I was wondering why they sent you here in the first place," said Carlos. "Sirius has an adequate cometary belt."

"But Sol is the only system with any kind of civilization this far from its sun. And I can count on better men to work with. Sol system has always had its fair share of cosmologists."

"I thought you might have come to solve an old mystery. The Tunguska meteorite. You've heard of it, of course."

Forward laughed. "Of course. Who hasn't? I don't think we'll ever know just what it was that hit Siberia that night. It may have been a chunk of antimatter. I'm told that there is antimatter in known space."

"If it was, we'll never prove it," Carlos admitted.

"Shall we discuss your problem?" Forward seemed to

remember my existence. "Shaeffer, what does a professional pilot think when his hyperdrive motor disappears?"

"He gets very upset."

"Any theories?"

I decided not to mention pirates. I wanted to see if Forward would mention them first. "Nobody seems to like my theory," I said, and I sketched out the argument for monsters in hyperspace.

Forward heard me out politely. Then, "I'll give you this, it'd be hard to disprove. Do you buy it?"

"I'm afraid to. I almost got myself killed once, looking for space monsters when I should have been looking for natural causes."

"Why would the hyperspace monsters eat only your motor?"

"Um . . . futz. I pass."

"What do you think, Carlos? Natural phenomena or space monsters?"

"Pirates," said Carlos.

"How are they going about it?"

"Well, this business of a hyperdrive motor disappearing and leaving the ship behind—that's brand new. I'd think it would take a sharp gravity gradient, with a tidal effect as strong as that of a neutron star or a black hole."

"You won't find anything like that anywhere in human space."

"I know." Carlos looked frustrated. That had to be faked. Earlier he'd behaved as if he already had an answer.

Forward said, "I don't think a black hole would have that effect anyway. If it did you'd never know it, because the ship would disappear down the black hole."

"What about a powerful gravity generator?"

"Hmmm." Forward thought about it, then shook his massive head. "You're talking about a surface gravity in the millions. Any gravity generator I've ever heard of would collapse itself at that level. Let's see, with a frame supported by stasis fields . . . no. The frame would hold and the rest of the machinery would flow like water."

"You don't leave much of my theory."

"Sorry."

Carlos ended a short pause by asking, "How do you think the universe started?"

Forward looked puzzled at the change of subject.

And I began to get uneasy.

Given all that I don't know about cosmology, I do know attitudes and tones of voice. Carlos was giving out broad hints, trying to lead Forward to his own conclusion. Black holes, pirates, the Tunguska meteorite, the origin of the universe—he was offering them as clues. And Forward was not responding correctly.

He was saying, "Ask a priest. Me, I lean toward the Big Bang. The Steady State always seemed so futile."

"I like the Big Bang too," said Carlos.

There was something else to worry about. Those mining tugs: they almost had to belong to Forward Station. How would Ausfaller react when three familiar spacecraft came cruising into his space?

How did I want him to react? Forward Station would make a dandy pirate base. Permeated by laser-drilled corridors distributed almost at random . . . could there be two networks of corridors, connected only at the surface? How would we know?

Suddenly I didn't want to know. I wanted to go home. If only Carlos would stay off the touchy subjects—

But he was speculating about the ship eaters again. "That ten billion metric tons of neutronium, now, that you were using for a test mass. That wouldn't be big enough or dense enough to give us enough of a gravity gradient."

"It might, right near the surface." Forward grinned and held his hands close together. "It was about that big."

"And that's as dense as matter gets in this universe. Too bad."

"True, but . . . have you ever heard of quantum black holes?"

"Yah."

Forward stood up briskly. "Wrong answer."

I rolled out of my web chair, trying to brace myself for a jump, while my fingers fumbled for the third button on my jumper. It was no good. I hadn't practiced in this gravity.

Forward was in mid-leap. He slapped Carlos alongside the head as he went past. He caught me at the peak of his jump, and took me with him via an iron grip on my wrist.

I had no leverage, but I kicked at him. He didn't even try to stop me. It was like fighting a mountain. He gathered my wrists in one hand and towed me away.

Forward was busy. He sat within the horseshoe of his control console, talking. The backs of three disembodied heads showed above the console's edge.

Evidently there was a laser phone on the console. I could hear parts of what Forward was saying. He was ordering the pilots of the three mining tugs to destroy *Hobo Kelly*. He didn't seem to know about Ausfaller yet.

Forward was busy, but Angel was studying us thoughtfully, or unhappily, or both. Well he might. We could disappear, but what messages might we have sent earlier?

I couldn't do anything constructive with Angel watching me. And I couldn't count on Carlos.

I couldn't see Carlos. Forward and Angel had tied us to opposite sides of the central pillar, beneath the Grabber. Carlos hadn't made a sound since then. He might be dying from that tremendous slap across the head.

I tested the line around my wrists. Metal mesh of some kind, cool to the touch . . . and it was tight.

Forward turned a switch. The heads vanished. It was a moment before he spoke.

"You've put me in a very bad position."

And Carlos answered. "I think you put yourself there."

"That may be. You should not have let me guess what you knew."

Carlos said, "Sorry, Bey."

He sounded healthy. Good. "That's all right," I said. "But what's all the excitement about? What has Forward *got*?"

"I think he's got the Tunguska meteorite."

"No. That I do not." Forward stood and faced us. "I will admit that I came here to search for the Tunguska meteorite. I spent several years trying to trace its trajectory after it left Earth. Perhaps it *was* a quantum black hole. Perhaps not. The Institute cut off my funds, without warning, just as I had found a real quantum black hole, the first in history."

I said, "That doesn't tell me a lot."

"Patience, Mr Schaeffer. You know that a black hole may form from the collapse of a massive star? Good. And you know that it takes a body of at least five solar masses. It may mass as much as a galaxy—or as much as the universe. There is some evidence that the universe is an infalling black hole. But at less than five solar masses the collapse would stop at the neutron star stage."

"I follow you."

"In all the history of the universe, there has been one moment at which smaller black holes might have formed. That moment was the explosion of the monoblock, the cosmic egg that once contained all of the matter in the universe. In the ferocity of that explosion there must have been loci of unimaginable pressure. Black holes could have formed of mass down to two point two times ten to the minus fifth grams, one point six times ten to the minus twenty-fifth Angstrom in radius."

"Of course you'd never detect anything that small," said Carlos. He seemed almost cheerful. I wondered why . . . and then I knew. He'd been right about the way the ships were disappearing. It must compensate him for being tied to a pillar.

"But," said Forward, "black holes of all sizes could

have formed in that explosion, and should have. In more than seven hundred years of searching, no quantum black hole has ever been found. Most cosmologists have given up on them, and on the Big Bang too."

Carlos said, "Of course there was the Tunguska meteorite. It could have been a black hole of, oh, asteroidal mass—"

"—and roughly molecular size. But the tide would have pulled down trees as it went past—"

"—and the black hole would have gone right through the Earth and headed back into space a few tons heavier. Eight hundred years ago there was actually a search for the exit point. With that they could have charted a course—"

"Exactly. But I had to give up that approach," said Forward. "I was using a new method when the Institute, ah, severed our relationship."

They must both be mad, I thought. Carlos was tied to a pillar and Forward was about to kill him, yet they were both behaving like members of a very exclusive club . . . to which I did not belong.

Carlos was interested. "How'd you work it?"

"You know that it is possible for an asteriod to capture a quantum black hole? In its interior? For instance, at a mass of ten to the twelfth kilograms—a billion metric tons," he added for my benefit, "a black hole would be only one point five times ten to the minus fifth Angstroms across. Smaller than an atom. In a slow pass through an asteroid it might absorb a few billions of atoms, enough to slow it into an orbit. Thereafter it might orbit within the asteroid for aeons, absorbing very little mass on each pass."

"So?"

"If I chance on an asteroid more massive than it ought to be . . . and if I contrive to move it, and some of the mass stays behind . . ."

"You'd have to search a lot of asteroids. Why do it out

here? Why not the asteroid belt? Oh, of course, you can use hyperdrive out here."

"Exactly. We could search a score of masses in a day, using very little fuel."

"Hey. If it was big enough to eat a spacecraft, why didn't it eat the asteroid you found it in?"

"It wasn't that big," said Forward. "The black hole I found was exactly as I have described it. I enlarged it. I towed it home and ran it into my neutronium sphere. *Then* it was large enough to absorb an asteroid. Now it is quite a massive object. Ten to the twentieth power kilograms, the mass of one of the larger asteroids, and a radius of just under ten to the minus fifth centimeters."

There was satisfaction in Forward's voice. In Carlos' there was suddenly nothing but contempt. "You accomplished all that, and then you used it to rob ships and bury the evidence. Is that what's going to happen to us? Down the rabbit hole?"

"To another universe, perhaps. Where does a black hole lead?"

I wondered about that myself.

Angel had taken Forward's place at the control console. He had fastened the seat belt, something I had not seen Forward do, and was dividing his attention between the instruments and the conversation.

"I'm still wondering how you move it," said Carlos. Then, "Uh! The tugs!"

Forward stared, then guffawed. "You didn't guess that? But of course the black hole can hold a charge. I played the exhaust from an old ion drive reaction motor into it for nearly a month. Now it holds an enormous charge. The tugs can pull it well enough. I wish I had more of them. Soon I will."

"Just a minute," I said. I'd grasped one crucial fact as it went past my head. "The tugs aren't armed? All they do is pull the black hole?"

"That's right." Forward looked at me curiously.

"And the black hole is invisible."

"Yes. We tug it into the path of a spacecraft. If the craft comes near enough it will precipitate into normal space. We guide the black hole through its drive to cripple it, board and rob it at our leisure. Then a slower pass with the quantum black hole, and the ship simply disappears."

"Just one last question," said Carlos. "Why?"

I had a better question.

Just what was Ausfaller going to do when three familiar spacecraft came near? They carried no armaments at all. Their only weapon was invisible.

And it would eat a General Products hull without noticing.

Would Ausfaller fire on unarmed ships?

We'd know, too soon. Up there near the edge of the dome, I had spotted three tiny lights in a tight cluster.

Angel had seen it too. He activated the phone. Phantom heads appeared, one, two, three.

I turned back to Forward, and was startled at the brooding hate in his expression.

"Fortune's child," he said to Carlos. "Natural aristocrat. Certified superman. Why would *you* ever consider stealing anything? Women beg you to give them children, in person if possible, by mail if not! Earth's resources exist to keep you healthy, not that you need them!"

"This may startle you," said Carlos, "but there are people who see *you* as a superman."

"We bred for strength, we Jinxians. At what cost to other factors? Our lives are short, even with the aid of boosterspice. Longer if we can live outside Jinx's gravity. But the people of other worlds think we're funny. The women . . . never mind." He brooded, then said it anyway. "A woman of Earth once told me she would rather go to bed with a tunneling machine. She didn't trust my strength. What woman would?"

The three bright dots had nearly reached the center of the dome. I saw nothing between them. I hadn't expected to. Angel was still talking to the pilots.

Up from the edge of the dome came something I didn't want anyone to notice. I said, "Is that your excuse for mass murder, Forward? Lack of women?"

"I need give you no excuses at all, Shaeffer. My world will thank me for what I've done. Earth has swallowed the lion's share of the interstellar trade for too long."

"They'll thank you, huh? You're going to tell them?"

"I—"

"Julian!" That was Angel calling. He'd seen it . . . no, he hadn't. One of the tug captains had.

Forward left us abruptly. He consulted with Angel in low tones, then turned back. "Carlos! Did you leave your ship on automatic? Or is there someone else aboard?"

"I'm not required to say," said Carlos.

"I could—no. In a minute it will not matter."

Angel said, "Julian, look what he's doing."

"Yes. Very clever. Only a human pilot would think of that."

Ausfaller had maneuvered the *Hobo Kelly* between us and the tugs. If the tugs fired a conventional weapon, they'd blast the dome and kill us all.

The tugs came on.

"He still does not know what he is fighting," Forward said with some satisfaction.

True, and it would cost him. Three unarmed tugs were coming down Ausfaller's throat, carrying a weapon so slow that the tugs could throw it at him, let it absorb *Hobo Kelly,* and pick it up again long before it was a danger to us.

From my viewpoint *Hobo Kelly* was a bright point with three dimmer, more distant points around it. Forward and Angel were getting a better view, through the phone. And they weren't watching us at all.

I began trying to kick off my shoes. They were soft ship-slippers, ankle-high, and they resisted.

I kicked the left foot free just as one of the tugs flared with ruby light.

"He did it!" Carlos didn't know whether to be jubilant or horrified. "He fired on unarmed ships!"

Forward gestured peremptorily. Angel slid out of his seat. Forward slid in and fastened the thick seat belt. Neither had spoken a word.

A second ship burned fiercely red, then expanded in a pink cloud.

The third ship was fleeing.

Forward worked the controls. "I have it in the mass indicator," he rasped. "We have but one chance."

So did I. I peeled the other slipper off with my toes.

Over our heads the jointed arm of the Grabber began to swing . . . and I suddenly realized what they were talking about.

Now there was little to see beyond the dome. The swinging Grabber, and the light of *Hobo Kelly*'s drive, and the two tumbling wrecks, all against a background of fixed stars. Suddenly one of the tugs winked blue-white and was gone. Not even a dust cloud was left behind.

Ausfaller must have seen it. He was turning, fleeing. Then it was as if an invisible hand had picked up *Hobo Kelly* and thrown her away. The fusion light streaked off to one side and set beyond the dome's edge.

With two tugs destroyed and the third fleeing, the black hole was falling free, aimed straight down our throats.

Now there was nothing to see but the delicate motions of the Grabber. Angel stood behind Forward's chair, his knuckles white with his grip on the chair's back.

My few pounds of weight went away and left me in free fall. Tides again. The invisible thing was more massive than this asteroid beneath me. The Grabber swung a meter more to one side . . . and something struck it a mighty blow.

The floor surged away from beneath me, left me head down above the Grabber. The huge soft-iron puppy dish came at me; the jointed metal arm collapsed like a spring. It slowed, stopped.

"You got it!" Angel crowed like a rooster and slapped

at the back of the chair, holding himself down with his other hand. He turned a gloating look on us, turned back just as suddenly. "The ship! It's getting away!"

"No." Forward was bent over the console. "I see him. Good, he is coming back, straight toward us. This time there will be no tugs to warn the pilot."

The Grabber swung ponderously toward the point where I'd seen *Hobo Kelly* disappear. It moved centimeters at a time, pulling a massive invisible weight.

And Ausfaller was coming back to rescue us. He'd be a sitting duck, unless—

I reached up with my toes, groping for the first and fourth buttons on my falling jumper.

The weaponry in my wonderful suit hadn't helped me against Jinxian strength and speed. But flatlanders are less than limber, and so are Jinxians. Forward had tied my hands and left it at that.

I wrapped two sets of toes around the buttons and tugged.

My legs were bent pretzel-fashion. I had no leverage. But the first button tore loose, and then the thread. Another invisible weapon to battle Forward's portable bottomless hole.

The thread pulled the fourth button loose. I brought my feet down to where they belonged, keeping the thread taut, and pushed backward. I felt the Sinclair molecule chain sinking into the pillar.

The Grabber was still swinging.

When the thread was through the pillar I could bring it up in back of me and try to cut my bonds. More likely I'd cut my wrists and bleed to death; but I had to try. I wondered if I could do anything before Forward launched the black hole.

A cold breeze caressed my feet.

I looked down. Thick fog boiled out around the pillar.

Some very cold gas must be spraying through the hair-fine crack.

I kept pushing. More fog formed. The cold was numb-

ing. I felt the jerk as the magic thread cut through. Now
the wrists—

Liquid helium?

Forward had moored us to the main superconducting
power cable.

That was probably a mistake. I pulled my feet forward,
carefully, steadily, feeling the thread bite through on the
return cut.

The Grabber had stopped swinging. Now it moved on
its arm like a blind, questing worm, as Forward made fine
adjustments. Angel was beginning to show the strain of
holding himself upside down.

My feet jerked slightly. I was through. My feet were
terribly cold, almost without sensation. I let the buttons
go, left them floating up toward the dome, and kicked
back hard with my heels.

Something shifted. I kicked again.

Thunder and lightning flared around my feet.

I jerked my knees up to my chin. The lightning
crackled and flashed white light into the billowing fog.
Angel and Forward turned in astonishment. I laughed at
them, letting them see it. Yes, gentlemen, I did it on purpose.

The lightning stopped. In the sudden silence Forward
was screaming. "—know what you've *done*?"

There was a grinding *crunch,* a shuddering against my
back. I looked up.

A piece had been bitten out of the Grabber.

I was upside down and getting heavier. Angel suddenly
pivoted around his grip on Forward's chair. He hung
above the dome, above the sky. He screamed.

My legs gripped the pillar hard. I felt Carlos' feet fum-
bling for a foothold, and heard Carlos' laughter.

Near the edge of the dome a spear of light was rising.
Hobo Kelly's drive, decelerating, growing larger. Otherwise the sky was clear and empty. And a piece of the
dome disappeared with a snapping sound.

Angel screamed and dropped. Just above the dome he
seemed to flare with blue light.

He was gone.

Air roared out through the dome—and more was disappearing into something that had been invisible. Now it showed as a blue pinpoint drifting toward the floor. Forward had turned to watch it fall.

Loose objects fell across the chamber, looped around the pinpoint at meteor speed or fell into it with bursts of light. Every atom of my body felt the pull of the thing, the urge to die in an infinite fall. Now we hung side by side from a horizontal pillar. I noted with approval that Carlos' mouth was wide open, like mine, to clear his lungs so that they wouldn't burst when the air was gone.

Daggers in my ears and sinuses, pressure in my gut.

Forward turned back to the controls. He moved one knob hard over. Then—he opened the seat belt and stepped out and up, and fell.

Light flared. He was gone.

The lightning-colored pinpoint drifted to the floor, and into it. Above the increasing roar of air I could hear the grumbling of rock being pulverized, dwindling as the black hole settled toward the center of the asteroid.

The air was deadly thin, but not gone. My lungs thought they were gasping vacuum. But my blood was not boiling. I'd have known it.

So I gasped, and kept gasping. It was all I had attention for. Black spots flickered before my eyes, but I was still gasping and alive when Ausfaller reached us carrying a clear plastic package and an enormous handgun.

He came in fast, on a rocket backpack. Even as he decelerated he was looking around for something to shoot. He returned in a loop of fire. He studied us through his faceplate, possibly wondering if we were dead.

He flipped the plastic package open. It was a thin sack with a zipper and a small tank attached. He had to dig for a torch to cut our bonds. He freed Carlos first, helped him into the sack. Carlos bled from the nose and ears. He was barely mobile. So was I, but Ausfaller got me into the sack with Carlos and zipped it up. Air hissed in around us.

I wondered what came next. As an inflated sphere the rescue bag was too big for the tunnels. Ausfaller had thought of that. He fired at the dome, blasted a gaping hole in it, and flew us out on the rocket backpack.

Hobo Kelly was grounded nearby. I saw that the rescue bag wouldn't fit the airlock either . . . and Ausfaller confirmed my worst fear. He signaled us by opening his mouth wide. Then he zipped open the rescue bag and half-carried us into the airlock while the air was still roaring out of our lungs.

When there was air again Carlos whispered, "Please don't do that any more."

"It should not be necessary any more." Ausfaller smiled. "Whatever it was you did, well done. I have two well-equipped autodocs to repair you. While you are healing, I will see about recovering the treasures within the asteroid."

Carlos held up a hand, but no sound came. He looked like something risen from the dead: blood running from nose and ears, mouth wide open, one feeble hand raised against gravity.

"One thing," Ausfaller said briskly. "I saw many dead men; I saw no living ones. How many were there? Am I likely to meet opposition while searching?"

"Forget it," Carlos croaked. "Get us out of here. Now."

Ausfaller frowned. "What—"

"No time. Get us out."

Ausfaller tasted something sour. "Very well. First, the autodocs." He turned, but Carlos' strengthless hand stopped him.

"Futz, no. I want to see this," Carlos whispered.

Again Ausfaller gave in. He trotted off to the control room. Carlos tottered after him. I tottered after them both, wiping blood from my nose, feeling half dead myself. But I'd half guessed what Carlos expected, and I didn't want to miss it.

We strapped down. Ausfaller fired the main thruster. The rock surged away.

"Far enough," Carlos whispered presently. "Turn us around."

Ausfaller took care of that. Then, "What are we looking for?"

"You'll know."

"Carlos, was I right to fire on the tugs?"

"Oh, yes."

"Good. I was worried. Then Forward was the ship eater?"

"Yah."

"I did not see him when I came for you. Where is he?"

Ausfaller was annoyed when Carlos laughed, and more annoyed when I joined him. It hurt my throat. "Even so, he saved our lives," I said. "He must have turned up the air pressure just before he jumped. I wonder why he did that?"

"Wanted to be remembered," said Carlos. "Nobody else knew what he'd done. *Ahh—*"

I looked, just as part of the asteroid collapsed into itself, leaving a deep crater.

"It moves slower at apogee. Picks up more matter," said Carlos.

"What *are* you talking about?"

"Later, Sigmund. When my throat grows back."

"Forward had a hole in his pocket," I said helpfully. "He—"

The other side of the asteroid collapsed. For a moment lightning seemed to flare in there.

Then the whole dirty snowball was growing smaller.

I thought of something Carlos had probably missed. "Sigmund, has this ship got automatic sunscreens?"

"Of *course* we've got—"

There was a universe-eating flash of light before the screen went black. When the screen cleared there was nothing to see but stars.

PLUTO IS BLACK!

Robert L. Forward

After all the talk about Dr Robert Forward, it's time readers met the man. This article was originally published in GALAXY with byline as "George Peterson Field"; at that time Bob Forward wasn't ready to come out of the closet and admit to writing for science fiction magazines. He thought his employers found him far-out enough without that association.

Since then he has been principal speaker at a number of science fiction writers' conventions, and has published speculative articles in SF magazine. A physicist by trade, his association with science fiction seems to have begun in high school when he bought Karen Anderson (then not Anderson and then not married to Poul) a lunch.

His publications include a serious proposal to Congress for an interstellar probe.

This article was the first SF publication describing the use of extreme gravitational fields near a rotating ultra-dense body. The mystery of the Pluto mass/size anomaly is still unresolved.

NOTE ADDED 16 YEARS LATER

It is amazing, but this wildly speculative article has remained valid for over fifteen years. As late as 24 March 1977, there was an article in Nature *entitled "Pluto: The Little-Known Planet," which pointed out that there was a significant discrepancy between the estimated diameter of 3000 km (*SCIENCE *194, 835; 1976) and the estimated mass of 0.11 Earth masses (*ASTR. *J. 76, 488; 1971). These numbers would give Pluto a minimum density of fifty times that of water.*

However, if the astronomical community had read my article when it was published in 1962 they would now know a lot more about Pluto. For like one of Swift's stories, which predicted that Mars had two tiny moons, my article predicts that Pluto has a satellite. But did they pay any attention to me and look for it? No!

It wasn't until 1978 that J. W. Christy of the United States Naval Observatory reported the discovery of a moon about Pluto. The astronomers are thinking about calling the new moon some fancy Greek name like Charon, but I think they ought to name it George (my pseudonym at the time) since for fifteen years the astronomers had been trying to to measure the mass of Pluto but were never able to do it properly. Finally they let George do it.

Yes, George did it (to me, this time). George is in a 154 hour, 20,000 km high synchronous orbit about Pluto.

Unfortunately for the premise of my article, that period and orbital radius for George tells us that the mass of Pluto is only about 1/380 of the mass of the Earth. That, combined with the present 2700 km estimate for the diameter of Pluto, gives Pluto a reasonable density of 1.5 times that of water.

Oh well, it was a good story while it lasted.

                         Dr Robert L. Forward
                         Malibu, California
                         18 August 1978

Pluto, the outermost planet of the solar system, was named after that dark, mysterious stranger, the Greek god of Hell. The name is apt, for this dark, mysterious planet has had the astonomers living in their own private purgatory ever since its existence was first deduced.

The astronomers have been able to obtain a few facts about the planet, but what is frustrating them is that by using these hard-won facts they can easily prove that such a planet cannot exist! However, despite all their theories, that baleful speck of light continues to glare down the telescope at them as if to say, "Wrong! Guess again."

It all started back in the 1820s when it was found that Uranus was not following a smooth elliptical orbit, but was staggering through the sky like a drunk. It was finally guessed that the erratic behavior was due to another planet still further out. Two mathematicians tackled the problem and independently calculated the orbit, position and mass of the hypothetical planet. With the position in the sky known, it was a simple matter for the astronomers to find the new planet—Neptune—which till then had been overlooked. As soon as Neptune was discovered, the orbit of Uranus was recalculated and this time the observations fitted perfectly—almost. There were still small differences between the predicted and the actual positions.

Spurred on by the success of the previous work, Professor Percival Lowell thought that there might be another planet still further out. He calculated that it should be four thousand million miles out from the sun, moving in an unusually elliptic orbit with a period of 280 years, and it should have a mass at least six times that of the earth. The same figures were later obtained by another prominent astronomer, Professor W. H. Pickering.

An object this large should be easy to find, so in 1915, Professor Lowell sat down at his moderate sized, but adequate, telescope and started looking. He died without finding it. It was there, but it was much fainter than it had a right to be and he had missed it. To be that faint, a planet that large would have to be painted black! The astronomers' private purgatory had started. Later searches with photographic plates also missed it, although it was later found that it had been photographed twice. Once it was masked by a bright star, and the other time the image fell on a flaw in the negative!

It wasn't until 1930 that Pluto was found. The radius, eccentricity and period of the orbit were almost exactly as Lowell had predicted. Because the orbital calculations were so closely verified, there was no reason to doubt Lowell's prediction that Pluto had a mass of at least six times the earth's mass, except that the size of the planet was impossibly small. It was so small that it still looked like a point through the telescope. It wasn't until 1950, using the 200-inch Palomar telescope, that an upper limit on Pluto's diameter was obtained. It was less than 3,600 miles, or smaller than Mercury. This would make the density of the planet hundreds of times greater than water! The earth is only 5.5 times denser than water, and osmium, the densest known material, is only 22 times denser. Thus, Pluto seems to be made of ultradense matter—except such densities should only be found in dwarf stars, neutron stars, and black holes—and those objects have the mass of a star, not a planet. Such a planet should not exist!

But it does!

The astronomers have tried everything in an attempt to make sense out of what they know (including fudging the numbers a little). There have been suggestions that Pluto and the small observed diameter may be due to specular reflection. (There was a similar effect present with the Echo balloon satellite.) But there are slow variations in the intensity, indicating that Pluto is rotating with a day of 154 hours, and one would expect rather sudden changes in intensity from the specular reflections. The other unusual thing about Pluto is its orbit. The orbit is so egg-shaped that it actually passes inside the orbit of Neptune, so that they would at various times in the past and future pass very close to each other. The astronomers feel that, due to the perturbations from the other planets, it is improbable that Pluto has been in its present orbit for more than 200 million years. This is only a small fraction of the age of the solar system; so apparently Pluto is a stranger which arrived in its present orbit from other regions of space.

There is one other nagging feature and that is the breakdown of Bode's Law for Neptune and Pluto. Bode's Law is an empirical formula for the orbits of the planets. The distance of the planets from the sun in AU is given by:

$$AU = 0.4 + 0.3 \times 2^n$$

where Mercury is at 0.4 AU and the other planets are given by the Bode formula with $n = 0$ for Venus, 1 for Earth, etc. The reason for its acceptance is best shown by the following table:

THE ORBITS OF THE PLANETS ACCORDING TO BODE

	Radius Using Bode's Law	Actual Orbital Radius in A.U.
Mercury	0.4	0.387
Venus	0.7	0.723
Earth	1.0	1.0
Mars	1.6	1.524
Asteroids	2.8	2.8

Jupiter	5.2	5.2
Saturn	10.0	9.54
Uranus	19.6	19.2
Neptune	—	30.0
Pluto	38.8	39.5

(Notice that Bode's Law does not predict a planet in Neptune's orbit.)

There is obviously something wrong out past Uranus. It is as if Pluto had come along, interacted with Neptune and pushed it into an inner orbit, usurping its proper place in Bode's Law.

A very weird planet indeed. What we actually know about Pluto is very little. But this little bit that we know points out that it may be very profitable to learn more about it. In the coming decades, as the Orbiting Observatories are put into operation, we will get to know it better. But until then it is interesting to speculate.

One of the most spectacular possible solutions to the mystery is to assume that Pluto really is a visitor from outside the solar system. Not just a frozen planet that happened to be collected by the sun long ago in its wanderings through space, but a device, a "gravity catapult" made by intelligent beings and placed in orbit around the sun . . . a "gravity catapult" being a generator of gravitational fields that can be used to accelerate spaceships to velocities near the speed of light.

Using Einstein's theory of gravity, the general theory of relativity, we can envision how such a gravitational catapult could be made, although we couldn't even begin to construct it with our present technology.

Einstein's theory of gravity predicts many unusual properties of gravitation. These effects are not well known since they are unobservable with our presently available instruments. So there was little reason to talk about them. The most interesting effect is that a rotating mass, such as a massive body, not only attracts an object toward it with its regular gravitational field, but it also "drags" the object around it in the same direction as its rotation. Thus a spaceship on orbit near the earth is helped along in its orbit (just a little bit) by the earth's rotation. In order to have any appreciable dragging effect on a space ship, a rotating planet has to be very heavy, and rotating rapidly; also the spaceship should be as close as possible to the planet's center. This calls for planets with high density, since they have all their mass concentrated in a small radius and the spaceship can get close to the center without hitting the surface.

Using these ideas of Einstein, we can envision how such a gravitational catapult could be made. It would require a large, very dense body with a mass larger than the earth, made of collapsed matter many times denser than water. It could be a spinning planet of dwarf star or neutron star density or it could be a spinning black hole or even two small black holes in orbit about each other. All of these objects would produce a large acceleration on a spacecraft passing at the proper distance from them. However, all the spherical masses have the problem that you have to get close to the surface before you get an appreciable drag effect, and if you get too close to the surface of an ultradense object you will be ripped apart by tidal forces. However, if the ultradense matter were in the shape of a ring, then it is possible to obtain the drag effect with minimum tidal forces. To be effective, the ring would have to be whirling in space like a gigantic, fat smoke ring, constantly turning from inside-out.

The forces the ring would exert on a nearby object, such as a spaceship, would tend to drag the ship around to one side, where it would be pulled right through the center of the ring under terrific acceleration and expelled from the other side. If the acceleration were of the order of millions of g's, then the velocity of the ship on the other side would be near that of light. The amazing thing is that because the acceleration is applied by gravitational forces, a person in the spaceship would feel very little. You are in free fall all the time! This is because gravitational forces act independently on each atom of the body at the same time and give each atom the same acceleration. Because there is almost no difference in the motion of the different parts of the body, there would be no feeling of weight—even at these very high acceleration levels.

A network of these devices in orbit around interesting stars would allow an advanced race to have an energetically economical method of space travel. Because, even though the ring would whirl a little slower after the spaceship had taken away some of its energy, it would gain that energy back when it decelerated an incoming ship. There, of course, would be no way to aim such a massive object, so to make sure that it can be used for more than one direction, it would be set to cartwheeling slowly (say with a 154 hour period?) so as to cover all parts of the sky.

Such a device could even by made elsewhere by some unimaginable technology and shot through space by a much larger device. It could halt itself by pushing against a massive planet (such as Neptune?).

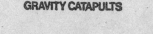

GRAVITY CATAPULTS

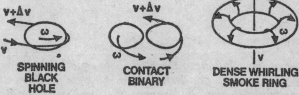

SPINNING BLACK HOLE   CONTACT BINARY   DENSE WHIRLING SMOKE RING

Maybe when we get to Pluto, we will find such a gravity catapult with a small artifical satellite around it. Inside the satellite will be a message from the Galactic Federation welcoming us into its membership now that we had interplanetary flight, and presenting us with the gravitational catapult for our use until we know enough to make one ourselves—a sort of "coming out" present!

FOUNTAIN OF FORCE

*Grant Carrington and
George Zebrowski*

*One of the solutions to the black hole equations—the real
equations, which are derived from Einstein's tensors and
are solvable only by a very few and very brilliant
people—suggests that black holes are exactly symmetri-
cal. What we see as an infinite sink, a black hole, becomes a "white hole", a source of matter and energy in
another time and place. The black hole and the white
hole are connected by a tunnel through spacetime. This
tunnel has irreverently been called a "wormhole".*

The math is complex, and only allows; it does not

*compel. That is, there is no requirement that wormholes
exist—but they might. The mathematics say that if a hole
spins rapidly enough, and is large enough, then what goes
into the hole in our universe might, just might, come out
elsewhere—and possibly elsewhen. There is no evidence
for the existence of this, but it is possible.*

*A number of stories on this theme have appeared; this
is one of the earliest, and still one of the best. It has been
completely rewritten to take account of new physics.*

*Grant Carrington and George Zebrowski are not gener-
ally thought of as "hard science" writers, but they can do
science when they try; as witness this.*

*Matter was disappearing from Einstein's universe,
streaming through holes punched into space by stars un-
dergoing gravitational collapse, returning to normal space
seconds, hours, or days later in time—sometimes between
the island galaxies, sometimes popping back into the same
galaxy only megaparsecs away. It was a universe pep-
pered with rat holes. Humanity's starships traversed these
spatial relics of gravitational collapse, charting regular
points of entry and re-entry in space-time's elastic fabric,
finding new wormways to maintain a reasonably useful
galaxy-wide system.*

Sita Rahman took readings from the microelectrodes
implanted in Fleming Mayhew's shaved scalp. She
stopped speaking and carefully turned a dial on the instrument console. "What does that feel like?" she asked.

"Like you're tickling a pleasure center with straw-
berry-flavored spaghetti." He looked up at her. She was a
short woman with closely cropped black hair and large
brown eyes, and she never looked into his eyes when she
was working.

"What's spaghetti?"

"An old Earth food."

"Still on that? I thought you were giving me some attention just now."

The light over the medical bay entrance flashed then

the door slid open, letting in the stocky form of Jack Bergier, nominal captain of the starship *Robert B. Leighton,* second in command to percept Fleming Mayhew.

"You look worried, Jack," Fleming said. "What's the matter?"

"Hans Pavel is missing. We just got the tach message." He handed Mayhew a slip of paper.

"What is it?" Sita asked.

Fleming looked at the paper. "They want us to go to Epsilon Lyrae immediately."

"The new rat hole there," Bergier said, "has swallowed two percept-starship teams already."

"Two?" Sita raised her eyebrows.

Bergier nodded. "The first was a young percept on his first cruise. They discovered the anomaly, reported it back to Vega IV, and started the standard exploratory approach. When they didn't report back within three days, Pavel was sent. He also took the standard approach, sending back a running account. The transmission cut off well above the point of no return."

"Maybe they went through and couldn't find a hole back. It wouldn't be the first time that's happened," Sita said.

Bergier shook his head. "Pavel was too experienced to do that. He wouldn't have gone in until he was sure it was a hole rather than a cyst with matter at the center. He would have said they were going in, and he didn't."

"And he was well above the event horizon?"

"I double-checked with Vega."

"How big was it?" Fleming asked.

"Five hundred kilometers."

"What?" Fleming sat up suddenly. "That's impossible!" Sita pushed him back down. "There's never been a hole bigger than ten kilometers before."

"It must have coalesced from smaller ones," Bergier said.

"The g-field near that thing would be huge. Maybe their gravitational shields gave out and tidal forces pulled the ships apart. They must have been crazy to send that kid in."

"He was the one who discovered it," Bergier said. "They didn't know what they had until Pavel went in."

"So they want us?" Sita asked. "You know we're tired."

"Fleming is the closest experienced percept. The next one is at least two days further away."

"And, if there's any chance of saving Pavel, time may be critical," Fleming said. "You don't have to go, Sita."

"If you went to hell, I'd have to go too. You're a piece of equipment that has to be in top shape. I wouldn't trust anyone else to work on you." She began removing the needles from the receptacles in his scalp.

"Put him to sleep, Sita," Bergier said. "He's got a lot of work ahead of him."

Two observer starships were waiting for the *Robert B. Leighton* when she arrived at Epsilon Lyrae.

"Look at them." Fleming smiled wryly. "We're the guinea pigs—and they're going to watch." He turned to Captain Bergier. "When do we start?"

"The *Swift* will send in a drone probe first. You'll follow it in."

Fleming nodded. "How soon?"

"You'd better be ready by twelve hundred."

An hour later, Fleming's eyes were covered with sensing pads, and earplugs played a sibilant wash of white noise into his mind. The microelectrodes had again been inserted into the scar tissue pockets of his skull and Sita Rahman sat nearby at the med console, monitoring his body functions and the precisely measured micro-flow of hallucinogens into his blood stream. The ship's computer waited in programmed patience until Sita connected it to Fleming's mind, then it began a stream of tests to certify that Fleming was prepared for complete merging.

A series of differential equations flashed across his mind. He stored them in the computer's temporary storage banks and activated the proper solution subroutines, which took the data and computed the answers while Fleming worked on other problems. At a critical juncture, the computer queried Fleming for the proper path to follow. Fleming activated a Runge-Kutta approximation in thirty-three steps. The computer compared Fleming's methods and delay times to the preferred answers in its banks and continued the tests.

Fleming ran problems in human psychology and motivation, radar sensing distortions and vectors, and other simulated situations. A minute after Sita had connected Fleming with the computer, it had compared his answers and methods with the desired results and weighed his failures and successes.

Satisfied, it projected a series of Hinton hypercubes onto Fleming's visual cortex. The multi-colored cubes rotated slowly, revealing distortion lines and plane surfaces bathed in light. Fleming concentrated on the cubes, traced the edges to a right-angled juncture, and followed the fourth perpendicular into four-space.

Every circuit in the ship was now his nervous system. The *Robert B. Leighton* became Fleming Mayhew's body. His eyes drank radar impulses; his ears heard the sighing of stellar winds; his voice was a laser beam flickering out to the nearby observational starships. The *Leighton*'s mini-black hole power plant was his heart, and the gravity screens his garments.

The computer fed him information on the black hole they were approaching, and Fleming computed that the g-force on an unscreened ship would be 1148 g's at a million kilometers, 45 million g's at 5000 kilometers, and 2 billion g's at 500 kilometers. Fleming made a very careful check of the ship's screens and the power that maintained them.

From far below the infrared to beyond the ultraviolet, his sensors showed him the splendor of the star that had collapsed upon itself, curving the fabric of space-time to permit matter to stream into another part of the universe, leaving only an ebony cave.

He was still too distant to perceive the hole in all four dimensions, but he could sense the stream of matter being drawn in, coalescing into a whirlpool of violently accelerated material, radiating at frequencies beyond the range of his human senses, a fountain of rainbow colors.

Fleming inhaled the spectacle, lingering over each of the streamers: hydrogen, radiating at the twenty-one centimeter band, a rich royal purple; helium, a vivid spring green; a mass of scarce oxygen atoms, swirling in a crimson nebula before disappearing; a sudden shower of X-radiation bursting out from the black hole like a fireworks display, as a piece of matter crossed the event horizon. The picture was unchanging, yet always different.

He could barely sense the beings who were caring for his human self, the soft creatures contained by the starship: dependable Jack Bergier, fear nibbling at the back of his mind; Sita Rahman, watching her instruments intently, ready to bring him out of the computer linkage if anything should go wrong.

There was another presence, beyond his starship shell, and Fleming reached out a tendril of thought to probe it. It was another percept, a cadet, observing from the *Ernest Swift*, a bright red thread of fear running through his mind. Fleming revealed his own thoughts to the cadet, showing his own fears and the controls by which he harnessed them.

Is Professor Weisberg still at the Academy? Fleming asked.

The stars twinkled with laughter. *Yes. Last week he slipped salt into the sugar dispensers in the faculty lounge.* The stars darkened. *Do you think Hans Pavel is safe?*

I don't know. They exchanged information about the wormhole, and Fleming showed the young cadet what he had just seen. He withdrew when the drone left the *Swift*, maintaining only a tendril of communication so that the cadet would be able to see how the older percept worked.

The drone spiralled toward the anomaly, lasering back its conventional measurements. Fleming followed it carefully. The gravitational flux increased as the drone approached the hole. No light could escape from it, but there was a slight blue shift in light coming toward the drone from the background of galactic stars and occasional bursts of energy from matter crossing the event horizon.

Then the mass detector went off-scale, and the drone was sucked in so quickly that Fleming was barely able to follow its path to the disappearance point.

Instead of taking the standard approach taken by the two lost starships and the drone, Fleming computed a shallow parabola for the *Robert B. Leighton*'s approach to the wormhole. The apex of the parabola was just above the hole's event horizon, the point of no return where nothing other than a faster-than-light tach beam could climb out of the hole's increasing gravitational well.

As long as the drone continued sending, the chances were good that the exit opened safely into some distant part of space-time. The signal would cease when the drone made the bridge-jump, but it would be picked up again when the sky was searched for the new point-source. Hole mapping would have been impossible without the modulation of the supra-light speed tachyon waves, except on a hit-or-miss suicide mission basis.

A tendril of thought reached out to Fleming from the *Ernest Swift*. He held it, strenghtening it into a pillar. *Hang on, youngster.* The stars were cold.

Warm nights in the pale crystal port of Nellean with a glass of smooth Altairean wine. The dancers of New Frisco with blue hair billowing about their ankles. Sita's cool touch on his arm in the mists of awakening. Sweat bathed his body and was absorbed by the sensing pads; fear was a vise around his brain.

As the *Leighton* gathered speed, Fleming's senses reached out ahead of it. A flare of white-hot brilliance blinded him as the *Leighton* lurched toward the anomaly like a toy on a rubber band. He stared into an ebony lake.

In a moment his eyes would fall in and sink like stones. Fleming cut in the forward field engines, driving the starship back. His eyes were flaming pools of agony and his four-dimensional perception was almost gone, but the ship's sensors were unaffected. The pillar of communication with the cadet was silent; the youngster was unconscious. The *Leighton*'s protective screens complained from the opposing forces playing with it. The pillar of communication disappeared as the cadet's physician disconnected him from his computer. Fleming reached out with laser tongues to talk to the other ships, relaying his own and the sensors' experience, even as the *Leighton* strained away from the hole, then accelerated rapidly as she broke loose.

Less than a minute and a half had passed since Fleming had been blinded. He relaxed now, letting his subconscious mull over what he had experienced.

Fleming's eyes were still burning when Sita unhooked him from the computer, although they were physically uninjured. He felt dizzy from the hallucinogenic inhibitors that Sita had injected into his bloodstream, but he was surprised at the clearness of his vision.

"What happened? Do you know what happened?" Captain Bergier's voice was insistent.

"Where did the drone come out?" Fleming asked.

"Can't you wait until he gets some rest?" Sita said angrily.

Fleming's vision rippled suddenly like the surface of a pond, hurting his eyes. "No, Sita," he said. "We've got to finish this thing off. Pavel's life may depend on it." To his surprise, his voice was remarkably steady, without the quaver to it he had expected. "There's nothing really different about the hole itself, except for its size. That might make the outstream unique . . ."

"In what way?" Bergier asked.

"It might come out farther away than any other outstream we've yet found. Quite a bit farther away."

"Outside the Milky Way galaxy," Sita said in a near-whisper. "What a fate. To be lost in the space between galaxies."

"Have we picked up the drone's tachyon beam yet?" Fleming asked.

Bergier examined a scanning screen. "Not yet," he said. "We're still searching the sky. We'll find it. There's no place in the universe from which we can't receive that tachyon signal."

Fleming closed his eyes and put his head back on the couch. "That's true," he said. "Unless the drone has left the universe we know."

"Then Pavel . . ." Sita started to say.

". . . is hopelessly lost, or dead. His shields might have failed and he's been torn apart. Otherwise he would have signalled back to complete the chart. Then he would have started searching for a return hole, or gone into stasis to come back using his star drive."

"But he might just be lost."

"Yes." Fleming looked at Sita's sorrowful face. "There's still another possibility, a real long shot, but possible, as far as we know. If Pavel's ship was only partially damaged and, if in the course of trying to pull away, the vessel came into the hole's ergosphere and stayed there for a time, then the entire history of the universe would have rushed past him in a short subjective time. All nature would collapse into a giant black hole, some 100 billion years from now. The time line of any conscious being caught in the ergosphere of any black hole connects to the end of time."

Bergier looked up from the screen he was watching. "The cosmos collapses, coalescing out of smaller black holes, maybe out of galactic center holes, and punches out as a white hole in a new space, a new fireball for a new expansion."

Fleming nodded. "Another universe, or a new cycle of our own, created by all the matter and energy streaming through the black hole finale of ours, expanding the fabric of new space, a fountain of force creating a new space for all the new potential of expanding material." *And later* he thought, *new rat holes will appear in that universe, as they do in ours, making one form of interstellar travel possible; but they will be the first holes in a sinking ship, holes connecting one part of the ship to another. Larger and larger holes will form, until they all coalesce into a giant black abyss which will be a new beginning of yet another universe.*

"Wait a minute," Sita said. "If Pavel went forward through time in the ergosphere, then he must still be *in* the ergosphere."

"If he is," Bergier said, "then we can reach him only by making a passage approach to go through, and we can't do that until the drone signal reaches us to let us know it's safe."

"I was talking about a possibility," Fleming said. "I don't really think he's there. It would take too much power to maintain a position in the ergosphere. He was probably drawn through, damaged or undamaged, even if he stayed in the ergosphere for a few moments."

"We've got the drone's signal!" Bergier said suddenly.

Fleming sat up. "Where is it?"

"I'll be damned! It's bridged to Andromeda!"

"Then Pavel is there too?" Sita asked.

"Wait a minute," Bergier said. "There's no additional message."

Fleming and Sita watched as Bergier peered at the screen on his console, his face bathed in the ghostly light.

"Pavel is there! He's using the probe drone's signal. He says he was damaged but went through safely, and there are large holes nearby that he thinks will connect back to our galaxy. He says there's no need for us to go through after him."

Andromeda! Even with current stardrives, it would take centuries to reach it. Despite the difficulties and dangers, wormhole charting had once again proved its value. Only a hole could reach Andromeda, and presumably other galaxies as well, with such speed.

His job was done. Fleming lay back and slept.

PAPA SCHIMMELHORN'S YANG

R. Bretnor

Long-time readers of science fiction will remember Papa Schimmelhorn, formerly the janitor in the Geneva Institute of Higher Physics, whose subconscious absorbed all the lectures and extrapolates to working gadgetry. Unfortunately, Papa missed three weeks of lectures due to a redhead from, I think, Berne, so that his knowledge of physics is incomplete.

When Mrs Pournelle and I were driving home from a convention in Canada, we stopped over to see Reg Bretnor, and by coincidence I had with me an old story col-

*lection containing a Papa Schimmelhorn. Naturally I
asked Reg why he didn't write one for this collection; the
result you see here.*

*Fair warning. You may not rely on anything said in
this story. And who cares?*

It was no coincidence that Little Anton returned from
Hong Kong to New Haven on the very afternoon that
Papa Schimmelhorn finished installing his anti-gravity
device under the hood of his 1922 Stanley Steamer touring car. For a week, Papa Schimmelhorn had been in
deep disgrace, if not with fortune and men's eyes at least
with Mama Schimmelhorn, his employer Heinrich Luedesing, Mrs Luedesing, Pastor Hundhammer, and two
deacons of the pastor's church, all of whom had caught
him *in flagrante* very much *delicto* with a part-time so-
prano named Dora Grossapfel up in the choir loft, where
they themselves certainly had no business being on a
lovely, warm Tuesday afternoon in June.

Old Heinrich, assuming a high moral tone, had suspend-
ed him for a fortnight from his job as foreman at the
Luedesing Cuckoo Clock Factory. Mama Schimmelhorn,
much less formally, had pried him off Ms Grossapfel with
her stiff black umbrella and had then applied it vigorously
to both of them. Ms Grossapfel had ruined her mascara
by weeping piteously, and Mrs Luedesing, mistakenly,
had taken her for the victim either of rape or of seduc-
tion. Then Mama Schimmelhorn had led him home igno-
miniously by the ear, prodding him all the way with the
umbrella, and hissing, "At more than eighty years—*ach!*
Dirty old man! Now you shtay in der haus. Nefer again
I let you loose all by yourself!"

So he had retreated to his basement workshop and to
the more congenial company of his old striped tomcat,
Gustav-Adolf, whose tastes and instincts were much like
his own, and had devoted several days to assembling and
installing the curious miscellany of valves, gears, tubing,
solenoids, and oddly formed ceramics which, in and

around a device resembling (though only when you looked at it correctly) the illegitimate offspring of a translucent Klein bottle, constituted the functioning heart of his invention.

The job done, he fired up the boiler and stood over it while it produced a proper head of steam. "*Ach,* Gustav-Adolf," he exclaimed, "how nice it iss I am a chenius! Imachine—no vun else knows dot for anti-grafity you must haff shteam, instead of elecdricity vhich gets in der vay. Und I myself do not know vhy, because it iss all in mein subconscience, chust as Herr Doktor Jung told me in Geneva when I vas chanitor at der Institüt für Higher Physics."

"Mrreow!" replied Gustav-Adolf, looking up from his saucer of dark beer on the cluttered Schimmelhorn work bench.

"Dot's right, und predty soon ve see how it vorks." Papa Schimmelhorn made some fine adjustments and peered at the steam gauge on the dashboard. He closed the hood and clamped it down. "Zo, ve are ready!" he exclaimed. Thinking of Dora Grossapfel's plump behind under easily removable stretch-pants, he climbed into the driver's seat. "*Ach,* such a pity, Gustav-Adolf! Imachine, my nice Dora among her predty clouds maybe at two thousand feet!" Heaving a sigh, he eased back gently on a sort of joystick he had installed where an ordinary car's gearshift lever would have been, and silently the Stanley Steamer began to rise—six inches, a foot, two feet. He turned the lever's handle left, then right, and the car turned with it. He tipped the nose up and then down. "*Wunderschön!* How do they say vith shtupid rockets?—all systems are go. Und now, Papa, all you do is vait vhile Mama simmers down, und vunce again ve chase die predty pussycats—"

In the background, a chorus of cuckoo-clocks began to sing the hour of twelve—and at that instant Little Anton, having parked his Mercedes 300-SL just around the corner, knocked at the basement's garage door.

"Vot iss?" Papa Schimmelhorn brought the car down to a gentle four-point landing, mentally reviewing the dames and damsels who, knowing that Mama was away for the day, might be expected to pay him a surreptitious visit.

The knocking was repeated, more emphatically. "I say!" called Little Anton. "It's me, your grand-nephew! Do let me in!"

"Lidtle Anton?" cried Papa Schimmelhorn, dismounting. "How nice you are back from die Chinesers, but your voice iss different in der accent. Vot has happened?"

"I've been listening to BBC, old boy. Open up, and I'll tell you all about it."

"*Donnerwetter,* der door iss locked und Mama has der key!"

Little Anton chortled. "Don't tell me a genius like you couldn't pick that stupid lock. You just don't want Mama to get any angrier. Well, all right then—"

In his mind's eye, Papa Schimmelhorn could see Little Anton crossing his eyes preliminary to reaching around the dimensional corner into that private universe to which only he had access. He waited. A moment later there was a click of tumblers and the door swung open.

"*Lidtle Anton!*" boomed Papa Schimmelhorn, embracing him and standing back again for a better view. "How you haff changed!"

And indeed Little Anton no longer was the callow youth who had left New Haven to seek his fortune when the sudden obsolescence of the Wilen scanner caused the Federal axe to fall, putting an end to young Woodrow Luedesing's dreams of industrial empire. He was perhaps a little plumper than before, but his smooth, pink features showed no signs of acne, his adolescent awkwardness had vanished, and he was attired, not in the rough, ill-fitting clothing he had worn from Switzerland, but in a creamy suit of fine Italian silk, shoes of the sort ordinarily afforded only by motion picture magnates and the Mafia, a pale silk shirt, an Old Etonian tie, and a gem-jade ring of the finest quality.

"*Ja!*" Papa Schimmelhorn shook his head admiringly. "Chust like mein own son, a chip from der old block!"

"Quite right, Great-uncle," replied Little Anton. "As you know, I'm a chenius too." From his sealskin wallet he took a business card.

Papa Schimmelhorn read it. *Pêng-Plantagenet, Ltd,* it said in English and Chinese, *Hongkong, London, Paris, Brussels, Rome, New York, Singapore, Tokyo, and throughout the world,* and in a corner modestly but decisively, *Anton Fledermaus, Director of Special Services.*

"That," said Little Anton, his new accent slipping for a moment, "means I head up their department of dirty tricks. It's a real tough job, Pop. We're the biggest conglomerate in the world, so *everybody's* trying to shaft us—Commies, Arabs, Japanese, you name it. I'm the chap who makes sure we keep ahead of them." He smirked. "I manage."

He related how Pêng-Plantagenet had hired him, promoted him, provided him a penthouse atop one of Hongkong's most expensive high-rises, and enabled him to learn not only better English but fluent Cantonese and Mandarin. "Yes," he said smugly, "*I've* changed, but—" He regarded Papa Schimmelhorn's huge stature, mighty muscles, and great white beard. "—you haven't changed a bit."

"Of course nodt!" boomed Papa Schimmelhorn. "Chunior, I tell you how to keep der vinegar vhen you are old—only by chasing predty pussycats!"

"*Mrreow!*" agreed Gustaf-Adolf emphatically.

"Und dot's nodt all—der old man shtill makes new lidtle tricks—" He gestured at the Stanley Steamer. "—I haff now an infention no vun else has made. Vait, und I show you—"

"I know," said Little Anton. "Anti-gravity. That's why I'm here."

"*Vhat?* How did you find out?"

"You can hide nothing from Pêng-Plantagenet."

"But only Mama knows—"

"And maybe a few dozen pretty little pussycats," said Little Anton, saying nothing about the affectionate and informative letters Mama Schimmelhorn had been writing him. "Anyhow, anti-gravity's something Pêng-Plantagenet can use. Who do you think worked up this big church social Mama's gone to? Who fixed it so there'd be lots of vodka in their punch. Papa, you're hired. We leave for Hongkong right away."

"But—but I do nodt vant a chob!" Papa Schimmelhorn protested. "I haff chust fixed der Stanley Shteamer, und I haff nodt yet taken my Dora for a ride."

"Look, you take off in that thing, and the Air Force is sure to shoot you down. Anyhow, Pêng-Plantagenet's hiring both of you—your car too."

"But I haff no passport!"

Little Anton smiled an Old Etonian smile. He reached into his pocket and pulled a passport out. "Oh, yes, you have. You're now a subject of Her Majesty the Queen. Like me. I guess you *still* don't get it—Pêng-Plantagenet can fix *anything*."

"*Nein*, I cannot leafe. Mama is already angry! If I go to Hongkong—" Papa Schimmelhorn shuddered at the thought.

There was a moment of silence. Then, "Papa," said Little Anton, "come outside and let me show you something."

Papa Schimmelhorn nodded grudgingly. "Okay," he grumbled, "but shtill I cannot go."

He followed Little Anton out of the basement and around the corner. There stood the sleek Mercedes, painted an Imperial yellow, complete with Hongkong license plates.

"Pêng-Plantagenet flew it here with me," declared Little Anton proudly. "But you've seen nothing yet—"

He threw the door open, and instantly a great change came over Papa Schimmelhorn. His blue eyes widened;

his whiskers quivered; something began to rumble in his throat. *"Pussycats!"* he exclaimed. *"Predty pussycats!"*

"From Pêng-Plantagenet," said Little Anton. "Nothing but the best." And he introduced Miss Kittikool (which he explained was her real name), a demure, ninety-five pound, nicely rounded package from Thailand, and a slightly larger but no less attractive Miss MacTavish, half Scotch and half Chinese, from Hongkong.

Papa Schimmelhorn swept them a splendid bow. He kissed their hands. He rumbled happily while they giggled and pulled his beard and marvelled at his muscles.

"Lidtle Anton," he announced, "I haff changed mein mind. This vunce I go to vork for Pêng-Panflageolet. Mama vould nodt beliefe me, so you must leafe a note. Tell her I go only to make a lot of money so she can buy new dresses, maybe a new umbrella. You vait a minute vhile I change."

"Good show, Papa!" Little Anton slapped him heartily on the back. "I knew you'd come through in the pinch." And the pretty pussycats carolled their own pleasure at the news.

Fifteen minutes later, he rejoined them, gloriously attired in a striped blazer with brass buttons, loudly checked trousers, an orange sports shirt, and open sandals. Then, after he had been cautioned on no account to attempt a takeoff, and after his grand-nephew had mysteriously relocked the garage door, he guided the Stanley Steamer, gleaming in its freshly polished British Racing Green, into line behind the Mercedes, having insisted only that Miss Kittikool ride with him.

All the way to the airport, he decorously drove with all four wheels on the ground, and with one hand less decorously exploring those inviting areas of her thigh accessible through the slit of her sea-green Chinese gown. A new and splendid jet awaited them, also painted Imperial yellow. As they approached, it extruded a wide ramp and, while the crew saluted, Little Anton unhesitatingly drove aboard, beckoning his great-uncle to follow him. But

Papa Schimmelhorn by this time was so exhilarated that he was unable to resist the temptation to fly the steamer straight into the door, a sight which subsequently sent two of the ground-control men to the psychiatrist.

As they entered the luxurious cabin, Little Anton nudged him covertly. "Would you like to know why Pêng-Plantagenet sent us all the way from Hongkong for you, Papa?" he whispered in his ear. "It's not just because of your anti-gravity device—it's because of your big *yang*."

"My *vhat*? Lidtle Anton, vhat are you saying? Und right in front of predty pussycats!"

"Don't worry," chuckled Little Anton. "It isn't what you think. Mr Pêng'll explain the whole thing. He'll tell you all about Black Holes and dragons, and how your *yang* fits in with anti-gravity."

On that flight to Hongkong, Papa Schimmelhorn enjoyed himself so thoroughly that he completely forgot his curiosity regarding Black Holes, dragons, his *yang*, and anti-gravity and was able to devote all his energies to Miss Kittikool and Miss MacTavish, both of whom agreed that he was unique in their experience; and even next day, during his first interview with Horace Pêng and Richard Plantagenet in their teak and sandalwood panelled offices on the thirty-third floor of the Pêng-Plantagenet Building, he found it difficult to concentrate on scientific matters.

Mr Pêng was a majestic, immaculately groomed Chinese with grey hair and an Oxford accent. His suit spoke of Saville Row, his tie of Brasenose College. Mr Plantagenet was a very tall, immaculately groomed Englishman with a medieval moustache, a bold Norman nose, an Oxford accent and a Brasenose tie. They greeted Papa Schimmelhorn with great cordiality, apologized because the press of business had kept them from meeting him at the airport, and enquired as to whether Little Anton's provisions for his comfort and entertainment had been adequate.

Papa Schimmelhorn, recalling how cozy bed had been with Miss Kittikool on one side and Miss MacTavish on the other, rolled his eyes and assured them fervently that their hospitality was absolutely *wunderbar*. "Chentlemen," he roared, "I tell you, it makes me feel like I am vunce again a young shqvirt, full of vinegar!"

"What did I tell you, sir?" whispered Little Anton to Mr Pêng.

Mr Pêng nodded, looking highly pleased, and Mr Plantagenet harrumphed with approval.

"Mr Schimmelhorn," began Mr Pêng, "we badly need your help. Expense will be no object. You will be rewarded richly—"

"Revarded? Don't you vorry. I haff a good chob vith old Heinrich, making cuckoo clocks, und here in Hongkong I am hafing fun, zo I am glad to help. Also, bedter you call me Papa instead of Mr Schimmelhorn, und I call you maybe Horace, und your friend, whose name somevhere I haff heard before, I call Dick."

Mr Plantagenet chuckled, and Mr Pêng inclined his head gravely. "Papa," he said, "your years and genius give you the right to choose the terms of address we shall use between us. Now I shall explain briefly the sort of assistance we require from you."

"Lidtle Anton has told you I am shtupid und a chenius only in der subconscience?"

"He has indeed informed us how your genius functions, but that is not important." Mr Pêng leaned forward. "Papa, do you understand all the implications of your development of an anti-gravity device? True anti-gravity is no simple Newtonian force. It bears the same relationship to normal gravity as anti-matter does to ordinary matter."

Two charming Balinese girls came in silently, dressed in their native costume and carrying trays of tiny sandwiches and tall, cold drinks, and Papa Schimmelhorn's eyes and mind began to wander, but Mr Pêng paid no attention. "This means," he said, "that only from an anti-matter universe can *pure* anti-gravitic forces be derived—and that you, somehow, have reached into such a universe. Now, there are three ways of making contact with the many universes contiguous with ours. One is by the use of parapsychological powers, like those so highly developed in your excellent grand-nephew. Another, which so far at least has been impossible, is by generating physical forces vast enough to manipulate those awesome phenomena called Black Holes, which come into being with the final collapse of a star or galaxy, and from which not even light can escape. Black Holes are themselves portals into anti-matter universes, where we believe anti-gravity originates."

"Now I remember," exclaimed Papa Schimmelhorn. "Vhen mein friend Albert vas alife at Princeton—ach, vhat a chenius! Such a shame he dies so young! Vunce vith him vas anoder man who vas alzo shmart. He vas called Oppi, and alvays he talked shtuff I did nodt undershtand about Black Holes in der shky."

"That must have been Oppenheimer, who first worked out the equations for them," put in Mr Plantagenet. "Did he explain to Dr Einstein?"

"Ja, but I am not listdening, dere is an undergraduate who cleans up for Albert and you vould nodt believe—"

"Perhaps his subconscious picked up the idea," said Mr Plantagenet.

"The third way," Mr Pêng continued patiently, "which actually was known and used in India and China in ancient times, is by combining the first and second, and this you seemingly have used."

Papa Schimmelhorn pinched the two Balinese girls as they went by, but Mr Pêng, thoroughly briefed by Little Anton was in no way annoyed. "Putting it roughly," he declared, "our own universe has become primarily a *yang* universe; otherwise Black Holes could not exist in it. At the other extreme, we would find *yin* or anti-matter universes. *Yang* and *yin,* the male and female principles, are the fundamental principles of all creation. Always they must balance; neither must preponderate too greatly over the other. When they are unbalanced, there is all sorts of trouble, from social unrest to Black Holes."

"How nice!" marvelled Papa Schimmelhorn. "Zo now I am der *yang* und maybe die lidtle topless pussycats und Miss Kittikool vill be die *yin*. Und I haff used my *yang* to make der dingus vork, efen if I don't know vhy?"

"Precisely," said Mr Plantagenet. "Very neatly put, old chap. Couldn't have phrased it more delicately myself."

"You have indeed used your *yang* to make it work," Mr Pêng went on. "You have used it to capture a Black Hole, conveniently a very small one, which now appears to be perfectly controlled within that Klein bottle affair in your car. This cannot safely give us access directly to a *yin* universe, but it may enable us to build a portal into another continuum, one which in ancient days was in constant communication with us and with which Richard and I are most anxious to restablish contact, for in it *yang* and *yin* are in perfect balance. This portal we will ask you to design—"

"Okay," said Papa Schimmelhorn, "I vill try."

"But before I continue—" Mr Pêng paused portentously. "—I want your firm assurance that no word of our project shall get out, either to the world at large, or to your wife, and most especially—and this I cannot emphasize too strongly because in due course you will meet them—either to Mrs Plantagenet or Mrs Pêng. They are—well, they're not in full sympathy with what Richard and I have in mind. What I am about to tell you, you may find very difficult to believe. You have heard of dragons, have you not?"

"St Cheorge und Fafnir und die chewels und die predty Rheinmädchen?"

Mr Pêng suppressed a shudder. "Ah, yes," he said. "But those are not dragons as we in China knew them. You see, dragons came to us from the special universe of which I spoke, a virtual mirror-image of what ours used to be. They are beneficent and very wise, and while they lived with us, in the days of the great Yellow Emperor, all China flourished. Then the decline of virtue, and especially the coarse anti-dragon sentiment in Europe, caused their complete withdrawal. You have only to look at the state of the world today to understand the consequences. I most especially am concerned. You see, Richard and I are not merely conglomerate taipans. For more than two millenia, my ancestors have been mandarins of the highest rank, and Hereditary Keepers of the Imperial Dragon Hatchery. For more than two millenia we have maintained our tradition, with all the appropriate ceremonies and sacrifices, in the hope that our dragons would return to us. You do believe me, don't you?"

"Vhy nodt?" said Papa Schimmelhorn. "If gnurrs come from der voodvork out, vhy nodt dragons?"

"Good. That explains my interest in the project. As for Richard, whom I met during our Oxford days, his motivations is quite as strong as mine. He is descended directly from another Richard Plantagenet, known as the Lion Hearted, and he is the rightful King of England—"

"Your Machesty—" murmured Papa Schimmelhorn politely.

"Thank you," said His Majesty. "Yes, after we became friends Horace explained the influence of dragons on our history. All that dreadful St George nonsense, and the other horrible myths and fairy tales. I at once saw the role they'd played in enabling the usurpation of our throne. Not that I have anything against the present usurper, who seems to be a very decent sort of woman, but I do want to set the matter right, you know. That's simple justice, isn't it? Besides, Horace and I have all sorts of plans. We shall re-establish the Chinese and British Empires. No one will be able to stand against us. My dear Papa, we shall rule the world!"

"Very much to its advantage," said Mr Pêng. "But that's beside the point. We've scheduled seminars for you with our foremost scientists and scholars—seminars which, I assure you, will not interfere with your—er, relaxation. They'll work with you until your intuition tells you you have the problem solved. In the meantime, Mr Fledermaus and our Chief of Security, Colonel Li, will see that you have everything you want." He and Mr Plantagenet stood up just as a tall and very military Chinese strode into the room. "Here's Colonel Li now."

The Colonel was middle-aged, but there was nothing soft about him.

"Gott in Himmel!" exclaimed Papa Schimmelhorn, as they shook hands. "Vot iss? Anoder Chenghiz Khan?"

"I do my best," Colonel Li answered modestly. Then, to Papa Schimmelhorn's surprise, he grinned. "My friend Anton tells me you're a man after my own heart. I too am fond of cats."

"That's right," declared Little Anton. "He knows every pretty little pussycat in Hongkong, and believe me, Papa, you'll be safe as long as he's around, no matter where, no matter what."

For the next two weeks, Papa Schimmelhorn enjoyed himself tremendously. In the late mornings and early afternoons, usually with the two pretty little Balinese on his lap, he endured lectures by a Swedish physicist, a Brazilian physicist, an impatient Nobel Prize winner from an unidentified Balkan country, two Taoist philosopher-historians, a Tibetan lama, a Hindu mystic in whose title the honorific *sri* was repeated one hundred and eight times, an eminent British archaeologist especially interested in dragons, and a rather puzzled science fiction writer imported from Southern California expressly for the purpose. As almost all the lecturers spoke either English, French, or German, only a few sessions had to be translated for his benefit. Occasionally, he would request works of reference which seemed irrelevant to everybody else, the *Book of Mormon*, the Eleventh Edition of the *Britannica*, the collected works of Alfred North Whitehead, of Herr Doktor Jung, and of Mary Baker Eddy, the *Bluejacket's Manual*, translations of the Mahayana and Hinayana Buddhist scriptures, and any number of others—and these he would scan rapidly. Occasionally, too, Mr Pêng and Mr Plantagenet would drop in on him, enquire as to his progress, and go away quite satisfied when he replied that eferything vas fine; he could feel it vorking inside der subconscience. He sent a picture postcard to Mama Schimmelhorn almost every day, views of Hongkong Harbor and of museums and ecclesiastical edifices, to illustrate the cultural aspects of his visit, which he declared took up what little time remained after his arduous workday developing special cuckoo-clocks with ethnic overtones for Pêng-Plantagenet's Southeast Asian trade. But from twilight on, he and Colonel Li and Little Anton devoted themselves to chasing pussycats. He and the Colonel became boon companions, and he was able to relax so completely that he never noticed such minor incidents as the occasional abrupt disappearance of some Slavic or Oriental or Middle Eastern type who apparently had been following them. At some of these, Little Anton simply crossed his eyes, gave them a push—and they were gone. No fuss, no muss. A few others were taken care of by friends of Colonel Li's, who employed less subtle, but no less effective, methods.

Papa Schimmelhorn's *yang* flourished, and his researches prospered. Among Hongkong's profusion of pretty pussycats, he eventually almost forgot Miss Kittikool and Miss MacTavish, neglecting them shamefully except when, hours after midnight, he came home to renew his energies with a few hours of sleep. Then suddenly he announced that he had solved the problem, and that the applied technology, costing only a few hundred dollars, could be completed in no more than another week.

Mr Pêng and Mr Plantagenet were, of course, delighted. They announced that the completion of the task would be properly celebrated by a splendid banquet at the Pêng mansion. Little Anton and Colonel Li were pleased, partly because commendations and rewards would be coming to them, and partly because the strenuous pace he had been setting was getting wearing. Only Miss Kittikool and Miss MacTavish, their noses badly out of joint at his faithlessness, failed to rejoice.

Five days went by, and every day Papa Schimmelhorn worked hard, with the dismayed assistance of Pêng-Plantagenet's engineers and scientists, assembling a very strange contraption. All sorts of seemingly unrelated gadgets went into it: the private parts of an old Singer sewing machine, a curiously interlaced webbing of copper wire and nylon fishing line, a spiral neon tube fabricated to his orders and filled with a semi-liquid, semi-gaseous substance he himself had brewed in the Pêng-Plantagenet laboratories. The net result began to look like a Japanese temple gate, or *torii,* made partly out of metal, partly of irridescent plastics, and partly of ectoplasm; and when Mr Plantagenet commented on its smallness, for it was four feet wide and scarcely large enough, as he pointed out, to accommodate even a little dragon, Papa Schimmelhorn slapped him jovially on the back and said, "Dickie, Your Machesty, don't vorry! ve hook it up to der anti-grafity machine und vith my *yang,* then—ho-ho-ho!—chust vatch it grow!"

Five days went by, and every night Papa Schimmelhorn went out on his *yang*-renewing mission, much to the disgust of Miss MacTavish and Miss Kittikool. Then, on the afternoon of the fifth day, the device was activated on a trial basis, but without being permitted to expand. Papa Schimmelhorn went up to it and peered through. He saw a different China and a different world. The fields were lush, the forests thick and green. Among the pure white clouds that adorned the sky, two handsome scarlet dragons were disporting themselves. And, on a boulder beside a waterfall, an ancient white-bearded gentleman in silken robes sat quietly reading. Obviously, he was a sage.

"Chust look!" cried Papa Schimmelhorn.

Mr Pêng and Mr Plantagenet crowded in to look. They gasped in amazement and delight.

The sage looked up. He stood. Gravely he smiled upon

them. Just as Papa Schimmelhorn flipped the switch turning the device off, he seemed to bow a welcome.

"Papa, you've *done* it!" Mr Pêng cried out.

"Of course I do it," answered Papa Schimmelhorn. "Tomorrow I haff it open all der vay und you can drife through vith maybe a horse and carriage."

Thoughtfully, Mr Pêng observed that a horse-drawn carriage might be the very thing, just in case that other China had avoided mechanization, and Mr Plantagenet remembered an elegant carriage and pair owned by a wealthy Dutch gentleman of his acquaintance, which he was sure he could borrow for a day or two. These arrangements were promptly made, and the balance of the afternoon was devoted to selecting appropriate gifts for whatever authorities might greet them: a Fabergé Easter Egg that had belonged to a Czarina, a nice copy of the Gutenberg Bible, carved emeralds from Ceylon, an original Titian, two Manets, a Gainsborough and a Turner, a tea service in platinum by the court jeweler to the late King Farouk, a one-minute repeater with two stop-second hands by Audemars-Piguet cased in the same metal, and a traditional cuckoo-clock featuring a whole choir of yodelling cuckoos, which Papa Schimmelhorn had thoughtfully brought with him in his carpetbag.

Regretfully, Mr Pêng explained that his wife and Mrs Plantagenet had, a day or two before, decided to take off on a shopping spree in London, Rome, Paris, and New York, in their own private jet. He and Mr. Plantagenet promised, however, that their absence would not be allowed to dampen the festivities that evening; and certainly it did not seem to, for everyone at the banquet was in excellent spirits and, as course followed rare Chinese course, many a toast was proposed to their success upon the morrow, to the triumphs that success was sure to bring, and to the genius who had made it possible.

The genius, who felt as though his *yang* had never been in finer fettle, divided his attention quite impartially between the dinner, the toasts, and the two extremely pretty pussycats who sat cuddled up against him. Colonel Li and Little Anton contributed to the general merriment by pressing innumerable drinks upon the sober scientists and scholars who had served as Papa Schimmelhorn's consultants, until even they became positively uproarious. Even Miss Kittikool and Miss MacTavish, though seated somewhat apart from the center of attention, appeared to have regained their good humor, giggling and whispering to each other vivaciously. The unfortunate absence of Mrs Pêng and Mrs Plantagenet was soon forgotten, even by their husbands, and a glorious time was had by all.

In New Haven, on the day of Papa Schimmelhorn's disappearance, Mama Schimmelhorn had returned from the church social much later than she usually did. She was quite tiddly, Little Anton's vodka having worked its wonders, and in a mellow frame of mind, almost—but not quite—ready to forgive her husband. Humming *Down By Der Old Mill Shtream,* she unlocked the front door. "I'm home, Papa!" she called out.

She listened. Her only answer was a hoarse *"Mrrreow!"* from the basement. *Maybe Papa has gone to shleep?* she thought as she went down the stairs.

She unlocked the workshop door, and Gustav-Adolf, meowing loudly, rubbed against her legs to tell her he was starving. She turned the light on. Papa Schimmelhorn was nowhere to be seen. The Stanley Steamer too was gone. She frowned terribly. Her black dress rustling, she strode to the garage door. It was securely locked.

"Zo!" she cried out. *"Again* you run avay. To shleep vith naked vomen vhen you should be thinking how maybe you do nodt go to Heafen vhen you die! Dirty ol—"

Then she spied the note Little Anton had left pinned to the wall above the workbench. She pulled it down.

Dear, dear Great-aunt, (she read)
I am so sorry that I missed you after coming all

the way from Hongkong, especially as I am taking
Papa back with me.

My employers want him to design some very
special cuckoo-clocks. They'll pay handsomely and
give him a huge bonus, and he'll be gone only a
short time. He told me that when he gets back he's
going to take you shopping for some new dresses
and a new umbrella!

> Affectionately,
> Your Little Anton

And scrawled below this was the simple message, I luff
you, Mama!! signed, Papa xxxxxXXXX!

She read the note twice. "Hmph!" she sniffed. "Zo
dot's how der opens und shtill iss locked. Lidtle Anton.
Der new umbrella I do nodt beliefe. But maybe this time
iss different. Lidtle Anton iss a goot boy now. Die
Chinesers haff taught him all about Confucius und how to
be nice to old people. Okay, I vait und see."

Her mind more at ease, she went upstairs again, fed
Gustav-Adolf liver, and settled down to drink a cup of tea
and phone Mrs Hundhammer; and during the next couple of weeks, whenever her suspicions were reawakened
they were lulled again by the arrival of a cultural postcard
from her husband or from Little Anton. It was not until a
few days after Papa Schimmelhorn announced his solution
of the problem that her tranquility was again shattered.

Her doorbell rang shortly after breakfast, and she
opened up eagerly, looking forward to a pleasant theological disputation with her two usual Jehovah's Witnesses.
Instead, on the front stoop stood a pair of the most elegant elderly ladies she had ever seen. Each was fairly tall;
each was ramrod straight; each—despite her age—was
still attractive. One was Chinese; the other, by the way
she dressed and held herself, could only have been English. At the curb behind them stood a gleaming Imperial
yellow Rolls-Royce with a chauffeur and liveried footman,
and Hongkong license plates.

"I beg your pardon," said the Chinese lady, speaking very softly. "Are you Mrs Schimmelhorn?"

Mama Schimmelhorn took in the situation at a glance. *"Ja,"* she said, "I am Mama. Vot hass he done now?" She stepped back so they could enter. "Come in and haff a seat, und right avay I bring der tea." Her black dress crackling, she bustled back and forth. "Alvays vhen he gets loose iss trouble vith naked vomen, sometimes vith only vun like Dora Grossapfel, sometimes vith four oder maybe fife. Only this vunce, vith Lidtle Anton who has been taught about Confucius—"

The elderly ladies exchanged glances.

"—this vunce I thought maybe he vill be goot. Vell, ve liff und learn—"

Reciting part of the long list of Papa Schimmelhorn's carnal sins, she served tea and biscuits, settled down with Gustav-Adolf on her lap, and permitted Mrs Pêng and Mrs Plantagenet to introduce themselves and tell their tale.

Only a day or so before, they informed her, they had been visited by two young women in the employ of their husband's firm, Miss Kittikool and Miss MacTavish, both of whom felt that—they were dreadfully sorry they had to tell her this—that they had been taken advantage of by Papa Schimmelhorn. So upset had they been that they had revealed the nature of the project for which he had been hired—Mrs Pêng did her best to explain the technicalities of Black Holes and anti-gravity and *yang* and *yin*—to engineer a breakthrough into another universe, where there were dragons and the Chinese Empire still flourishing.

Mama Schimmelhorn stood up. *"Donnerwetter!* Die *yang* and *yin* I do nodt undershtand, also Black Holes except like maybe in Calcutta. But Papa—dot iss different. Vhen it iss nodt naked vomen, it iss time-trafel, und gnurrs, und sometimes X-rated cuckoo-clocks. Such monkey business. Vell, now I put a shtop!"

"We were hoping you could," Mrs Plantagenet said

fervently. "I assure you that I have no desire to become Queen of England. I couldn't possibly cope with that dreadful Labour Party at my age. Besides, Richard keeps talking about crusades against the Saracens, and though I dare say they deserve it, it does seem a bit late in the day for that sort of thing, doesn't it?"

"Primula's quite right," declared Mrs Pêng. "I myself certainly do not want to be Empress of China, surrounded by eunuchs and slave girls and palace intrigues and all that rubbish. Of course, Horace has promised me that he doesn't want the throne, but there aren't any other candidates, and—well, you know how men are."

Mama Schimmelhorn indicated grimly that indeed she did.

"But worst of all," Mrs Pêng continued, "he wants to bring the dragons back again, even though he knows I can't stand snakes and lizards and all those horrible crawly things. You see, in ancient China his family had charge of them, and they became quite devoted to the creatures. Can you imagine having the sky full of dragons, Mrs Schimmelhorn?"

"Dragons?" Mama Schimmelhorn snorted. "*Herr Gott,* iss bad enough vith seagulls und die filthy shtarlings! Efery day on der front porch—you vould nodt beliefe!"

"Exactly," said Mrs Plantagenet, putting her tea-cup down. "We'd better phone and find out what sort of progress they've been making. I'll charge the call to my account."

"Der phone iss in der hall," said Mama Schimmelhorn.

Five minutes later, her guests returned with grave faces. "Your husband has already constructed his device and is about to give it a preliminary testing," Mrs Pêng announced. "According to Miss Kittikool, however, he doesn't plan to make the breakthrough until late tomorrow afternoon. If we hurry, we may still have time. Will you come to Hongkong, Mrs Schimmelhorn?"

Mama Schimmelhorn's expression would have done credit to a Grand Inquisitor. "Ja, I vill come!" she told them. "Ve finish up der tea, und I call Mrs Hundhammer to come und feed mein Gustav-Adolf, und ve shtart right avay." She picked up her umbrella. "Papa," she proclaimed, hefting it, "*this* time vhen I catch you I make you vish I am chust a dragon inshtead of Mama Schimmelhorn!" '

Fifteen minutes later, black hat firmly on her head, hands folded tightly over the umbrella's handle, she rode between her new-found friends in the back seat of the Imperial yellow Rolls, headed for the airport. She was in no way impressed by the luxury surrounding her. Her mind was fixed on one objective, and she smiled grimly as she contemplated it.

For security reasons, Papa Schimmelhorn had installed his interdimensional gate inside a huge godown owned by Pêng-Plantagenet; and there, early next morning, he arrived with Little Anton and the two pretty Balinese to find Colonel Li already on duty at the doors and his employers awaiting him in the Dutch taipan's borrowed equipage beside the Stanley Steamer.

Once, as a youth in Switzerland, Papa Schimmelhorn had spent a pleasant summer driving a horse-drawn charabanc full of twittering female tourists from one romantic Alpine spot to another, and as the taipan's coachman had prudently been escorted home, he at once offered to take the reins. As soon as he had made sure that steam was up, he kissed the Balinese goodbye, showed Colonel Li the lever that dilated the gate, and he and Little Anton climbed to the box.

The gate expanded. The other China appeared there before them. The sleek, black, powerful horses pawed the ground and snorted. Papa Schimmelhorn shook out the reins and clucked them forward. "Zo!" he cried out. "Dragons, here ve come!"

They moved through the gate at a brisk trot, but now the landscape no longer showed the rock, the sage, the waterfall. A wide, smooth road took shape before them; it looked like porcelain, but on it the horses' hooves made virtually no sound. It did not, like most roads, simply wait for them, but changed form and direction much faster than it should, and the surrounding landscape altered with it. They were passed by crags and pines, by bamboo groves and orchards full of flowering trees—and suddenly they noticed that they were not alone. Behind them and to either side, vehicles escorted them, vehicles that called to mind at once the majesty of a Bugatti Royale and the glowing purity of fine Sung Dynasty celadons. They had no wheels, and floated silently a foot or so above the ground—and overhead, now, half a dozen discoid aircraft hovered just as silently. Bells sang their deep brazen song into the air—

"They appear to have achieved a considerable technology!" said Mr Plantagenet apprehensively.

"I never expected anything like *this*!" whispered Mr Pêng. "Dear me, I hope they're friendly!"

But Papa Schimmelhorn just took off his Tyrolean hat and smiled and waved at all of them.

Then suddenly the road took an abrupt turn and ended at a meadow between arcs of glorious flowers; and at its end a palace stood—a palace of unreflecting glass and porcelain, faceted in the most abstract and complex simplicities. An enormous yellow dragon was stretched out comfortably in front of it; and around him, and to either side, the meadow was thronged with dignitaries—gray-bearded sages, high mandarins in their embroidered robes, stately men and women who (Mr Pêng observed *sotto voce*) could only have been tributary kings and nobles. Between them, near the dragon's head, stood an empty throne carved of a single block of jade, carved intricately in ancient and more ornate times.

The horses spied the dragon. Eyes rolling, ears laid back, they balked; they plunged and reared; they paid no heed when their coachman tried to quiet them. Then suddenly the dragon looked at them out of his great golden eyes, and they stood still, tense and sweating, totally mo-

tionless. Several functionaries came forward, to take their
bridles, to help Mr Pêng and Mr Plantagenet alight, to
offer Papa Schimmelhorn a polite hand down, which was
cheerfully ignored. Behind them, other officials stood,
looking by no means as cordial and holding short metallic
rods with control buttons on them.

"They've got lasers, Papa!" whispered Little Anton.

"Ja wohl!" answered Papa Schimmelhorn. "Chust like
in *Shtar Vars*. But do nodt vorry. Somehow I vork it
out."

The functionaries parted as obligingly as the Red Sea
had for Moses, and through them strode a very tall
Chinese, magnificently robed, who stood eye to eye with
Papa Schimmelhorn. He addressed himself to Mr Pêng,
who simply couldn't take his eyes off the dragon.

"I, sir," he declared, in very strangely accented Mandarin, "am Prince Wen, the Prime Minister. I marvel at
your insolence in coming here. Using this person's ex-
traordinary talents and endowments you have crossed for-
bidden frontiers. We have been observing you for
centuries—" He gestured at the discoid aircraft. "—and
we have even retained an understanding of your barbaric
tongue. The dragons were indeed wise to have abandoned
you. In your universe, *yang* and *yin* are perilously out of
balance. Now you endanger ours. Had I not been ordered
otherwise, I would at once have disposed of you and your
illicit gate. Have you no idea of the dangers involved in
tampering with Black Holes?" He shuddered. "But the
Daughter of Heaven is too merciful. She has decreed that
she must judge you personally."

He bowed three times toward the palace. Bells rang.
Trumpets sounded.

"*D-daughter* of Heaven?" quavered Mr Pêng.

"Of course," answered the Prime Minister. "In our universe *yang* and *yin* are in perfect balance. This is Thurs-
day—therefore you will appear before the Empress. Had
it been yesterday or tomorrow, the *Son* of Heaven would

have examined you. Only on Sundays do they rule China and the world together."

"N-naturally," remarked Mr Pêng.

The Prime Minister smiled cruelly. "I promise you that, once she sees how you have trespassed here, flaunting your unbalanced *yang* in our very faces, she will be quite as merciless as I."

Again the trumpets sounded. A crowd of courtiers and of ladies-in-waiting emerged from the palace's jade doors, moving in a pavane of abstract, highly ordered patterns. In their midst, robed in richly ornamented but curiously diaphanous brocades and wearing a spreading headdress of gold filigree adorned with pearls and jade, strode a Personage. Now in her late middle years, she had been and still was beautiful, but her eyes were cold and clear and calculating, and on her face was an expression of iron determination.

Papa Schimmelhorn, unable of course to understand the conversation, had been amusing himself by contemplating the ladies-in-waiting as they came out, rather lasciviously because some of them were very pretty pussycats indeed. Now, looking on the Empress, he gulped. That expression was only too familiar. He had first seen it on the face of Mama Schimmelhorn when he was courting her, and blinded by her girlhood pulchritude had failed to grasp its meaning. Mama's eyes were gray; the Empress' were black. Mama was a Swiss, originally a blonde; the Empress, quite as tall as she, Chinese. But that was unimportant. Papa Schimmelhorn knew instinctively that they had much in common, and suddenly a panic premonition told him that he should run away. But there was, obviously, nowhere to run to.

Cymbals clashed. Wind instruments cried out like unseen sea birds. The Empress advanced through the pavane and mounted to her throne. Just once, she clapped her hands. There was instant silence. Then she addressed Prince Wen in a strange, singing, fluting language; and he replied at length in the same tongue, interspersing his comments with strong crystalline notes of emphasis whenever he gestured toward their visitors.

Finally he turned. "I have recommended your instant dissolution," he declared. "Painlessly, of course."

"That is unfair!" Mr Pêng cried out. "At least you out to let us present our gifts and our petitions!"

"It *is* unsporting!" put in Mr Plantagenet.

The Empress silenced them. She spoke again in the alien tongue.

"I have been ordered to consult the great Chu-t'sai," Prince Wen announced, pointing to the dragon. "The Daughter of Heaven wishes him to decide your fate."

He and the Empress spoke again, addressing their remarks to Chu-t'sai himself. The dragon listened. With enormous dignity, he stood. He stretched his great neck over the courtiers' heads until his twenty-foot-long head was directly in front of Papa Schimmelhorn. For a long minute, while Little Anton trembled in his boots and even the Prime Minister held his breath, they regarded one another. Then Papa Schimmelhorn, with a chuckle, reached up and rubbed Chu-t'sai's mighty chin, and winked—and, never changing his expression, Chu-t'sai winked back.

"P-p-papa," stuttered Little Anton as the vast head drew back again. "Did you see what he did?

"*Natürlich,*" replied Papa Schimmelhorn. "Ve undershtand each oder. He iss like Gustav-Adolf. I think maybe he iss a Dirty Old Man dragon."

Suddenly, then, Chu-t'sai himself spoke in the singing, fluting language, its words and notes pitched several octaves lower. He spoke only for a moment, but the Empress nodded.

"The great Chu-t'sai," translated Prince Wen with ill grace, "says that we must wait. It is fortunate for you that we, so much more advanced, learned to converse with dragons a thousand years ago. I shall find out how long the waiting is to be—"

But before he could put the question, Little Anton

nudged Papa Schimmelhorn. *"Listen!"* he whispered. "Do you hear what I hear?"

Papa Schimmelhorn listened. So did Mr Pêng and Mr Plantagenet. Unmistakably, on the road behind them, a powerful car was racing at full speed—and now everyone was staring past them in its direction.

Tires screamed on curves. The engine roared.

"Richard," said Mr Pêng apprehensively. "That—that sounds to me like Mrs Plantagenet's Ferrari."

"It does to me too!" moaned Mr Plantagenet.

"Did you tell Colonel Li that they were on no account to be admitted?"

"Horace, I didn't. After all, they were in *Europe!* Why didn't you?"

"I—I never even thought of it," admitted Mr Pêng.

There was a final screech of brakes. The throng parted. The bright red Ferrari slid to a harsh stop beside them. In it were three old ladies, all looking extremely angry. The door flew open, and the first out was Mama Schimmelhorn. She ignored everything and everybody. At her expression, even the great Chu-t'sai snorted dolefully. Her umbrella at the ready, she advanced against her husband.

"Hah!" she roared. "Again you get avay, to chase bad girls und play vith dragons und Black Holes and shpoil Little Anton so he forgets about Confucius!" She seized Papa Schimmelhorn firmly by the ear, and started applying the sharp point of her umbrella to his brisket by way of punctuation.

"Mama! Mama! *Bitte schön,* nodt in public, in front of eferybody! Only look—on der throne iss die Empress of China!"

"To her you should apologize!" Mama Schimmelhorn continued unrelentingly. Coming to shteal her dragons und her dancing girls! *Ach,* do nodt argue—chust vait till ve get home—"

Meanwhile Mrs Pêng and Mrs Plantagenet had descended on their own husbands rather more genteelly, but with equal resolution; and the Empress, gazing at the scene, turned to Prince Wen and said, in the singing tongue, "The great Chu-t'sai was right. Though they are of course still barbarians, their *yang* and *yin* may not be as hopelessly out of balance as you thought." She pointed at Mama Schimmelhorn. "At least, her *yin* certainly seems to be as effective as his *yang*. We'll keep them for a time at least, and find out their reason for coming here. Of course, we will make sure that their gate is closed and never built again. But who knows? Perhaps we may be able to help them become truly civilized."

So for three days Mr and Mrs Pêng, Mr and Mrs Plantagenet, Papa and Mama Schimmelhorn, and Little Anton were entertained imperially, with only the slight condescension inevitable in dealing with barbarians. Banquet followed banquet, feast followed feast, one magnificent spectacle followed closely on another: dances, dramas, and rituals almost unbelievable in their splendor dazzled the visitors, but most impressive of all was a ballet performed for them by the great Chu-t'sai and his wives high in the air during a thunderstorm. (Rather patronizingly—and to the annoyance of Mr Pêng, who of course knew it already—Prince Wen pointed out that dragons, by virtue of their perfect *yang* and *yin,* had natural anti-gravity, and that that was why Chinese dragons were always depicted without wings.)

Mr Pêng and Mr Plantagenet were permitted to present their gifts, which were very graciously received, much being made of the Fabergé Easter Egg and especially of Papa Schimmelhorn's cuckoo-clock which the Emperor himself averred would thenceforth hang in the Imperial bedchamber. They were also allowed to introduce themselves formally to the entire court, after which—partly because of the family credentials Mr Pêng and Mr Plantagenet presented and partly because of the marked favor shown Papa Schimmelhorn by the great Chu-t'sai—their status improved noticeably, even Prince Wen mellowing a bit.

Mr Pêng and Mr Plantagenet were awed and delighted by all they saw. Mrs Pêng, Mrs Plantagenet, and Mama Schimmelhorn got along famously with the Empress via two or three interpreters, though Mrs Pêng found it difficult to concentrate when she looked up and saw dragons watching her through the window. Little Anton, having been assigned a pair of pretty pussycats so that his *yang* would be in better balance, had a ball. Only Papa Schimmelhorn failed to enjoy himself; constantly surrounded by young women of surpassing beauty, he was never permitted out of range of the umbrella, and once or twice when he tried to sneak away, he was stopped effectively by enormous female attendants.

Not until the last day were Mr Pêng and Mr Plantagenet given permission to submit their petition to the Throne, and they did so with the utmost politeness and strictly according to protocol as defined by Prince Wen.

The audience was, of course, conducted on the meadow, so that Chu-t'sai could comfortably participate. He and the Imperial couple listened. Then they took counsel, speaking in hushed voices.

Finally, the Empress proclaimed their decision. She and the Emperor and the great Chu-t'sai all recognized the singular virtue of Mr Pêng and Mr Plantagenet, particularly in a world so gone to seed. They realized that Mr Pêng was fully qualified to function as Hereditary Keeper of the Imperial Dragon Hatchery, if his world had only had one, and that Mr Plantagenet would have made a marvellous King of England. She spoke of how impressed they were by Papa Schimmelhorn's genius and his tremendous *yang,* unparalleled since the days of the Yellow Emperor. However—

She paused and the great Chu-t'sai uttered a deep and mournful sound.

"However," she went on, "because the balance of *yang* and *yin* in your own world is so grievously impaired, and because it obviously will be very difficult to make the place habitable again, the Chu-t'sai has regretfully denied permission to any of his relatives to return there with you."

Mr Pêng's face fell. Mr Plantagenet looked stricken.

"And as for your Black Hole and its illicit gate," she said, "much as we dislike dismantling so great and rare an accomplishment, for our own protection we must do so the instant you return—"

Mr Pêng and Mr Plantagenet started to protest, but she held up her hand.

"—and, as a condition of our letting you return, we must have your solemn promise that you, at least, will never try to reconstruct it. We are going to give you many gifts to take back with you, but after you have promised you shall receive, from the great Chu-t'sai, the most precious gift of all, which shall be your responsibility and the sacred responsibility of your sons and daughters. Do you promise solemnly?"

Mr. Pêng looked at Mr Plantagenet. Mr Plantagenet looked at Mr Pêng. "We promise, Daughter of Heaven," Mr Pêng said sadly.

The Empress smiled. "Very well." She gestured, and four servitors came up carrying an enormous covered hamper, which they set down before Mr Pêng.

"That is the great Chu-t'sai's gift to you," the Empress said. "It is lined with silk and with the softest down. It holds a clutch of eight dragon eggs, together with the latest scientific instructions on their proper care. A great honor has been paid you."

Mr. Pêng bowed profoundly, and thanked the Empress, the Emperor, and the great Chu-t'sai for their trust in him and their munificence.

Then the Empress clapped her hands, and there was music. The audience was at an end, and everyone turned to a late luncheon served there on the meadow, after which the rest of the Imperial presents were brought out, boxes in ebony and lacquer, wrapped in silks of an unimaginable richness, and loaded into the carriage and into the Ferrari.

"We hate to see you go," the Empress said, "but I assure you it's for the best."

The most cordial farewells echoed from every side, and Papa Schimmelhorn embraced the great Chu-t'sai's right nostril. *"Herr Drache,"* he declared, "I vish I shpeak your langvidge."

The great Chu-t'sai whiffled at him softly.

"Ja!" said Papa Schimmelhorn. "I bet ve could tell each oder plenty of shtories—" He saw Mama's eye transfixing him, and patted the huge nostril once again with a sigh. *"Auf wiedersehn!"* he called back over his shoulder.

The carriage started down the road; the Ferrari followed; the escort fell in to either side and overhead. The road and landscape unrolled before them, faster, faster—

Then, as abruptly as they had left it, they were back inside the godown, with only a very tired and worried Colonel Li waiting to welcome them. As the Ferrari's rear bumper cleared the gate, behind them they heard a soft implosion, and for an instant the air seemed to scintillate and crackle. They turned—and the gate was gone. Only the Stanley Steamer stood there, a thread of smoke and the smell of burning insulation issuing from its hood.

There was a long, long silence, which Mr Plantagenet finally broke with a *harrumph.*

Mr Pêng turned to him dolefully.

"Cheer up, old lad," said Mr Plantagenet. "We *do* have the dragon's eggs, you know. When they hatch out we'll have proper dragons!"

"Richard," answered Mr Pêng, "do you know how long dragon's eggs take to hatch? *One thousand years*— and even though our Chinese thousand is often an indeterminate number, it's still going to be a dismally long time."

The Pêngs and the Plantagenets very kindly invited the Schimmelhorns to spend a few more days in Hongkong as their guests, but Mama Schimmelhorn refused, saying she was ashamed to be seen with Papa in polite society. She insisted they drive directly to the airport; and this they did, delaying only long enough for Little Anton to retrieve Papa Schimmelhorn's carpetbag and stow it in the Stanley's trunk, for Mama to accept a substantial check (made out in her name) from Mrs Plantagenet, and for their presents from the Empress to be put aboard.

During the drive, not a word was said, even Little Anton remained silent, and the only sound was the occasional sharp tapping of the umbrella's point against the back of the driver's seat. The Imperial yellow jet was awaiting them with its ramp down, but this time Papa Schimmelhorn knew he could not fly it in. His drive up the ramp was positively funereal.

Despite the courteous and considerate crew, the splendid service and superb cuisine, their return was by no means a fun flight—and the fact that Colonel Li, in a mistaken effort to do his friend a final favor, had assigned the two pretty Balinese as hostesses did nothing to improve the atmosphere or alleviate Papa Schimmelhorn's despondency. All the way, Mama Schimmelhorn sat grimly in her seat, never breaking silence except to elaborate on the misdeeds of Dirty Old Men, and how promising youths like Little Anton would do well to pay them no attention and think rather of Confucius.

They landed at New Haven. Mama Schimmelhorn tipped each of the crew fifty cents. The ramp extruded. They climbed into the car.

A tear in his eye, Papa Schimmelhorn cast one last lingering look at the pair of Balinese, and mutely shook Little Anton by the hand. Luckily, he had presence of mind enough quickly to palm and pocket the small piece of paper his grand-nephew passed to him.

"Ve drife shtraight home," ordered Mama Schimmelhorn, and he obeyed.

"Ve put der car in der garage," she told him, unlocking

the door, waiting until he had driven in, then locking it again and pocketing the key.

"Und now ve go upshtairs und open up die presents from die Empress."

Papa Schimmelhorn picked them up and followed her. There were two long boxes in cases of figured silk, fastened with silken cords. There was a large square box similarly wrapped. Mama Schimmelhorn opened the long ones first. Lacquered, each contained a scroll on silk, with carved ivory ends. She unrolled the first. It was a classical Chinese ancestral portrait of Papa Schimmelhorn seated in a great teak chair and garbed in the handsome robes of a jade-button mandarin and Assistant (Honorary) Keeper of the Imperial Dragon Hatchery.

"*Ach!*" she exclaimed. "Dot iss how you should look—nodt alvays leering und vinking und, thinking about naked vomen."

She unrolled the second. A counterpart of the first, it showed her in the role of the high mandarin's wife, appropriately attired, except that her black hat was set firmly on her head and that her right hand, relentlessly, held her umbrella. On her lap, the painter had depicted Gustav-Adolf, whom Mrs Pêng and Mrs Plantagenet had described carefully to the Empress.

"It iss beaudtiful!" murmured Mama Schimmelhorn. "Ve hang vun each side of der fireplace."

Then she opened the third package, and out of a box of ebony took a large bronze *ting,* an ancient sacrificial vessel of great rarity and value.

"Vot iss?" grumbled Papa Schimmelhorn. "To cook die beans?"

"Shtupid!" she snapped. "It iss to plant maybe petunias. Now go downshtairs und get your bag, und bring up poor Gustav-Adolf."

Papa Schimmelhorn departed gladly, and as soon as he determined that he and Gustav-Adolf were indeed alone, he read the message Little Anton had passed to him. It said,

Dear Papa,
There's another present, just for you. It's from the
Emperor and your dragon chum. I sneaked it out in
my own little universe so that Prince Wen wouldn't
catch on.
It's out of one of those air-cars of theirs, and I've
translated what it says on the outside.
Have fun, old boy!

Love,
Anton

Papa Schimmelhorn hurried to the trunk. Behind his
carpetbag, there was a plain cardboard carton with
Chinese characters, and under these was the translation:

Imperial Air-Car Factory (it read)
Anti-Gravity Unit
To Be Installed In Steam-Propelled Vehicles Only
(1.3 Dragonpower)
Warranted Black-Hole-Free

Quickly he put it back again and closed the trunk. He
hoisted the carpetbag to one huge shoulder and Gustav-
Adolf, who had been sniffing at the Stanley Steamer, to
the other. As he went up to rejoin Mama Schimmelhorn,
he did his very best to look downcast and shame-stricken.
But he didn't make a very good job of it.

He was thinking of fluffy white clouds at two thousand
feet, of warm summer breezes, and of Dora Grossapfel's
stretch-pants.

GLORIA

Gail Kimberly

After Papa Schimmelhorn, one needs balance. Fortunately that is provided by this story making use of the time-distortion properties of black holes.

Gail is one of the newer writers of science fiction. Her previous publications include a straight science fiction novel, Flyer; *a book about the childhood and adolescence of the historical Count Dracula; and a novel of madness and Jungian psychiatry.*

You can't say she isn't versatile.

In the ghostly vault of the Milky Way there is a grave-stone that can be seen, sometimes, by starships that travel there. It is a cross that hangs in the blackness of space and burns forever.

There were thirty-five or forty attending Mass that morning; crowds of hairy, horned Ouitians kneeling in the foam pews. Several more than there had been yesterday.

Father John Simon sighed, proffered the holy wafer to Mary who waited alone at the altar rail, then placed one upon his own tongue. None of them were here for the Mass, he knew. They weren't here to learn about God and Jesus and the Christian life. They still held their belief in whatever it was . . . a ball of fire, or some such pagan image.

"Dominus vobiscum."

"Et cum spiritu tuo." Mary's voice was the thrum of a tree-frog in the silence.

"Ite, Missa est." He held out his hands toward the congregation. But they wouldn't leave, of course. They were waiting to hear what had brought them.

Father Simon turned and left the plastiplex dome that served as his church. He had set up a makeshift vestry by placing a screen in front of a semicircle of bushes and it was here, as he removed his vestments, he considered the situation. The Fathers of the Galactic Mission had failed. They had preached in the deserts of the planet Tatic; in the crowded cities of Paisly; among the farmers of Feim and the wild creatures of Ectogan. The Taticians clung fast to their stone idols; the citizens of Paisly were still godless hedonists. On Feim the four-armed, two-headed natives refused to worship Christ in the form of a human being, even when they were assured that God had no shape, and after Father Ramirez had carved a statue of Him with four arms and two heads.

The savages of Ectogan had accepted their gifts and had seemed interested in learning about God, but they were cannibals. When the Fathers had tried to dissuade them from this practice, they had killed three of them. The remaining five missionaries had managed to give the bodies Christian burial before escaping from Ectogan.

The cruciform starship, its transparent outer shell blazing with lights, leaped among the stars and drifted there for a long time, a firefly among flames, until the five priests on board decided not to return to Earth. After all they were missionaries, and even martyrs if need be, and so they landed their vessel on Cithira.

A winged tribe there gave them their first success. Beautiful, intelligent people, who accepted the Fathers and their God with warmth. When they had ordained two new priests among these people and decided to push on to another planet, Mary had come with them. Her parents had wanted the child to be their gift to God, to be raised by the missionaries and taught to become one of them herself. Reluctantly, the priests had brought her along with them to Ouito.

They set their starship down in the crater of a dead volcano, and this was their gathering point for weekly meetings. Then Father Breen had flown his land shuttle toward the mountains, to set up his plastiplex dome there. Father Sogorsky had gone with Father Ramirez to the cave cities scattered along the seacoast. Father Pirelli had chosen a cluster of islands near the equator of the small planet, and Father Simon had decided to work here among the hunters in the forest. Mary had stayed with him, of her own choice.

Then, about an Earth-month later, Father Pirelli had disappeared. When he didn't show up for their weekly meeting, the others searched for him in their shuttles and made inquiries to the Ouitian Central Government. Then Father Breen vanished. At the time of the last meeting, Father Sogorsky had shown up alone to report that Father Ramirez was also missing, and there had been no help from any of the Ouitians in trying to find any of them. Later today he was to join Father Simon, along with Father Ramirez if he had shown up by that time, and they would try to decide what to do now. Clearly, Ouito was a dangerous place.

Father Simon removed his alb and emerged from behind the screen. The Ouitians still knelt inside the transparent dome, their silver-grey bodies in attitudes of prayer, but with who-knew-what thoughts in those horned heads. Mary sat on the ground outside, arms around her knees, her wings rolled into tight blue sticks on her shoulderblades.

"Do they come today, the Fathers?"

"Yes, Mary. I think we'll leave this planet tonight."

"Then why do you go back in there?" She turned her delicately boned face toward the tent and rolled yer yellow eyes at the Ouitians. "This is hell, Father."

He nodded. Once, on Cithira, he had shown her a twentieth century illustration of Satan in one of his old books. The horns and cloven hooves of the Ouitians did look Satanic, but they had double snouts and tiny mouths in their reddish-brown faces. Mary considered them all to be devils, and said so frequently. She stood now, with a grace Father Simon found delightful, and looked up at him for his answer.

"Because we don't know yet that we *are* leaving. Things should go on just as usual. Father Ramirez might be with Father Sogorsky today. The disappearances might be explained yet."

"Maybe," Mary said doubtfully, "but if the others are not dead, why don't they communicate?"

"They might be too far away for their radcoms to work. We don't know yet, Mary."

The girl still looked doubtful, but Father Simon brushed past her and through the doorway. She was following, he knew. She always perched on the bench beside him when he played, just as she followed him everywhere, always wanting to be beside him. Mary, whose Cithiran name sounded like a flute song. He had named her when he had baptized her, but even he knew that "Mary" was too mundane, too Earthlike a name for her. "Dryad" might have suited her or, he thought wryly, "Salome". She was one of the crosses he had to bear . . . as a priest and as a man old enough to be her grandfather . . . a doubly heavy cross in this lonely and frustrating existence. He settled on the bench at the organ and drove away his thoughts with a long note.

The Ouitians waited silently for the music; Father Simon conscious of them as he played. This was their bribe; the reason they came to the church at all. They were an intelligent race, but although they built dwellings and made tools and even clothing, there was no other resemblance to humankind. Father Simon had learned enough of their language to communicate with them, but he was a long way from fathoming their mental makeup. The inhabitants of the forest were hunters who lived in caves, that much he knew. He had never been permitted to visit their caves, or even see one. The Ouitians had been drawn from the forest first because of curiosity, and now because of the organ music, and so he played for them . . . a Bach sonata and then, because of his own mood today, a Bartok concerto.

As the last notes of the concerto faded he could hear their gruntings, and turned to see them writhing in the pews as though in convulsions. It was time to stop. The music had a physical effect on them, he didn't know what or why, only that after a certain length of time listening, they always did this. Mary rose from the bench, looking worried.

"Come now, Father. Enough."

He nodded, and followed her slender form down the aisle, and as he went he raised his voice to be heard above the noise of the Ouitians. "Mass tomorrow as usual. Bring your children with you!" He had asked so many times about the children he had never seen, and had tried to let them know how much he would like to get closer to them, and to share their lives. There had been no response.

He and Mary waited near the land shuttle until the Ouitians left the church and had disappeared into the forest. Then they climbed inside the ship and went to meet Father Sogorsky and . . . please God! . . . Father Ramirez, at the starship site.

"I gathered fruit for our dinner, Father. Eat something."

"I can't."

"They will be here soon."

"Of course they will. I'm not worried. I'm just not hungry." But he was worried . . . very worried.

"What could happen?" Mary asked, going over ground they covered each time a priest disappeared. "We had permission from the Planetary Federation to come here. The Ouitians have been friendly." She was perched on the edge of a chair in the starship's lounge, watching Father Simon pace furiously.

"Then why have the four disappeared?" he asked himself, her, the room. "Something's either holding them prisoner or has killed them. They haven't even communicated . . . just vanished completely."

Both of them looked toward the port, but it was already dark and they saw only reflections of themselves. Late, Father Simon thought. Much later than it should be. But still they waited, talking together, speculating, until the buzzer on Father Simon's radcom startled them. He pulled it from the breast pocket of his shirt. "Yes?"

Father Sogorsky's voice was faint. "They're dead, John. All dead."

"Who? Where are you?" Father Simon's voice was tight and anxious, but the faint voice on the radcom went on talking without pause.

" . . . being killed off. They hate us. Get away now!"

"Where are you?"

"Hiding from them. Wounded. It has to be the music. Drives them crazy. Affects their—"

"Where are you?"

"B3-45-NR, I think. Around there. Just got to my shuttle to meet you. They attacked."

Father Simon was already heading for the passage, with Mary behind him. He turned to her and spoke over Father Sogorsky's voice. "You're not coming."

"No."

But he had forgotten she was winged, and as he brought his shuttle down at the indicated point he could see a burning mass that must have been Peter Sogorksy's vehicle, a deserted beach, and a flash of blue wings below him. He set the shuttle down on the sand and Mary soared to a rock close by.

"I couldn't stay alone there," she called softly. "If anything happens to you, I don't want to live."

For only a moment he took a different meaning from her words, and his heart jerked painfully. Then he remembered that he was her only protector now . . . her only means of escaping the planet if danger threatened. "Ssssh!" he told her, and played his pulselight among the rocks, searching for Father Sogorsky. He didn't want to use the radcom. The sound of his voice might be heard, or the buzzer of Father Sogorsky's instrument. But surely the injured priest could see the light, and he must be here somewhere.

When they finally found him he was unconscious, his clothing torn, his face battered and bloody, one of his hands crushed. Mary helped, and together they carried him toward their shuttle.

Father Simon opened the cargo door and hoisted the man inside. When he turned, he saw the Ouitians running toward them across the beach. He had no weapon . . . missionaries didn't carry them . . . but the Ouitians carried knives and spears, and several had rocks.

Father Simon held up his hands. "Stop this murdering!" he shouted in Ouitian. "Stop! We came with love!"

Mary stood frozen beside him. The Ouitians paused in front of them, then a knife flew through the air, and Mary made a soft, painful sound and crumpled to the ground.

He scooped her up in his arms and placed her inside the shuttle, then jumped in after her and closed the door. The Ouitians surged forward and surrounded the vehicle. Grimly, Father Simon clambered into the drive seat and maneuvered the controls. The shuttle lifted and sped away.

He managed to get the shuttle inside the starship himself, and activated the compucontrol himself, and as the ship rose, he got Father Sogorsky into the webbing and strapped him in. It was too late for Mary, but he lifted her delicate body out of the shuttle and strapped her down, too. She would go with him on this last journey.

Free at last, he said the words to her he never could have said, and bent and kissed her lips.

In the days that followed, after Father Sogorsky died, Father Simon struggled with grief, frustration, and rage. These finally formed themselves into one strong desire, and he knew that he would not give up God's mission . . . that he would glorify Him even in death. His life had to be worth something, and his life's work had to have some meaning, and the missionaries who had died so futilely had to be memorialized. He turned the starship toward Cygnus X-1.

Objects falling into a black hole seem, to an outside observer, to be falling forever. To space travelers approaching the vicinity of Cygnus X-1 there is a peculiar formation that appears. A cross, brightly lit, that burns forever among the stars.

SINGULARITY

Mildred Downey Broxon

I first heard of Mrs Broxon when I received a curious postcard signed "Bubbles". Since then she has been a Vice President of Science Fiction Writers of America, a passionate teller of tragic Irish tales, the author of a dozen unprintably ribald ballads, and the genius who introduced the writers to a marvelous drink called Athol Broze.

She is also one of the best of the new generation of science fiction writers, as I think this story will prove.

1

Autumn struck early. Spahi stood in the foothills on first snow. The low brush held no hiding place for thrani; his prey must lurk in the half-shadowed ravine. The thrani were driven to the lowlands by the first mountain snows; already, for many days, the higher slopes gleamed white. The beasts would welcome hunters. Such was their destiny; what thran, after all, would wish to be reborn an animal?

Twilight brought gusting of chill wind. Spahi shuttered his scale-plates and closed two of his eyes, leaving open one for color vision and one for light-dark. He crouched on the snow and retracted both pairs of feet and two arms. With his other two hands he held his spear. "Come, thran," he whistled. The sound blended with the wind; there was no motion in the ravine. In a while, if the thran did not emerge, he must go after it. But if it were afraid to come out, its meat would be only food, without bravery to feed his children.

It was a long, cold wait. He was glad he had left his children home with another hunter who had made her kill early. Younglings would fret at waiting, and here in the foothills, on the snow, he could not let them out of his pouch to run.

The sky darkened. Spahi opened both light-dark eyes, shutting out his color vision. There—he could see a moving shadow at the edge of the ravine—

This thran was huge. Its armor-plating would roof huts and make shields; it could also deflect Spahi's spear. But this was not his first hunt. He knew where to strike.

He stepped closer. The beast had freely come forth, and must be met with honor. "Come, thran," he whistled. "Come, and be reborn a person." The thran saw him, hesitated a moment, then charged. Good; it was brave. Spahi stood his ground, his spear braced, and aimed at the soft spot encircling the eyes. His spear pierced the brain. He stepped aside as the thran was carried forward by its own momentum. A short way past him the animal fell, rolled, and snapped feebly.

"Well done, thran," said Spahi. The beast shuddered. Its blood pooled dark on the snow. In the moonlight Spahi saw the edges begin to crystallize. He set to work with his best knife, hacked off the larger armor plates, then cut the air-filled insulation layer beneath into strips and uncovered the dark meat. He piled chunks onto the largest plate, cut a hole to attach a cord, and formed a sled.

The hard, bright stars of winter had not risen. Some later summer constellations yet shone in the sky. Early, it was, for first snowfall. But the old bard had predicted a cold, dark winter.

The ill-omened constellation, The Coward, crouched on the horizon. Spahi wondered if it were auspicious to kill a thran while *that* was in the sky.

Spahi dragged his burden home, his last pre-winter task complete. Soon it would be time to huddle indoors and fashion armor, while cold winds screamed outside.

2

Closer to Epsilon Eridani than its seventh, farthest planet, the Watchguard satellite waited. In two hundred and forty years it would complete one orbit. Placed by the original Exploration team, it waited to report any disturbance that might indicate spacefaring alien life.

Most known alien races were pre-scientific, such as those on Epsilon Eridani II, Mancken's World. The probe, when activated, was programmed to fling a capsule Earthward through whitespace.

Years passed; the probe traversed some twenty degrees of orbit. Planets revolved about the star, satellites about their planets, in an age-old dance. Comets streaked through the system, brief brilliant visitors, but the probe ignored such tenuous collections of ice and dust.

Eventually the Watchguard detected a faint wobble in

the farthest planet's orbit. As programmed, the satellite switched from standby and began recording. The pull became more definite. Watchguard responded; a cryogenic capsule, its information chilled to near absolute zero, sped toward Earth. Though in normal space the distance was 3.30 parsecs, in whitespace, with chilled data, it would be covered in one Jump. Only supercooled information could survive the severe randomizing effect of whitespace.

3

Carl Thorstensen, just back from a mental-health leave, sat in the Administrator's office. The psychiatrists had sent him home to Scandinavia to rediscover his cultural roots. Of the four xenologists on Carl's latest expedition, two were left permanently impaired, and one was dead.

Alienation was an occupational hazard. On his second assignment, Carl had been forced to take over for Harston, his senior xenologist, when she decided that five fingers were unaesthetic, and carved off her thumb and forefinger so that she might more closely resemble the natives of Mroglay. When she began on her nose and ears—well, Harston had a desk job now, far away from stress or public contact. Plastic surgery could only do so much.

This latest mission, too, had been disastrous. But after sailing up fjords, letting the northern sunlight tan his face, sleeping on the cramped shelves that passed for beds, breathing fresh air and eating real food, Carl no longer dreamt of blue-glowing oceans where sunlight shimmered overhead. No more did he taste with his skin or scorn the tiny air-breathers who wished to speak with him. No, he had recovered, and was fully human. He was lucky. Martin still could not talk, and Savros had flung herself into the waves, after they thought she was cured.

He pushed the past aside. Nina Leclerc was here as well. He hadn't seen the small Haitian woman since graduation. She'd been Savros' roommate, at the Academy.

Nina had been called back from her own vacation: a refresher course in astrophotography. She never went home.

No point in thinking of Haiti. Her grandmother was dead now. There was no sign of the curse she'd vowed to send Nina, when she fled to the stars. Nina was safe in Exploration, no matter the ceremonies on her seventh birthday.

The Administrator spoke. She was a tall woman in her mid-forties, attractive, save that the right side of her face was motionless, and her left arm was drawn tight against her body. A casualty of Exploration, retired to a desk job.

"You are assigned to a Scout II—the *Brendan*—for a six-month expedition to the Epsilon Eridani system. Our records show that you worked together successfully in pilot training."

"What is our assignment?" Nina said. "My orders indicate I am to observe a short-lived astronomical phenomenon."

"And mine," said Carl, "are to observe and record native culture on Epsilon Eridani II, Mancken's World. A Scout seems a bit small for this sort of assignment. Will we have two or four crew?"

"The urgency," the Administrator said, "is due to the astronomical situation." She turned toward Nina. "That, of course, is your department."

Astronomy and physics; the hard, clean sciences—yes, that was her life now. Not that stinking hut in the hills, with the screaming chickens, the blood, and the fat old woman who told Nina that she held the Power and must succeed her. Nina, aged seven, had vomited. Her mother, afraid to resist, dragged her to the hills each week for instruction until she was old enough to escape.

"What is the short-lived phenomenon?" Nina said.

"The Watchguard satellite in the Epsilon Eridani system sent a whitespace capsule. Analysis reveals that the system will be traversed by a black hole of some four solar masses, moving at 200 kilometers per second. It will disrupt the largest gas giant—Epsilon Eridani 5—and graze the star, causing stellar-matter loss and flares. We have been given a rare observational opportunity."

Carl spoke up. "But Mancken's is inhabited."

"Yes," said the Administrator. "As a xenologist this is your last chance to observe the natives. We would send a larger team, but our budget for pure research is limited."

Carl gripped the arms of his chair. "Won't you try to evacuate?"

Nina recalled the first time she'd noticed him in the Academy. It was at the Cygnus X-1 report. Many expedition members had been recent alumni, and were known to the underclassmen.

She'd watched Carl sit white-knuckled as the death announcements were made. The usual offer followed: Those who wished to leave the Academy could do so now, without reproach. The Academy would try to find them groundside jobs.

She'd expected Carl to join the handful of dropouts, but, to her surprise, he stayed. When she asked Savros about him later Savros said she thought he was overly sensitive for a xenologist.

But Carl stayed, took pilot-training with Nina, and graduated. And it was Savros who later went alien and died.

Carl stared at the Administrator and repeated his question. "Won't you try to evacuate?"

The Administrator shook her head. The paralyzed right side of her face twisted her expression. "We have neither time nor resources, nor have we anywhere to settle the natives even if we could transport them. If they were exposed to Jump-drive they would suffer genetic damage in any case, and could not reproduce any more than can Explorers. No, we can merely record what we can of their culture."

Put like that, it sounded logical. But a whole sentient

race faced destruction; so few there were, amid the sterile stars.

He saw Nina watching him; her expression held contempt. Damn her! Just once he'd like to see her ruffled. Even her first Jump, during pilot training, hadn't bothered her, while he himself had been violently ill. She'd cleaned up after him. He pressed his lips together. "All right, where do we start?"

After two weeks of hasty preparation, Nina and Carl shuttled to where the *Brendan* hung in Lunar orbit, gleaming like a golden barbell. One sphere held the engines that would jump the craft and its occupants in and out of grey-space. In the other sphere were sleeping quarters, the galley, and the laboratories.

Jumping was a calculated risk. If the engines malfunctioned, a Jump too high into greyspace, much less one into whitespace, would destroy the delicate codes in the cells' nuclei. Explorers who met with malfunction returned hideously changed; most died soon. Xenology students tried to communicate with them, as an exercise. No one had yet succeeded.

Carl had an almost-superstitious fear of Jump engines, and thought about them as little as possible. He knew only where the governors were and how to switch them on for a pre-programmed Jump. But short-lived humans must rely on them; how else could they reach the stars?

The shuttle neared the *Brendan* and docked on the bar connecting the two spheres. The ship's umbilical tube snaked toward the airlock.

Carl gathered his personal gear and stepped aboard the ship that would be home for the next few months. Nina, silent as usual, did the same.

Carl's hands and feet tingled. Jumping had begun. The *Brendan* leapt from "normal" blackspace in and out of greyspace, again and again. Carl fought nausea.

Six Jumps to go. *It's going to land us in the black hole,*

we'll be sucked in—six more Jumps and they could enter the system, place their observer in orbit around the fifth planet, then coast in under conventional power.

Five—four—three—*isn't it too grey out? We'll go random!* Two, one. Then space was black, and Carl stopped twitching. The K2V gleam of Epsilom Eridani contrasted with comforting darkness. The *Brendan* drifted outside the orbit of the fifth, largest planet. The rest of the trip to Mancken's World would take weeks at normal speed.

Mancken's World, a gold-brown crescent, spun past the porthole; Nina had started the *Brendan* spinning, for gravity. Carl was planetside in the shuttle. She had five standard days for uninterrupted observations. She scarcely noticed being alone. Other humans were an annoyance.

Nina compared her newest observations with previous readings. According to computer projections, the black hole was approaching at a narrow angle to the ecliptic. Soon it would near E.E.5, the gas giant. Nina doodled a diagram: an arrow pointed straight toward the star. The approach should be spectacular.

She looked again out the porthole. The planet was quarter-lighted by its reddish-orange sun. Through cloud rifts she glimpsed an occasional sparkle of ocean: fewer oceans than Earth had, and many of them frozen. She thought of the lofty, ice-locked mountain ranges. A solar flare would melt their glaciers.

She wondered idly whether some effort might have been made to save the natives had they developed writing or advanced technology.

But she was not a xenologist, and the natives were not her concern. Everyone eventually died. These folk were doomed by a combination of time and physics.

4

Spahi was carving spirals on a thran-armor shield—a plate from the thran he had last killed—when a youngling approached and stood nearby. Ill it was to interrupt an artist. Spahi finished the whorl, set down the piece, and opened all four eyes in attention.

"Spahi," the youngling whistled, "the bard would speak with you."

"What on?" he said. The bard was old, and often disapproved of Spahi.

"She said that only you who talked with the sky-folk before could talk with them now."

"The sky-folk? Again?" They had come when Spahi was much younger. He had watched others try to communicate, and had, when asked, whistled into their machine, indicating what he meant—though he was not sure they understood his gestures.

"The bard says come."

Spahi laid down his tools carefully, put his sleeping children into his pouch, and strode outside. He did not wait to don an insulating garment. It was yet daylight and early in the season. However, he retracted two legs and all four arms against the chill, and left only his color-vision eyes open. This promised to be a singularly cold winter.

He scrunched over snow, deeper now than when he'd killed the thran, and walked to the bard's hut, at the edge of the settlement. She was indeed aging. Even on such a mild day smoke billowed from the roof-vent. Spahi recognized a plate from his own thran patching the roof. As fit tribute to her station he had brought her the largest and best armor from the back.

The bard stood inside the doorway, huddled in insulation, as if she had taken a long, cold walk. Down to the ship, perhaps?

"May the tales comes easy, and may you tell them soon to the gods," Spahi greeted her.

"The sky-folk are landed again, earlier than they said. This time they have a thing that talks, but it speaks badly and I cannot understand it. You were young when last they came, Spahi."

"That I was." He did not add that she had tried to prevent him, a youngling, from speaking with starfolk; best that old quarrels be forgotten.

"This time there is but one offworlder. Would you see what it wants?" She shivered. "The outdoor light hurts my eyes, and the day is cold. Find what it wants, Spahi,"—she was still in command, "and then come to tell me."

The youngling waited outside the hut. "I will show you where it landed," he whistled. "Please let me come along."

The craft was not much larger than a hut; it was made of gleaming metal instead of stone. So much metal! Spahi recalled his childish wonder. It was somehow different from the first craft he had seen—he yet remembered every detail, even the markings on the side. Another artist must have fashioned this one. The pattern was not particularly pleasing. Perhaps to these folk it meant something.

The door opened, and a short device of sticks or bones was lowered.

A star-being climbed down. It wore a gleaming suit. "I am not afraid," the youngling murmured, as if to remind himself.

"Nor should you be," said Spahi. "It comes from the sky, and there you too would go, if you became its prey."

The youngling drew in all his limbs and squatted in a lump. Cold, or afraid? But he was young yet.

The creature carried a device some one-sixth as large as itself down from the ship and placed it on the snow. The object whistled. Spahi looked at it curiously. Was someone in the box? If so, he had a very bad accent; perhaps he was a foreigner from across the mountains. And he must be very small.

The sky-creature ran hands over the device; it whistled again, and Spahi tried to understand. The speech halted and rasped: "I come . . . no fight. My . . . tribe . . .

here . . . before. I understand . . . your language . . . cannot make sounds."

"Oh," said Spahi slowly, to be understood, "I have met your kind before. I talked into another box, when I was young, like this one." He indicated the youngling, who opened one eye.

The creature adjusted the box again. "Good. Is . . . this . . . correct?"

"Not quite," said Spahi. He repeated "Is . . . this . . . correct?" with proper inflection. The next phrases were clearer.

"I have never been here before. Others came before me to learn. I would learn how you live. I would hear your stories and see your artwork."

"I," said Spahi, "am a metalworker and shield-carver. I fashion fine spears and ornaments. But what would you learn from us? You come from the sky, you use strange metal, you speak with the gods. You should tell *us* stories; you are the far traveller."

The creature did not answer for a moment. Then, "Where do far-travellers learn their tales? My time is short. I must see what I can of your world before I leave. The folk beyond the mountains—"

"Are ignorant barbarians," said Spahi. "Half their thrani are wasted in the hunt, they have no bards, and their shields—" he made a whistle of disgust— "are not carved. When they die their highest hope is to become like us." Spahi remembered meeting a cross-mountaineer one summer near the pass; he had not looked much different from Spahi himself, but the two did not speak.

He remembered his promise. "First I must speak with the bard."

5

Carl Thorstensen stood by the door of the bard's hut and stared out into orange twilight. Through the mask that supplied his additional oxygen—Mancken's atmosphere was too thin for prolonged human comfort—he could smell pungent smoke. He was surprised at how well he and Spahi had been able to speak. Could he have done the same, were he an inhabitant of a bronze-age culture, faced with a creature who spoke through machines? And Spahi had met humans only once before, when he was a youngster.

The natives' appearance was strange: plated ovoids some one and one-half metres high, with four shieldable eyes, four lightly armored legs and the same number of arms, all retractable to minimize exposure to cold. Mancken's folk—from this tribe at least—were intelligent and not specially xenophobic. Carl wondered if they were the first intelligent life to evolve on E.E.2. Their dim K2V star had burned a long time. They might be the last of several races. No one would ever know.

Carl shivered. Those incredible mountains! Higher than any on Earth, they loomed against the dark. He considered climbing them. What an expedition that would be—gale-winds screaming on the peaks, bitter cold, thin atmosphere—he did not wonder that the various local cultures were isolated. Even in the height of summer, those peaks never shed their snow. In the stratified snowfalls must lie pollen-written records that could be deciphered by experts—had time not run out.

Recorder in hand, he stepped inside the hut. Stories were promised for tonight.

The hut was crowded; the inhabitants saw him and rustled. They moved to make room by the fire, near where the old bard sat huddled.

The hut was small, ground-hugging against gale force winds. Over the central fire, a hole in the domed roof opened to let smoke escape. The roof itself was made of overlapped plates, similar to the plates on the natives' bodies, but each a metre or so across. Piles of spongy material stood against the walls; the bard and a few of the others sat or leaned on chunks of it.

Spahi had brought his children, Carl saw. He kept them with him almost constantly—he must have an older mate, then, who had already done her share of child-rearing. He set the two down by the fire; they were smaller replicas of their father, no bigger than Carl's hand. They sat quiet, all four eyes open.

Carl thought he saw, by the door, the youngling who had accompanied Spahi earlier in the day, but it was hard to tell individuals apart.

The bard spoke to her people. "Long ago, when Spahi was a youngling and you, Nikar, were raising your very first children—" A creature with cracked and dulled plates rustled near the fire— "beings came from the sky. One has returned this day and would hear stories; a traveller, gathering tales to bring the gods."

Carl spoke, awkward with the simulator. "It is not the gods who sent me. My own people wish to know stories of your world."

"Are you a bard, then, that you can remember after one hearing?" The old one's voice was sharp.

"No. I have something here that will listen, and remember, so that your stories will never die." Never die, indeed. Forgotten in some storage system, source material for xenology students in last-minute search for thesis material—a dry, cold immortality. Carl noticed the shocked silence in the hut. The occupants looked at him, all four eyes open.

Spahi spoke first. "Who would wish not to die?"

The bard joined in. "You claim I would not die. Would I live on, cold and stiff, near-blind and in pain, my house roofed and my meat killed by others, forever? This is curse indeed. I will tell you nothing."

Immortality, Carl realized, was not a universal desire. "No, you yourself will die—" how true!— "but others will tell your stories. In this box there is a sort of bard," how else to explain? "who will remember."

"I will die, though, as will we all?" The old bard was still suspicious.

"Yes," said Carl. "I guarantee it."

She relaxed; her plates fluffed out to let the warmth flow against her body. "Very well, then. Listen, bard in the box. I speak a story."

"In summer, when rivers wake from winter sleep, when stars are paler than their frost-bright brothers, and the sun, in pity, stays longer than the night, at that time, long ago, did great thrani walk the land, even before the first snows gleamed the hills. Their herds were huge, and they were chased by hunters stronger and swifter than any who live today." She paused.

Things were always better in the good old days, thought Carl. Or was this an ancient tale of changing climate?

"Thrani sought the hunters with joy, to be reborn and speak, not wander mute in animal darkness. For if an animal slays a thran, then thran remains but an animal. With joy the hunters also sought them, for the thrani flesh was full of courage. Swift-speared and quick-knifed, they killed them and brought them home. They fulfilled their promise that the thrani be reborn. If a thran killed a hunter, well, the hunter would be a thran for a life-time, but a great thran, to be killed by an even greater hunter and thus reborn a person.

"In those days lived one hunter who would not go on the chase; she feared the thrani, and feared pain. Some said she had fed on coward's meat.

"Summer passed, and days grew short. Still the fearful one would not hunt, and her children cried until her former mates took pity on them and fed them; at last their father took them, though he was caring for children of his own.

"Riverbanks hardened, and in the mornings ice rimmed the streams, breaking only at midday. It was yet summer, but the gods grew angry. The people armed the cowardly hunter and drove her into the hills; they would not let her bring down the cold before its time.

"She hid in the bushes, afraid, yet she could not go

back. The king of all the thrani waited there. Some say he
was a mighty hunter who had died—some say her father—who now awaited his reward. He had waited long,
and was tired. It was her destiny to kill him, and his to be
reborn. But she was soft from idleness, and her spear
missed, wounding the thran. If fled and cried, "Am I now
old, and tired, and yet cannot die, because of this
hunter?" The gods raged: the thran deserved better. They
flung the woman into the heavens, undying amid the stars.
They found the thran where it lay weeping, killed it, and
made a mighty feast in their great hall. The woman, still
cold, watched us from the summer sky, but the thran,
killed by the gods, is a godguest. Its frozen blood spreads
across the heavens, the bright path you see among the
stars.

"The children and their father, and his children, left
this land and went over the mountains in disgrace to shel-
ter amid lesser folk.

"Since that time the thrani do not come from the hills
until the first snow, and only brave men and women hunt
them. The snows are early now, summer is brief, and winter is cold and long. So ends my tale of the coward who
will never die."

The old bard sat back, ruffling her plates again, spreading the warmth across her aged body. "With two bards in
a hut, each should tell a tale."

What bard? thought Carl. Oh. The bard-in-the-box.
Dammit, he wanted to think of the implications of the
story—but it was all on tape, now, and he must not of-
fend. He looked at Spahi, who made no sign. Carl could
not speak without the simulator, and even then he was
clumsy. What could he tell them? He ran through his rep-
ertory of tales. Nothing he'd learned from the cetaceans;
their imagery was wrong for an ice-locked world with few
oceans. He would prefer not to think of the cetaceans;
memories were still too fresh. One of the stories of the
folk Harston, the self-mutilating xenologist, had wanted to
emulate? But those were strange, multi-level schizoid

things, perpendicular to reality; hard for a sane person to understand, let alone remember. (Why then could he recall them so well?) He settled finally on something he knew, and spoke to them, haltingly, of battlefields, Valkyries, and Valhalla. Battles, he noted, evoked less enthusiasm than the hunt, so he changed the story accordingly. Evidently these folk were so isolated from their neighbors, and so dependent on each other, that full-scale wars were rare and even feuds uncommon. What point in killing a person, if he would only be born again, in your own tribe? He wove a wondrous tale of herds of stampeding tigers—lavishly described and embellished—and Valkyries swooping down to gather the fallen and set them to feasting and battle in the hall of the gods.

Even the bard admitted, grudgingly, that she would hear more at some time. But now the hour grew late.

As if on signal the company arose. Spahi gathered his children, stowed them in his pouch, and inquired where Carl would spend the night.

Carl was tired. "In my ship." he picked up the simulator.

"I will walk with you, lest the snows slide beneath your feet," said Spahi. They stepped out of the hut. Overhead the stars were bright and clear. Carl could see Sirius glaring brilliant overhead. "Is that how it is, among the gods?" Spahi asked.

Carl shrugged. The gesture was not only meaningless, but indiscernible under his suit, but he could not operate the simulator while walking on snow in darkness. By the time they reached the shuttle, Spahi was holding back a respectful distance. Carl waved goodnight and climbed the ladder, sealing the door behind him. His suit was cold, and burned his fingers when he took it off. He could spend a few precious hours in sleep, now. Then a quick trip to the village over the mountains, perhaps stops at others, an aerial scan—he could do little in depth, not on a world as fragmented as this, in the time he had. He felt he would return to Spahi and to the old bard, at the last.

6

Nina watched the bright speck of the shuttle wink into view. On the radio, Carl had sounded tired and discouraged.

The shuttle arced between the two spheres of the *Brendan*; Nina felt a slight vibration as the umbilical tunnel connected.

She'd been without company for some time; until radio contact she had not spoken in days, and her voice was rusty. She heard Carl clamber into the hallway toward the living-and-lab sphere. He struggled out of his heat suit, stowed it, and came forward.

He stepped into the galley area. She was amazed at the weight he'd lost. Concentrated rations and overwork always did that, of course, and it was cold on Mancken's, but in five days Carl, ordinarily thin, had become gaunt. His cheeks were shadowed and the blond stubble of his beard gave him a derelict appearance.

She cleared her throat. "How was it, planetside?"

He looked at her without answering and went to the food area, running his fingers over the selection buttons. "Cold." He chose something and carried it to the table. He lifted the cover and looked, without enthusiasm, at the steaming mass.

"Ah—did you get many good records?"

"Stowed on the shuttle. Unload them after I get some rest. Too tired." He stirred his food as if it were a specimen to be examined.

Nina rose and tossed her own tray into the cleaner. "You're back in time for the spectacular. Events around the big planet are getting interesting now; in twenty-four hours it should break apart." She washed her hands and leaned against the counter. "We'll be in position for some direct observations, but the orbital observer should give us the best pictures. The outermost moon is showing signs of perturbation. Before closest approach, of course, the satellites will have been torn loose, and the atmosphere will have begun—"

"STOP IT!" Carl stood and threw his tray across the galley. "You goddamn ghoul! Do you think all this is happening so you can publish an article?"

Nina watched him stalk toward his sleeping cubicle. She'd only said what would happen. Why was he crying?

Carl thought of Nina, calmly describing the destruction of a world as if it made no more difference than—*than what?* An ant hill, after all, is important to the ants. And a world—there are billions of stars, and most have planets.

He sat in his cramped sleeping room, the panel firmly shut. He was exhausted, and, after five days, he stank. He peeled off his coverall and headed for the cleaner. He did not encounter Nina.

As he slept he dreamt of chill, red-lit plains. Behind them wind-driven clouds brawled over black peaks. Somewhere in the sky a face watched as he stood cold and alone, waiting for the world to end. Morning would never come.

After his rest period Carl sought Nina to make amends; shipmates must at least be polite, and he was ashamed of his outburst.

She was in the astronomical lab, of course; she almost always was. He rapped on the panel; it slid open a crack and Nina looked out. She stood, silent and braced.

"I'd like to apologize," Carl said. "I was tired. I am overly involved with my own project, and I suppose—"

"I cleaned up the galley," she said, without expression.

"If I might observe—you said, today—" Carl stood in the doorway.

Nina slid the panel back and beckoned him inside.

The observatory had one large porthole that scanned, alternately, the planet or the stars, as the *Brendan* rotated. A clear bubble containing a drive-mounted telescope protruded through the outer hull. A whirring motor kept the telescope pointed at the same patch of sky. Attached to the telescope was a camera, and the desk was piled with black-on-white negative prints. Carl bent over and examined one. Ink dots, some large, some small, some a bit smeared.

Nina riffled through the stack. "Here." She pointed to a dot surrounded with specks. "An earlier photo of Eridani 5, the gas giant. The smaller dots are its satellites, four of the six. Two are occluded."

She selected another photo. "This was taken three days ago. The farthest satellite's orbit is shifting, see?"

Carl could detect little if any difference. Now there were five satellites visible, and all had moved. It was hard to tell.

Nina picked up another picture. "Here, I'll show you one taken two hours ago. I'm switching to color now, and the satellite station has begun sending in continuous data—"

Carl bent over the color positive. The gas giant, fifth and largest planet in the system, hung golden against the black of space. In the background shone a few bright stars.

Nina showed him a computer printout. "This is a projection, looking down at the planet. See how the orbits are perturbed? And this is how it will be when the most distant satellite is finally pulled away."

"Where will it go?"

"It can't be captured by the hole. It will most likely wander; it may leave the system altogether."

Another photograph spat from the camera. Carl studied the first one; then Nina brought over the second.

"The planet itself is starting to bulge."

The sphere did look oblate.

The camera clicked again. Nina extracted another print. "It's begun to draw off atmosphere."

Glowing gas streamers spiralled into space.

"Next, the liquid high pressure layers will be stripped

away. They will evaporate immediately. At the last, the core, released from pressure, will explode."

She turned again toward the camera.

"How long is left?"

"About five hours to zero. We've never seen this happen, of course, but according to calculations—"

He stopped her. "Was there ever any detailed study made of E.E.5?"

"The first Exploration team catalogued its satellites, recorded what physical data they could, spectroscopically analyzed the atmosphere—"

"No one's ever been there, though," Carl said. "Not on the planet, but perhaps on one of the larger satellites? Or is there too much radiation?"

"No. It's not like our Jupiter. It's smaller, more like Saturn, but without the rings. There is one satellite of about 0.5 Terran mass, but it's never been explored. Not with an inhabited Terrestrial planet in the system." She sounded bitter. "Priorities, you know. The xenologists get first choice."

Some theorized that intelligent life forms might dwell on gas-giants. But even if they did, contact and communications would be almost impossible. The gravity, radiation, and totally alien psychology—Carl had thought, sometimes, how it might be, to live adrift in a methane-ammonia atmosphere.

Nina attached magnetic clips to her paperwork and pictures, and checked the office for stray objects. "I'm going to stop the spin, now. I want to observe this on direct visual. No one has ever seen what we are about to. Did you leave anything loose?"

"I don't think so." Carl went to look. Some galley items needed securing. As he stored them, he thought of the dying planet, even its satellites untrodden.

What did Spahi's people call it? It was an early evening object now—they would be able to watch its destruction. A fuzziness, a thin patch of bright mist—what would it look like planetside, and what would they think?

Carl took an anti-nausea pill and returned to the observatory. Nina had been awaiting his return; she neutralized the spin.

The *Brendan* hovered in synchronous orbit over Mancken's terminator. Carl looked out the viewport with the aid of a small refractor. Nina busied herself with calculations, readings, and ever-more-frequent photographs.

"The upper atmosphere just went. That will change the pressure—the inner liquid layers will peel off soon."

Carl did not want to watch, but he could not stop himself. Even weightless he could imagine the gravitational pull, the tidal forces—his blood would pool, his flesh would stretch and tear—

But no. The victim was a planet, gas and liquid, not known to be inhabited. If it were—the turbulence, swirling through layers of ever denser gases, mixing the ecolayers, pulling and confusing the beings who floated there—Carl became dizzy. He looked again out the porthole and saw a tiny glowing patch.

Nina preferred the latest picture. Ribbons of gas, glowing from molecular collision, whirled about an invisible point. Most swirled off and dispersed, but some were pulled into elliptical orbit about the singularity. The orbiting gases glowed ever-brighter, overheated, fluorescing now, eerie blue—

"It's happening," Nina said. "You might want to shade your eyepiece."

For a moment Carl looked away from the telescope. *The wrenching, tearing* . . . The planet flared, exploding, spreading starlike brilliance.

Nina held out a photograph. "There," she said. "The glow is captured matter spinning toward the event horizon. From now on, we should be able to visualize—Carl? Are you all right?"

Shaking, he stared at the photographs, then back at the small new star in the porthole. "How close will it pass to Mancken's?"

"Nowhere near. Mancken's will be at quadrature. It will, though, pass very near the sun." She pulled another photo, studied it, and clipped it to the board. The camera spat a few more pictures. "To think I saw it myself! It was magnificent!"

Carl was tired, horrified, and fascinated. Such raw power! When it reached the sun . . .

7

The sky-creature returned sooner than expected. Hospitality made Spahi leave his work, clean his hands, and hasten to the landing site, guided by the excited, jabbering youngling.

The old bard had not stirred from her hut for days. It was clear the gods wished her stories soon.

He stood on the snow and waited for the creature to emerge. It did so as it had the last time, burden-laden, backing down from a doorway. The creature's movements were jerky, and it dropped a piece of equipment. Once on the ground it stumbled and wavered a bit, then came forward.

"I have more expeditions to make, more tribes yet to visit, but I thought I would return here—"

"Have you already gone beyond the mountains?"

"Yes."

Spahi waited.

"Oh. You want to know what they are like? The ones I met are much like you; some were afraid, and I did not stay. I left gifts."

"And the others? There were others you could talk with?"

"Some. The languages are much different from place to place, but I had the records of the other expeditions. Here, look. Have you seen anything like this?" The creature reached into a pouch on its suit and drew out a package. It fumbled it open, thick-fingered, and showed Spahi a spearpoint, dark grey metal save for the bright chiseled spirals.

Spahi touched it: the point was sharper than any he made, and it was long enough to pierce thran-hide. It was beautiful, and unlike the red metal he worked. He had never wanted any object so much. He handed it back. "I have never seen its like. It came from beyond the mountains? Where?"

"Four passes over."

Spahi could never cross four passes, not with the short summers.

"I am collecting works of artistry," the creature said. "I would like to have one of your shields, as well."

One of my shields? To go with that spear-point? Spahi was flattered. The sky-folk did not even hunt. "Come back to my hut, then," said Spahi, "and choose."

"Not now. I have more travels, but I will return in time."

In time for what? The creature ascended to its craft. Spahi turned back to the village, and the youngling followed.

The shuttle flew over a snow-choked mountain pass. On either side moonlight gleamed the higher peaks. Winds spun snow-clouds to sparkle in the silver light. The air in the narrow pass was turbulent; Carl fought to keep his craft free of the menacing walls, the steep and jagged, snow-bare cliffs.

No wonder there was little commerce on this world. The winters were so long—yearly the snow crept down from the mountains and receded ever-more-slowly, as an advancing tide, or so the bards said.

But soon flames would melt the encroaching glaciers and blast the breath from living lungs. The shuttle swerved. Carl forced himself to concentrate.

Too late. Another current, buffeted from mountainsides, snatched him, and whirled him toward the valley. The shuttle brushed the tops of some low shrubbery. He tried to steer for the open spaces, but another wind-gust smote.

Time and space ran out as he fell toward sparkling snow. Metal crunched, then all was silent.

His harness had saved him serious injury. He took inventory. The initial sharp chest pain faded, but then he began to shake. When he reached to release his safety harness he could not use his right hand. Why did the shuttle lie at such an angle?

One way to find out: go look. *If I don't get offworld I'll die, melted in solar flares, or, even sooner, frozen.* His hand was throbbing now. He refused to believe it was broken. The pain would go away.

It throbbed harder, swelling in the glove. *All right, dammit!* Carl released his harness with his left hand and undid his suit-latches. His hand was turning purple. Broken or sprained, he could not use it. When he tried, the fingers refused to move, and bone-ends grated.

He blinked away the sworls of green/blue dark. He must immobilize the injury. He reached, left-handed, for the medikit behind his seat, fumbled it open and found the hand templates. He activated the foam cylinder. The bones would not be set, and he could not use his hand, but the grating pain would lessen.

This was not the time for pain medication. Later, after the shock wore off.

He was glad he'd been wearing his heatsuit; he doubted he could have donned it now. *No one is coming to get me.* No one could. Nina was on the *Brendan,* but he had the shuttle.

His thought of Nina, cool, dark, contemptuous, decided him; he would tell her later. He fumbled the door open and stepped onto the snowy surface of Mancken's World.

One crumpled landing ski should pose no problem. With digging and righting—or carefully-aligned blasting—he could fly back now; but without in-space repairs he could never land again. Time was short enough to scratch future planetside missions. *You've broken your toy; if you take it home, Mommy won't let you use it again.*

One-handed he could not make repairs. The pain shot to his elbow, and sickened him. He climbed back aboard the shuttle and radioed the ship.

"*Brendan* to shuttle. Come in."

"Nina, Carl here. I want to send up some time-compressed tapes to the computer, so I can wipe mine for further recordings."

"*Brendan* to shuttle, fine." Then, "Carl, are you okay?"

"I'm fine. Stand by for transcription." There was no further communication save a signal indicating that the tapes had been sent and received.

Carl sat in the pilot's chair awhile. The shuttle's radio was too big to carry, and nothing smaller could reach the *Brendan*. If he wanted more time planetside he must set out for help alone. He clipped a knife and his rocket-launching sidearm to his suit, packed supplementary oxygen and food, and climbed down.

The first few metres were educational. The shuttle blast had melted the snow into crust; here, in the undisturbed drift, he sank hip-deep with every step.

The shuttle already seemed far uphill. The bright moon was setting, and darkness, save for the small, faster-speeding satellite, was complete.

He floundered back to the shuttle. Using a pry-bar, he pulled two metal plates from the broken landing ski.

He had to return to the seductive warmth of the shuttle to cut the harness straps from one seat, before he could fashion a crude pair of sliding snowshoes.

He burned holes in metal, the torch held in his teeth while his broken hand steadied the work. He also pried loose the long metal ski-edge. He would need a pole.

Long was it since he had snowshoed, and never had he skied. Now, with overburdened pack and injured hand, it was a slow downhill slogging, falling, getting up, falling again. He thought of the lofty peaks and despaired.

What does it matter if I lie here and die?

The snow isn't so bad, as long as the thrani stay away, and my plates don't stick—*what?* Where am I, what— I've got to go on. He fell. I can't get up. I'm too tired, and the pain—

He listened to the humming of his heatsuit. Eventually the low sound blotted out the wind.

Mancken's revolution is 30.7 Earth hours, and nights, at high latitudes in winter, last 2/3 that time. It was still cold and dark when Carl awoke. His hand was swollen and throbbing, his mouth was dry, and his bladder was full. The thirst and urgency could be alleviated, but he dared not take any pain medication. How long had he slept? He had no way of knowing. His muscles were stiff; it had been several hours.

The constellations had wheeled about the sky; it must be nearly morning. Only the dim light of the smaller moon and some scattered starlight illumined the slopes. Carl's eyes were dark-adapted now. He must press on, must try to reach the village, where he might find help; his only alternative was to climb back to the shuttle and leave this world forever.

If he headed downslope he would eventually reach the village. He wondered how far he must travel; he'd only flown this pass once before, and in the dark he could discern no landmarks.

The metal snowshoes were light, yet his muscles protested. He was unused to the shuffling gait, and he often tripped. Each jolt, every misstep, hurt his hand as much as if he had broken it anew. After a time he noticed nothing but snow, pain, and fatigue. He set the suit-alarm to remind himself to eat, and slogged downslope.

The snow had frozen and refrozen. He could hear the crunch as he broke through crust, could see the large glittering crystals. Did they glitter more brightly now? The sky was paling. He stopped, awed, as always, by the beauty of mountain sunrise.

The highest peaks glowed pink, while the shadows remained deep purple. The pink ran slowly down the
slopes, leaving the peaks white, as if from a colored rain.
As Carl watched, his suit-alarm rang; time to eat. He was
nauseated from pain and fatigue, but if he did not ingest a
certain number of calories he would collapse.

He sat, opened some concentrated rations, and slid
them through the helmet-latch to thaw. The wind that
gusted briefly through the opening brought ice.

Sunlight spilled into the valley as he munched tasteless
food and sipped stale water. How could he have ever
thought this sun dim and cold? It was glorious, a welcome
sight after a long night alone in the dark.

He rose and slogged downhill. It was not until evening
that he sighted the thran.

8

Nina, aboard the *Brendan*, listened to the speed-sent
tapes; woundup blather. Then she broke radio contact.
Carl had been terse even for him. She wondered why he
had bothered to relay information instead of using more
tapes; was he gathering that much material? She had
nothing much to do until the next photograph, and the
shipboard silence was broken only by the whirring telescope drive and the pinging camera-timer.

What was Carl finding planetside? She cued one of the
transcribed tapes, slowed it to normal, and switched it on:
rustling in the background, perhaps a fire-crackle, some
tonal whistling that might be speech. A more mechanical
whistle, in reply, could be Carl's simulator.

Somehwere the computer held Mancken's language-
key. She could program it to translate, though machines,
faced with unfamiliar idioms, made ludicrous errors. She
sat back, instead, and listened to the variance of whistles
and breath-sounds as if they were a symphony.

During briefing she'd seen pictures of the aliens. She
had looked at them as she had the orbital photographs of

Mancken's World: interesting, but irrelevant. The natives would soon be dead, their planet irreversibly altered, their sun shrunken to a cinder.

The whistling rose and fell; a story was being told, with alien values and heroisms. She could appreciate the musical pattern—

It was not music, though, and not mere pattern. This was a language of living beings. Carl grieved for their fate. For a moment she, too, felt loss. Silly, of course.

She was a scientist, and nothing could affect her, not even her grandmother's curse.

The next photograph should be ready. She switched off the tape. Living creatures, after all, were planetary parasites. The slightest axial wobble could plunge them into an ice age or an intolerable draught. Only the march of the planets and the slow wheeling of the Galactic Year were lasting reality.

Even so, the music of living Mancken's speech haunted her, as fear had haunted her for years.

What could Grandmother have sent, to follow me even now? She slid the panel of the observatory closed and leaned against it, at home with her familiar machines.

9

Spahi sat in the bard's hut with his children and the youngling. The old bard was failing. The wind howled outside, calling her.

She lay near the fire. The youngling and children watched, that they might learn not to fear death. Spahi was there because he had been summoned. The old bard moaned. The sound blended with the wind.

"Spahi, we have often disagreed."

He maintained respectful silence.

"Yet you have done my bidding, and dealt with the sky-folk, when I was too aged. You taught them some of our speech, told them of our ways, brought them to bardic fires."

Spahi said nothing. Was this a reprimand?

"Spoke I to them stories, tales of old times, and they said—the sky-being and its bard—that they would remember when I died. I have not told the last tale of my life. Would you remember it, Spahi? It is important."

The old bard spoke of the time when the sun, attacked by scavengers, lashed out in agony and killed its children. Spahi was not memory-trained as was a bard, and the old one's voice was weak. Surely this was but a tale. The old bard's whistling grew fainter than the wind. She paused to draw ragged breath, and said, "Spahi—there is no bard with us?"

"No," said Spahi, ashamed that her mind was wandering.

"No sky-creature, no bard in a box?"

"No."

"There is no point in finishing the story. You will see what happens soon enough. I am tired."

She would say no more, and soon her breathing stopped. Spahi gestured to the youngling, who went to her and closed all four of her eyes, shuddering at his first touch of death. Spahi next took his children forward and showed them the old bard, explaining that she was with the gods. Then he reached up to tear the largest thran-plate from the roof.

Air currents swirled sparks from the fire toward the stars. The old bard was free now. Spahi and the youngling took the withered body, placed it on the fire, and left the hut. The fire roared for a time, then died down, and the last sparks floated toward the heavens.

10

The thran was huger than Carl had imagined. He knew how difficult such vicious, intelligent beasts were to kill; to slay one, among Spahi's folk, was to become adult. He fumbled at his pack-straps, cringing at the pain, and gripped his rocket pistol in his good left hand.

Theoretically the weapon was multi-purpose; the projectile, which accelerated even after firing, was less-affected by varying atmospheres and gravities, and could be fitted with exploding warheads.

Exploding warheads in this case had not seemed necessary, but looking at the thran, he wondered how the natives ever killed them, with their crude weapons.

The thran charged. Its feet splayed over the snow. Plated like Spahi and his kind, its huge jaws were studded with fearsome teeth, and its four small arms tipped in clutching claws. Carl tried to aim.

A claw ripped Carl's suit. He felt bitter cold against the skin of his left arm—the good one! Clumsy on snowshoes, he stumbled. The thran, carried by its own momentum, staggered on a few metres, then wheeled. As it steadied itself for another rush, Carl dropped to on aching knee, steadied his rocket-pistol, and fired.

He'd been a good shot at the Academy; he did not miss. The projectile spatted against the thran's armor, almost without effect. The beast bellowed and rushed him again.

Carl let it come as close as possible, then aimed. Too late. Again thran claws raked him; this time they drew blood. He fired again, too quickly; this one skimmed off the plates to crater a snowdrift.

The eyes. Spahi had mentioned the eyes. Carl had four shots left before he must reload. Pain and cold were making him shaky, and his aim would be affected. The four eyes were clustered in a small area of thinner plates. And the eyes, of course, connected directly with the brain.

He aimed and fired. The projectile creased the thran's head, singeing the plates. The thran bellowed. Carl fired again, and once more missed the eyes. Two more shots, and, with his right hand immobile and his left arm freezing, he doubted he *could* reload. He was wasting his ammunition. Spears. Spahi claimed to have slain many a thran with spears, but Spahi was an experienced hunter, and an armorer as well. Carl had never hunted. Wild animals on Earth were protected.

He had no crafted spear-tip, nothing but the jagged metal edge on his improvised ski-pole.

The thran waited now, wary. *At a rudimentary level it does calculate and plan.*

It seemed willing to wait all night. Carl's unprotected arm was almost frozen. He must provoke an attack. Two shots left; best to waste one, or rather invest it. He shot deliberately away from the vital centres, striking the thran on one foot. It bellowed and rushed at him.

Carl steadied the pole in the snow and pointed it two-handed—never mind the agony—at the thin space encircling the four small eyes.

The thran came closer, blotting out the sky. Its beaked-and-toothed mouth snarled. It was huge, magnificent, far too big to kill. Carl steadied his lance and aimed for the eyes.

The thran struck. The shock buckled the metal rod and screamed through Carl's broken hand. A sickening crunch of metal through bone, a spurt of blood—theirs too was red—and the screams of a mortally wounded beast. Carl released the spear, and the animal stumbled past, blinded and dying.

Even so it thrashed a long time. Carl waited until the great jaws stopped snapping. He had killed his first thran! He threw back his head and howled.

His first kill! Now he was adult. He pried off the largest back-plate and grasped the yielding insulation. He stripped some loose and wrapped it around his bleeding arm. Beneath it was dark, fresh meat. Thran meat! He pulled off a chunk—difficult, with such tough muscle—and crammed it into his helmet.

Helmet? Why was he wearing a helmet? The meat was still hot, though garnet-crystals were already forming on the snow.

He gorged and slept. It may have been pain, alien protein, or raw meat; he awoke befouled and hurting. What had come over him? He knew better than to eat alien food. He scoured his helmet with snow, as best he could, and took the largest thran-plate, the one he had pried loose. If he did not get out of the mountains soon he would die. He could never climb back to the shuttle.

If I leave the meat, the thran has died in vain. But the damn thing had tried to kill him. In any case, the meat would keep in the snow, and he could use the plate as a sled.

He bored holes with his belt-knife, attached straps, and loaded the plate. It was a long journey; he fell many times, and wished he had taken off in the shuttle when he could. But if he had, he could never return, and he was the last observer.

The insulation slipped, and the cold made Carl's left arm almost useless. The sled slewed and bumped over hummocks. He had to tug it over rises, with one numb arm and one ruined hand, but at last, far off, he sighted Spahi's village.

Smoke rose from most of the stone huts. A denser cloud hung where the old bard lived.

It took Carl one entire Mancken's day to cover the remaining distance. At the last, near the village, Carl realized he must abandon the sled, and his survival kit—food, simulator, and recorders. He stumbled on alone.

Spahi was trying to replicate the spear-point the sky-creature had shown him, but his metal bent too readily. What had the foreign craftsman used? He would like to test that point against a thran.

The youngling entered his hut and stood waiting to speak.

"Yes?" Spahi put down his tools. "What do you wish?"

"The sky-creature," the youngling began.

"Back so soon?"

"It does not have its craft; it is alone, and cannot speak. I think it is hurt."

"Where?"

"By the old bard's hut, the first place it reached, crawling."

Crawling? Injured? The sky-creatures, then, were no gods. Spahi put his children in his pouch and set forth.

He felt momentary sorrow at the sight of the unroofed hut. He and the bard had often disagreed; he was ashamed that he had, at time, mocked her.

The sky-creature lay huddled inside the roofless shell, one arm wrapped in thran-insulation. It bore none of its devices.

"Are you ill?" Spahi whistled.

The creature made an alien sound and gestured at the empty hut. "The old bard died," said Spahi. "What happened to you?"

The creature pointed to the mountains. One hand, Spahi saw, was encased. He had not seen that thick covering before. The creature tried to stand, but fell. It began to shake.

I must get it to warmth, and feed it, thought Spahi. Do they eat the same as we? He and the youngling helped support the sky-creature, and took it to his hut.

Spahi settled it as close as possible to the fire. He hoped it was not ill; he knew nothing of how to care for such a being. Its arm, he saw, had been slashed in several places. Sky-folk had no plates, and must be easily injured. This one was losing fluid—how serious might that be? With such a fragile covering mishaps must be common. He wished the creature would wake, so he could ask.

He summoned the youngling, who was crouched, watching. "You know the creature cannot speak without aid. Do you remember what its device looks like?"

"I believe so," the youngling said.

"Go, then, back to the bard's hut, and follow the trail as far as you can. If you find aught that might be the creature's, bring it here. I do not know what it needs, and it cannot tell us."

"It is cold, winter, and there may be a thran."

"Have you no compassion, no fear? The sky-creature

may die. Do you wish it reborn, knowing you failed to
save it? Would you see its ghost in our village's next
child?"

"No." The youngling edged toward the door. "I will
search."

"Do so carefully," Spahi said. He would go himself, but
he must stay with the helpless creature.

It slept a long time, and made strange sounds, whether
its own speech, or cries of pain, Spahi could not tell.

The creature needed different air, Spahi knew, greater
warmth, and perhaps different food. Spahi was no healer.
He watched and worried.

Carl awakened in semi-darkness. His mouth was dry and
hot. His right hand throbbed and his left arm ached.
What had happened? After killing the thran, he remembered little. He tried to sit up; dizziness sparkled. Not
only was he feverish, he had not eaten in far too long.

A shape leaned over him. Spahi? Yes, this was his hut.
On the walls thran-plate shields shone beside metalwork-
ing tools. Carl tried to form a whistle.

"Sky-creature," Spahi said, "you are awake. You were
found at the old bard's hut. You might have died there. I
know you cannot speak; I have sent the youngling to find
your devices."

Carl sank back and nodded, wondering if Spahi understood the gesture. Perhaps in context. He must have
abandoned all burdens at the last and crawled. He
remembered nothing but cold white pain.

If he had his simulator he could speak with Spahi, explain the problem. Or if Spahi could understand visual/
verbal symbols—he himself was of little use, one
hand broken, and the other arm felt inflamed. He hoped
he had immunity. His body, at least, was reacting to the
infection, but he would have preferred a good broad-spectrum antibiotic. Maybe even a pain pill, now that he was
home.

Home?

All his equipment and supplies were lost in the snow, abandoned while he was delirious.

"As you slept, I wondered," Spahi whistled. "You seemed injured. Is it normal with your kind, to lose so much fluid? You have little protection."

Carl pointed to his arm, shook his head—no, that gesture was meaningless—and held his arm close to his body, rocking back and forth.

"It is not normal, then," Spahi said. "Is there aught I might do?"

Carl shook his head again, hoping the gesture would now be understood in context. If only his supplies would arrive. If not, he realized, he could not even radio Nina what had happened. He would die here of infection, starvation, or alien protein. And in any case, everyone on Mancken's was doomed.

He was afraid, then disgusted. Spahi had saved his life, or tried to; yet he would die with the rest of his people, while Carl was frightened to share their fate.

He was glad that he could not speak; he might have babbled. He watched the fire flicker against the thrani plates.

II

Nina, shipboard, could not contact Carl; the shuttle did not answer. The black hole approached, circled now by debris from Five. Interplanetary dust and meteoroids joined the dance into dissolution, glowing past the visual spectrum into x- and gamma-rays.

The musical speech of the natives haunted her, though she had never replayed the tapes. *It could as easily happen to Earth, and as little would she grieve.* She would never miss the sterile, modern townhouse in Port au Prince or the very European convent school; still less would she miss her forced visits to her grandmother in the hills—*the chickens, and the blood—*

She opened her eyes. The telescope was still there, its camera yet clicking. Time grew short. *Where was Carl?*

She extracted the latest photograph. The auroral effects were still spectacular, fluorescence swirling into—what? There was nothing but gravity, and spin. Only the tracks of the phenomenon showed on her photographs.

Photo-graph. Light-writing. Here light, gravity-crushed, could never escape—

The *Brendan* rotated, bringing Epsilon Eridani into view. A sun, life-and-warmth giving. Nina remembered reaches, and sand, then shuddered, picturing first a tidal bulge, then ribbons of gas drawn from the star's very substance, and the flares engulfing Mancken's World. It was merely astro-physics, proceeding as calculated. *But why an inhabited system? And where is Carl? It is late and dangerous!*

12

Carl lay in Spahi's hut for days, speechless. He felt his fever rise, then drop, as he developed antibodies. Did thrani claws bear poison? He dreamed, hot-mouthed and aching, until the youngling returned with his sled.

"He must have killed a great thran, for this plate is the largest ever—larger even than the one you gave the old bard for her roof."

"It was mainly an accident," Carl mumbled, then heard the whistling. He could speak! He adjusted the simulator. An idea occurred. "It was, indeed, a great thran, so great that it blotted out the stars. Injured and alone, I slew it. It lies dead on the mountain."

Spahi and the youngling flattened their scales. "You wasted it?"

"No. It is frozen. I could not carry it, wounded as I was, to the village. You might redeem the thran, if you help me. I must repair my broken ship. I will teach you to work metal and show you the tools."

"You killed the thran, then, near your ship?" said Spahi.

"No. Two days' journey down the mountain." Carl paused. "But if you help me I will give you the metal spear-point."

Spahi bristled. "I do not ask payment to save a thran or to help a friend. I would learn, though, what you can teach."

Carl was ashamed. He had cheapened friendship. He was weak; he needed more rest. But time was limited. "Come with me in the morning," he said, "I will need help. Both my arms—" He thought he saw amused tolerance, from those who had spare limbs.

"We will pull you uphill on the thran-plate sled," said Spahi. "To the thran you killed, and onward, to your ship. We leave at first light."

Carl, Spahi, and the youngling set into the pass, dragging Carl's equipment on the thran-sled; occasionally Carl himself, overwhelmed with weakness, became cargo.

He hardly noticed when they came upon the body of his thran. Reproachful, Spahi and the youngling looked at him and indicated the amount of ruined meat. "So much of a noble thran, to be wasted," Spahi said.

Carl said nothing. The two natives carefully butchered, wrapped (in mesenteric and pleural membranes), and stored the good meat in a snowbank, leaving the huge head as a marker. They offered Carl the largest teeth as trophies.

They spoke little on the rest of the ascent. After blizzard-impeded struggles they reached the shuttle, and Carl was able to show them what must be done. His thran-mauled arm was healing, but his right hand was still useless.

Metal repair on a low-gravity planet at high altitudes, with bronze-age apprentices, was memorable. Spahi and the youngling had never used welders, and were unfamil-

iar with the properties of the new metal. Carl despaired of
finishing the task. His supplies would run out, or the job
would be botched. But Spahi and the youngling were eager and intelligent. Eventually, after false starts and tools
dropped in the snow, they finished. The shuttle once
again stood straight, on newly mended skis; only the
black marks scarring the paint showed where mending
had been done.

Carl offered Spahi and the youngling a ride to the village, but they refused, saying they wished to gather the
thran meat, and the distance was not great. Tired and
weak, Carl did not insist. He watched the two figures—
one large, one small—dwindle into the blizzard.

They went out of their way to help me. I know their
world is doomed, and no attempt will be made to save
them. They braved the winter mountains for a stranger—
and for duty to their prey.

He felt sick, and was unsure whether it was due to hun-
ger or residual infection. He launched the shuttle into orbit, to intersect with the *Brendan.*

13

Nina was frantic. Carl's first radio message in nine days
had not explained his delay. He sounded weak and confused. She feared brain damage from exposure.

Still, she was not prepared for the sight of him as he
staggered into the living quarters. She had expected
gauntness and filth, but not wasting illness. One arm of
his heatsuit was ripped.

"Carl—let me help you out of that—"

"I'm all right." He tried to fend her off and winced.

She saw the foam splint. "You're hurt! Here, don't be
ridiculous." He swayed and almost fell. She stood under
his arm, bracing him on her shoulder and steadying him
as she led him to the locker. She supported his right side,
and it was not until she helped him undress that she noticed that his left arm, not only his suit, was gashed—red

with infection. She discarded the suit—fortunately they carried spares—washed him, and inspected his wounds. The cuts on his left arm were swollen, their edges gaping. They should have been closed at the time. Now they would require surgical unscarring. His right hand, at least, was properly foam-splinted—that injury must have happened earlier. By now the foam was dirty and split, and the skin on Carl's left arm showed signs of frostbite. He was flushed and gaunt, his ribcage sharp, his wrists and ankles almost fleshless.

Still supporting him, she slid him into his bunk. She looked down at him, already collapsed into sleep, and opened the panel between their rooms, lest he need her in the night.

Waking on crisp bedding, Carl first noticed the gravity; he felt too heavy. Why was he warm and clean? Then he moved. *His hand!*

That, and the ache in his left arm, brought him awake. He lay in a dimly lit oblong room, crowded and narrow. Next to his bed, though, the panel was slid back—how did he know there had been a panel?—and his bunk lay close to another.

He moved his right hand over his head and rolled over. Someone slept in the adjoining bunk. He reached out his left hand—never mind the pain of stretched skin—and touched soft flesh. A woman!

She turned in her sleep. "Carl?"

Who was Carl? There was something he should do now. His breathing was faster and he was operating by instinct. He reached out with his right hand, but it was encased in plastic. His left arm brushed the covers, scraping raw, bandage-sprayed flesh. Pain stopped him. With a groan he fell back and covered his face with his right arm. Soon he slept.

After Carl woke her, Nina did not sleep. She watched him. He would need febrifuge, more broad-spectrum antibiotics, perhaps stronger painkillers, and that hand must be set.

She kept thinking of him as a patient. She need not have opened the panel, merely turned on the intercom; or she could have worn clothing to bed. What had she hoped would happen? She and Carl had never been close.

When later she used the boneviewer to set his hand, though, she could have caused him a bit less pain.

As Carl convalesced from his injuries, he spoke little to Nina. He prowled the *Brendan*. Would he were again on the planet's surface, in the cool snows—his fever made him thirsty. His body seemed awkward, gangly.

The small brown female, Nina, followed him everywhere, asking him questions he could no longer answer. She fed him medicine, as if he were a youngling. She did not seem to understand that there was something he must do.

The black star. If he were eaten by a star, he would become one himself. As would she, who loved stars, who studied them. Time was short, and he must return to his own people at the last.

Though the panel was no longer left open between their quarters, the lock was flimsy. Carl waited until Nina slept, after a longer-than-usual work shift. He tried to sense if her breathing were slow and regular. At times now, he could hear things past the limits of sound—

He slid the panel open. Nina lay, small and alien, on her narrow couch, curled on her side. He struck her once, then again.

After the first blow she awoke, but too late. He carried her down the corridor and wrestled her into a heat-suit. She too should be prey for the dark star.

Nina let herself be dragged from the shuttle.

There was no point in resistance. Carl was mad. She had known that for days, but she'd never thought he might become violent. At least he'd remembered to put her in a heat-suit.

Snow coated the ground; the winter twilight was orange. Nina had stood on many other planets, but the skyraking mountain peaks, the dimness, and the cold frightened her; that, and her knowledge of what approached from space.

Two natives came across the snow. They looked much like the pictures she had seen; one was large, one much smaller, possibly young. If she could speak to them, she might call for help—but Carl had the simulator, and she did not know their language.

The taller alien spoke in musical whistles. From the tape she'd heard, she recognized the cadences.

Carl, carrying his simulator, responded, then turned toward her. "This is Spahi, who saved my life. He has two children, the size of your hand, whom he carries with him. His companion, curious about off-worlders, is a youngling. He will never have a name. He went out in the snow and the dark, menaced by wild animals, to find my survival kit. He and Spahi helped repair the shuttle, and tried to nurse me after my bout with a thran, when I suffered from exposure and infection. I reached their village crawling, and they took me in."

In the middle distance, Nina saw a huddle of low domed huts; smoke curled from their tops. She did not want to meet these people—these aliens. She never wanted to see a hut again.

"I killed the thran with a spear, the traditional way. Now I might have a name. But my people are to die, and they do not even know what awaits. I must tell them."

"Carl, no!" Nina heard the simulator whistling, and knew she was too late. She watched the two aliens, expecting a violent reaction. The larger one—Spahi, she supposed—whistled, pointed to the few sprinkled stars, and then to itself.

Carl, through the simulator, whistled more urgently, and gestured toward the shuttle; Spahi walked away,

toward the village. The smaller one—the youngling?
—tarried.

If she could only reach the shuttle while Carl was dis-
tracted—but the deep snow would make her clumsy.

"A black star will eat our sun?" the youngling asked.

"Yes. This woman knows, but she cannot speak to you.
She studies the stars."

"Spahi will neither go with you, nor send his children,"
said the youngling. "He says that to be eaten by a star is
to become a star, and live with the gods."

"But you will all die," said Carl. "And none will
remember you."

"Who can forget the stars?" The youngling turned to
go.

"Wait! The ice will melt, the ground will shake, and
the air will burn. You will all die. Dying hurts." *Dying
hurts*—how do I know? Has it happened to me before?
*Air turned to fire, the sun devoured, its cooling embers
scraps after a feast. Who ate the sun? The blood-mouthed
wolf—and the gods themselves are dead.*

A small, silver-suited figure rose and ran for the
shuttle. Carl leapt after it. *Prey!* He threw her to the
snow; she raised a knee and struck. He was enraged; he
throttled her.

She fought loose and ran into the twilight, into the
falling snow. Carl watched her and snarled. She, who had
dismissed Mancken's World—*where was that?* as irrelevant—she would die out there in the snow, frozen, devoured by thrani, or scorched by solar flares.

He looked down at his hands. *What was he doing?* He
was human, as was she.

The youngling watched nearby. "Come with me," Carl
said. It backed away. "Come and live."

It looked at the shuttle, and whistled, "I would rather
the stars ate me. I understand the stars." It retreated further.

"Then, take this to Spahi, as a hosting-gift." Carl unfastened his pouch and tossed the spear-point into the snow. The youngling scrabbled for it, then ran.

Carl watched him go, a frightened figure fleeing into twilight. He stumbled back into the shuttle and slammed the door against the wind.

Nina was out there in the dark. He stared again at his hands. He had tried to kill his shipmate. He was going alien; there was no question. But not gently alien like the folk of Mancken's World; he was a berserker.

He had to find Nina, bring her back. She would not dare return by herself, after what he had done. But if he went out searching, she might circle back to the shuttle and strand him here. If the shuttle were disabled, she would have to wait for him, and he could explain, apologize—

He opened the control panel and surveyed the mass of circuitry. Something vital, but small; no, not the ignition, that could be bypassed. But the fuel-feed control—he snapped out the unit. Small enough to carry, no larger than one of Spahi's children. Without it, takeoff was impossible.

He closed the panel again. While she tried to locate the trouble he would have more time to get back, to talk with her.

He slipped the unit into his pouch and went out in search.

Nina fled into the dark, without direction. Anywhere to escape Carl. He had trapped her on an alien planet, in the dead of winter.

Even worse, she knew what would soon happen.

The snow crust was not quite strong enough to hold her; she broke through from time to time, stumbling blind, hip-deep in drifts. She had to get away and plan her strategy.

She was unarmed, but there was a rocket pistol on the shuttle. If she could get back—as long as Carl was not there—

The low, scraggly brush afforded little cover. She crouched, looking for the glint of the shuttle. The stars gave little light—

There! A flash of yellow as the door opened, then closed again. He was coming after her! He could track her in the snow! She ran again, gasping, floundering.

"Nina!" the voice came over her suit radio.

"Nina, this is Carl. Come back. I'm all right now. Come back. Can you hear me?"

She dared not answer. She'd watched him change. For the first time since Haiti she was afraid of another human being. She ran in silence until almost exhausted. When again she plunged through the crust, she felt not frozen ground, but empty air. Then the snow-cornice crumbled and she fell onto gravel, ice, and a trickle of water. After one bright red moment of pain, she could not feel her legs.

She lay in the icy stream trying not to cry out, for fear she would be heard. She had no idea where Carl was. He might be very near. She must hide beneath the treacherous overhanging banks, anything to be out of sight. *But her legs wouldn't move.* It couldn't be from the cold, not this soon, not with her heatsuit.

Gripping the rocks of the stream bed with her gloved hands, she dragged herself out of the water.

Nina wouldn't answer on the radio.

There were forty hours left, thirty-five to activate the Jump drive and flee the system. He had to find her. If only he could keep from going alien again.

You're finished, Carl. You never dare ship out on another mission. Twice now. The first time was bad enough, but this time you almost killed—you can't trust yourself a third time.

He circled until he saw her tracks, leading away from the shuttle into the hills; light impressions on the crust, then larger marks where she broke through and fell. But it was dark, and her tracks were crossed by those of thrani and villagers. Carl was no woodsman. He stood, confused.

From time to time he called on his suit radio, but there was no answer.

After the twenty-hour night, dawn rose. Ten hours of daylight; then, the last twilight would fall.

He thought of Spahi, but he and the youngling would not help. "If the sky-creature fled, it must have a reason," Spahi said. "Such is its right. Perhaps it wishes to become a star. You said it studied stars?"

"She will not answer when I call her," Carl said. "She may be hurt."

"If it wished to speak to you, you have a device it could use. So it must not wish to speak with you."

"It was afraid," the youngling said, staring at Carl. "If your own folk are afraid of you—" He left the thought unfinished.

Twilight fell, and Nina knew the time was growing near. She was certain, now; her back was broken, and her spinal cord snapped. Paraplegic. She could never again go to space.

Twilight was deepening. Only hours remained. She switched on her suit radio.

"Nina! Where you you?" She was still alive! He could take her back to the *Brendan,* they could both escape.

"Never mind." Her voice was weak. "You're still planetside."

"I couldn't leave you."

"You will have to. I am injured, and I am not coming back. You must get our records home."

"I don't care, now."

"I'd rather die than live crippled. Do this for me: get the data to the Academy. Don't let our work go for nothing."

Carl considered. "I'll quick-feed it to the *Brendan* and send a whitespace capsule."

"Do you have time? Besides, my last observations aren't—finished—yet. I hadn't completed—the records —they're not cold-stored."

"I can't leave you here to die."

"I won't go back to a desk job. Do you want to die here too? Do you know how it will be? When the flares hit it will be night. First we'll see auroras, then the wind will start, as the atmosphere is sucked away; and the air will burn. Do you want to stay for that? And all our work, all the memory of your precious natives, my observations, gone for nothing? I don't think you can find me in time. You have to get back to the *Brendan,* ready it for Jump, store my records. Get off-planet, Carl. Do one last thing right."

"Nina, I can't—"

"Get the hell out! All I had was my work. Let Nina Leclerc make one final contribution."

Her radio clicked off and she would no longer respond.

Twilight deepened. Carl sat and thought, then re-installed the fuel-feed regulator.

Aboard the *Brendan* he collected all the data Nina had left and fed it safely into chilled storage, with his own records. The *Brendan* spun, and Epsilon Eridani itself came into view. The porthole darkened, and Carl could faintly discern the solar disk. Disk? It was flattened now, bulging. Soon tidal action would pull flares out into space—

He knew what that would mean on the planet. Winds, as the atmosphere boiled away, winds wild enough to flatten stone huts. *And who rides the wind?* Then heat and radiation would follow. Nina had explained it all.

Nina. She'd done nothing wrong. She couldn't help being cold. Cold. The thought of her, huddled somewhere on Mancken's World. He'd followed her last wish.

What kind of man am I? He headed for the engine sphere. Carl knew little of Jump engines, but what little he knew was enough. He was able to make the final adjustments; they were not, after all, particularly delicate.

The *Brendan* would reach Earth much faster in white-space.

14

Spahi had summoned the tribe to gather at the old bard's house. The ship was gone, now; he watched it go, then tracked the frightened, abandoned sky-creature to its hiding place in the creek. He carried it to the hut; it could not speak with him, but it knew the stars, and should be with the rest of them at the last. It might speak with the Black Hunter.

Those who had names gathered around the hut, leaving the younglings and children within.

The sky-being was, as a courtesy, put with the adults. Spahi, on the outermost rim of the circle, hefted his coveted metal spear-point. If the gods approved his guest-gift, they might make him into a very bright star.

He heard the sky-creature whimpering.

Nina lay surrounded by alien shapes. They had found her in the creek—how, she did not know—and, when they carried her toward their village, she saw the shuttle was gone. Just as well. Better a quick, clean death.

But she was afraid. How would it feel to die this way? She knew the process—howling winds and thinning atmosphere.

A black, dead star. I gave my life to the study of stars; now the ghost of one comes for me. Then she knew what her grandmother had sent for her.

She screamed as the sky danced in flame.

15

The Academy cadets filed in for the report on the Epsilon Eridani expedition. Some upperclassmen had known Carl and Nina personally.

An Administrator came onscreen. Partially paralyzed,

her left arm and the right side of her face was drawn tight. What expedition had grounded her?

"The Scout II *Brendan,* sent to observe a short-lived phenomenon in the Epsilon Eridani system, has met with one fatality and one—singularity. Nina Leclerc, Astronomy, is missing and presumed dead. The xenologist, Carl Thorstensen, returned through whitespace with the data." The cadets shuddered. "Xenology majors are to gather immediately after this assembly for a clinical conference.

"Astronomy will hold a memorial service for Leclerc.

"Any cadets who wish to resign may do so without prejudice." It was the usual offer. Only a few cadets stood to leave. The upperclass xenologists and astronomers departed, either to conference at the Explorers' Hospital, or to Leclerc's memorial service.

They knew what could happen, but they still wanted the stars.

TWO POEMS

Peter Dillingham

When I began collecting material for this book, I had no thought of including poetry. Then there arrived, at weekly intervals, a series of short poems about black holes, all from a man I'd never met. I sent no replies—and the poems kept coming—and eventually there were two I liked. I hope you will too.

CYGNUS X-1
    Hell's huge black spider . . .
                                Robert Southey

Not swan but spider
Latrodectus mactans
The primal widow
Black
Time marked
Devouring her mate
Sucking its life juices
Snared in a web of
  gravity
Swathed in silk of gravity
Silken shroud of gravity

THE SALESMAN WHO FELL FROM GRACE WITH THE UNIVERSE

To: M.
Re: Time and Mileage Report R78463

Although the extraordinarily circuitous way
in which it was delivered
violated long established field communication policies,
we were far more disturbed to discover
a number of serious and uncharacteristic discrepancies
in your last Time and Mileage Report,
discrepancies that unaccountably increased in magnitude
the farther you traveled from the home office.

To be specific:
you recorded having arrived at a point
300 kilometers from your destination
194 hours, 33 minutes and 49.6681 seconds
after embarking on your most recent sales trip;
an unimpeachable witness, however,
observed that it actually took you
194 hours, 33 minutes and 50.1129 seconds
to reach that point in your journey.
The discrepancy may seem minor,

being only a matter of .4448 seconds,
but it marks the beginning of a significant trend.

Subsequently, for instance,
you reported being only 180 kilometers from your
destination
194 hours, 33 minutes and 49.6692 seconds
after your departure,
while our informant noted that the elapsed time was in
fact
194 hours, 33 minutes and 50.1141 seconds—
a discrepancy of .4449 seconds.

Your next entry indicates that you had proceeded
to within 90 kilometers of your destination
after being in transit a total of
194 hours, 33 minutes and 49.669854 seconds.
Our observer, however,
recorded your total travel time to that point as
194 hours, 33 minutes and 50.1150 seconds—
a discrepancy of .445146 seconds!

We might have been inclined to overlook
such admittedly slight discrepancies
were it not for the final entry on your report,
namely, that you finally arrived at your appointment
194 hours, 33 minutes and 49.670200 seconds
after beginning your trip.
Our informant, however,
testified that in point of fact
you never reached your destination,
and, that, as of 195 hours after your departure
from this office, you were still at
a certain roadside tavern of highly questionable repute
known as Gus' Hole-In-The-Wall Bar and Grill,
located some $30 + (3 \times 10^{-8288})$ kilometers
from our client's establishment.
From subsequent reports by our observer,

it would seem that you have decided to take up
permanent residence
at Gus' Hole-In-The-Wall Bar and Grill.

We need not remind you that this particular call
was considered of the utmost importance and urgency
in view of our competition's concerted efforts in the area.
Regretfully, therefore,
we must insist upon your immediate resignation.

Although our action may seem precipitous
in view of your long years of outstanding service to the
firm,
as you well know, ours is a company
that has always required and received
absolute integrity and dedication from its field
representatives.
The singularly aberrant nature of your behavior in this
instance
has raised grave doubts regarding your true character
and leaves us no alternative
but to demand your resignation.

We will need your signature on the attached documents
and their return at your earliest convenience.
Upon receiving them, we will forward your final check,
which includes, we believe, a most generous severance
award,
to Gus' Hole-In-The-Wall Bar and Grill,
unless, of course, you advise otherwise.

With sincere best wishes for success
in your future endeavors ...

Hi, E,
so glad you've come through.
Welcome aboard.
I think you'll like working here.

THE NOTHING SPOT

Dian Girard

Dian Girard is not a full-time writer, and consequently there is far too long an interval between her stories. Although her principal character is a rather dippy housewife of the twenty-first Century, a dumb-blonde type who always manages—but just manages—to cope with the future, the real life Dian is nothing like that. She's a supervisor in an impressively large company, and her husband is an engineer/designer of computers.

I am addicted to Cheryl Harbottle stories. I don't see how anyone can fail to be.

Ping! Cheryl Harbottle sat up, startled. She looked around the room for the source of that odd little noise. Nothing seemed to be wrong. The lighting panels were still glowing at the Midday-Summer setting and the Woodland Sounds background tape was still giving out with soft coos, twitters, and the sound of rustling leaves.

Her eyes finally came to rest on the new decorator lamp. Humph. That must be the problem. The darned thing was burned out or something. It looked funny.

Cheryl got up and walked over to peer at it. There was nothing in the middle where something should have been, she thought, wrinkling her slim brows. There really was nothing. All of the wires were in place, but the bright glowing ball in the middle was gone. What was worse, she couldn't see through where it was supposed to be. The air looked sort of fuzzy, or distorted. It was almost like looking into rippling water.

Cheryl bent closer to peer at it, and something grabbed her nose. She yelped and jumped back. Then she rubbed the end of her offended member and stared at her lamp. Well! She had the distinct feeling that it shouldn't do that. She walked around to look at the other side. There was barely enough room for her to edge around into the corner behind it.

The lamp was a sort of pole-like arrangement. One end was moored in the ceiling and the other was stuck to the floor. The middle blossomed out into an elaborate mesh of gleaming wires in a big cage arrangement.

Cheryl poked an experimental finger at the nothing in the middle. About two inches from the center something took hold of it. She pulled her hand back rapidly and pursed her lips. What she needed was the instruction book. Of course, there wasn't one. She hadn't seen an instruction manual for anything in years. Well, the computer ought to know something.

She sat down in front of her Insta-Think home terminal, flicked it on, and asked for a catalog. The alphabetic listing on the screen rolled by slowly and she stopped it at "lamps, decorator." That was how she'd bought the fool thing in the first place. The computer obligingly switched to its collection of 60-second advertisements. Eventually, after watching what seemed like an endless array of lighting fixtures in all sizes, shapes, styles, and colors she saw her lamp. "New Lighting Concept," the ad proclaimed in fiery letters. "Capture the Sun in Your Living Room!"

Cheryl pressed the MORE button on the terminal and the system cycled into the full three minute sales pitch. Not that it told her much. Some vibrant baritone informed her that she'd be the envy of the neighborhood and pointed out the benefits of "metal-sheen polybutyrate," whatever that was. She pressed the MORE button again when the ad was over and got an expressionless voice that talked about hydrogen, ignition and containment systems, energy pulses, and electromagnetic balance. The picture on the screen was a maze of interconnecting lines with squiggles, boxes, and numbers. Out of sheer spite she pushed the advance button once more, but all she got was a picture of long strings of mathematics and a theory lecture that made no sense to her at all. Cheryl switched off the terminal irritably and swiveled around to look at the broken lamp.

Well, it probably would be best to turn it off. Then she might as well call Repair. Let them handle it. Damn, she'd only had the fool thing for a week. That was the trouble with the modern world—nothing was made right any more. At least there was a thirty day warranty, she thought tiredly. She should have bought one of those cute little antique lamps with the glass bulb.

She got up and walked over to switch the lamp off. Nothing. As a matter of fact, the nothing was still there. She flicked the switch on and off again, but the funny little distortion in the middle stayed right where it was. A little experimentation with a writing stylus proved that the pull was still there too.

Cheryl frowned. Odd, very odd. Something was working, but how was it working with the power off? She pushed the stylus at it again and this time let the lamp grab it. The stylus moved smoothly forward and to her horror it disappeared into the lamp. Gone, finis, kaput.

Ridiculous!

Cheryl circled the lamp warily, her eyes wide. She picked up a china figurine she'd alway hated and offered it as a sacrifice. There seemed to be a little difficulty dragging it through the wire maze, but eventually the figure was gobbled up. That was sort of gratifying, actually.

Keeping an eye on the nothing spot Cheryl began to carefully bend some of the matrix wires out of the way. Eventually she had a clear opening to the center, which didn't seem to affect the spot at all. She had a feeling she'd just voided her thirty-day warranty, but she'd gone too far to stop now. She offered the lamp her morning paper, and watched with a sort of clinical detachment as the pages curled inward, compressed together, and turned into a funnel which slowly disappeared into the nothingness. Where the devil was it going? Big things just couldn't be put inside of little things. On the other hand, maybe the spot was bigger on the inside than it was on the outside. There had to be a limit though. With a slightly fiendish smile she picked up a large plastic fern, pot and all.

Now that really was too much! When the potted fern was gone she offered up last season's overcoat, an old pair of shoes, her husband's tacky old fishing hat, that awful painting Louise gave them at Christmas, and an extra pair of salt shakers. At differing rates of speed they all vanished down the insatiable maw of the lamp.

She'd fix the damned thing. Cheryl pried the matrix wires further apart and began to bend them back and forth. Eventually they snapped off and she shoved each one ruthlessly into the spot. In less than twenty minutes she managed to feed most of the lamp to itself. Not even a burp. All she had left were the two bare poles, top and bottom, which she couldn't pull loose. And the spot, of course. Cheryl thought wistfully of the old saying, "crawl into a hole and pull the hole in after you." This hole obviously wasn't going anywhere. It completely ignored the fact that most of its parent structure was gone and hung there about five feet from the floor. She could see a good two inches, top and bottom, between it and the poles. It was balanced somehow.

"With no visible means of support," Cheryl said out loud, with just a touch of panic. She could see it a lot better now. Well, she could see what she couldn't see a lot better. It seemed to her, when she bent carefully to look, that there was a tiny black speck in the middle of the distortion, but she couldn't be sure. She got a ball of cord from the twins' room and dangled the end enticingly over the spot. The cord straightened and moved gently forward. She experimented a little bit, pulling the cord out and letting it be caught again. Eventually, however, it was grabbed for good. It moved inexorably forward. She braced her feet, leaned back, and pulled. No good. The cord kept moving and the spot stayed put. She unrolled some more cord and tied it firmly around the big armchair. The spot ate up the slack and the armchair began to inch its way across the room. When the cord shortened enough that the chair began to lift into the air she decided the experiment had gone far enough.

Unfortunately Cheryl was better at tying knots than undoing them. She ran around the apartment frantically, but by the time she'd turned up a pair of Saf-T-Shears in the den the spot was administering the *coup de grâce*. Cheryl watched helplessly as her Komfy Kushion chair, with Genuine Imitation Tufted Vinyl upholstery, slowly deformed and funneled its way into the spot.

Migod, there was no stopping it! It seemed to be immovable, and it had the appetite of a growing teenager. Cheryl felt a sudden cold shiver. What if one of the kids bumped into it? She gulped and wished she hadn't destroyed the cage that had fenced it in. Cheryl dashed into the bedroom and stripped one of those awful orange polkadot blankets off of the bed. She could at least wrap it up so no one would blunder into it. There wasn't any cord left, but a little rummaging turned up two ugly ties belonging to her husband. Back in the living room Cheryl carefully gathered one end of the blanket around the lower pole and tied it firmly with a green plaid tie. Then she folded the blanket up over the tie, around the spot, and gathered it to the top pole, leaving plenty of slack in the middle. She secured it with the other tie and adjusted a frivolous bow as a sort of farewell to the spot. There it was, helplessly swathed like a pot-bellied mummy. Cheryl drew a deep sigh of relief.

Her relief was short lived. The blanket folds began to arch inward until she was staring at an acrylic hourglass. The waist narrowed, disappeared, and the top and bottom of the blanket started to strain toward the center. Eventually the fibers gave up with a sickening "rrrrripp!" Cheryl found herself looking at two strips of orange polkadot garnish, one on each pole. And a slightly askew purple and red striped bow. The spot shimmered contentedly.

Cheryl ran to the computer terminal to call Repair and then stopped suddenly. Repair what? Not the lamp, it was virtually gone. The spot didn't need repair, it was working just fine. Residence Maintenance? Was it a Maintenance problem if you had a bottomless pit in your living room? They might even accuse her of putting it there, and sue her for lowering the property value.

She stared glassy-eyed at the little monster. Maybe she should rope off the corner, put up caution signs and warning blinkers. Cheryl giggled with just a touch of hysteria. How about charging admission? "See the eighth wonder of the world! Watch the Harbottle Spot devour Cincinatti!"

On the other hand . . . Cheryl calmed herself and frowned at the spot. It ate things up, did it? Finally she marched over to the computer terminal and keyed in a number. When she got her connection she said, "Hello, this is Mrs Harbottle in 1743, B Level. I want to discontinue my rubbish disposal service. I've made other arrangements."

Now all she had to do was find some tasteful drapes that would go with the rug . . . and those orange polkadots, of course.

FOR THE LADY OF A PHYSICIST

Michael Bishop

I'm not sure I understand this poem. I'm not even sure why I liked it. I did, though, and I hope at least some-body else will.

The introductory quotation is real, and in the final essay of this book I'll have more to say. Meanwhile, a poem written by a black hole.

"Although Bekenstein's hypothesis that black holes have a finite entropy requires for its consistency that black holes should radiate thermally, at first it seems a complete

miracle that the detailed quantum-mechanical calculations of particle creation should give rise to emission with a thermal spectrum. The explanation is that the emitted particles tunnel out of the black hole from a region of which an external observer has no knowledge other than its mass, angular momentum and electric charge. This means that all combinations or configurations of emitted particles that have the same energy, angular momentum and electric charge are equally probable. Indeed, it is possible that the black hole could emit a television set or the works of Proust in 10 leather-bound volumes . . ."
—*S. W. Hawking, "The Quantum Mechanics of Black Holes"*

in Scientific American *(January, 1977), p. 40.*

If I with her could only join
In rapturous dance, loin to loin,
Deep space itself would soon discern
Galactic rhythm in our burn.
Our bodies stars, our debts all void,
Then would we waltz and, thus
      employed,
Inflate with megacosmic thrust
Through night and death and sifting dust.
Godlike lovers, we would hang
Beyond the cosmos whose Big Bang,
All the mad millennia past,
Was but a popgun to our slow blast.
And as we reeled with raw élan,
Pulsing plasma in vast pavane,
We would shame the Pleiades,
Relume the Magellanic Seas,
Deliver all our Milky Way,
Ionic flux too fierce to stay,
In supernova, and so rehearse
Our own expanding universe.
      But my small body is no star,

Albeit something similar:
A blind pool vacuuming into it
All the lambency it's not fit
To redirect and render rife.
The woman I would take to wife
Sees only blackness in my eyes,
Rapacious ebon, hungry skies,
An O-gape gravid with desire
To aggrandize itself in fire;
And so her light sweeps down the hole
That is the maelstrom of my soul.

Therefore, I have become for her
A dark, entropic murderer,
Whose chiefest virtue is his pull.
Then, while my strength is at its full,
Let me draw her to my embrace,
Collapse her will and show my face.
With her my Beatrician guide,
We'd tunnel with the thermal tide
Into the arms of Betelgeuse—
With Quasar sets and Marcel Proust
Emergent with us, glory-bound,
Detritus of God's Lost & Found.
Thus, though we cannot create light
From love, yet we will vanquish night.

THE VENGING

Greg Bear

When humanity goes to space, we will carry our own attitudes with us. When we examine black holes—assuming
they do exist, and are not mere figments of mathematical
imagination—we will do so as scientists looking at inani-
mate objects.

But there are 100 billion stars in our galaxy, and many
of them have planets. It is certainly not impossible that
some of those planets will be inhabited.

And those we find in space may not share our attitudes
at all. In this story a newer writer, Greg Bear, examines
black holes from an alien viewpoint, and finds—

1

"Waltz if you will, woman," Kamon thought bitterly, "your husband will be dead soon and all your lands and holdings scattered to state officials like seeds to parrots." He watched from the parapet as the dancers executed their moves to strains of Ravel's "La Valse." Three small moons hung above like etched glass streetlamps, one at the horizon over labyrinths of hedgerows, another to the west topping the Centrum Minara, and a third at zenith, the largest. Their light made the polished dance-floor tiles gleam beneath the swirling gowns and white breeches.

"Enjoying the view, I hope," an old woman said, stepping up quietly behind him. She was dressed in a plain black robe—an Abstainer by dress and manner. Kamon turned his head to acknowledge her presence, then turned back.

"It is a bit limited," he said, his voice clipped with the accents of non-human teachers.

"You can see the whole floor from here," the woman said, knowing very well what he meant.

"The *subject* is limited," he clarified. "They are all mindless in their pleasures, don't you think?"

"When I was young I enjoyed such pleasures, and I wasn't exactly mindless. Though I was foolish. To be sure, I was foolish."

"I find it difficult to believe the Anna Sigrid-Nestor was ever foolish."

"Kamon, you're getting old, too. You know how foolish the young are. They have no sense of impending death."

"On the contrary, Baroness. I have been aware of death since I was a few brief months old. Or do you forget that no juvenates exist for my species?" He turned one fluid blue-green eye on her and kept the other on the dance floor.

"Your karma, perhaps," Nestor said with a shrug. "Are you keeping an eye on Edith Fairchild, or just dreaming of assassinations and seizures?"

"That you are privy to my affairs does not give you the right to be glib," he said sharply. "Your position is not so strong that you can feel completely secure against me."

"You're a wretch, Kamon." She walked past him and leaned on the parapet, turning away from his pale leather-tan face and three-lipped mouth, which articulated so many languages so well. Teeth like a lamprey, she reminded herself. Mind to match, vicious by design.

I am not a species bigot, but dear Deos, she thought, I despise his class of Aighors. "I'm privy, and I'm compelled to silence because of our pact, but I grow tired of the support of your kind," she said. "So I've come to announce a rescension."

"That will not be advantageous—"

"Quiet until I've finished. I count the Honorable Disjohn Fairchild as a fine friend and an excellent human. I'm disgusted with myself that I'd even think of letting self-interest negate my duty toward a such man. His kind is rare, Kamon. You're proof by example."

Kamon bowed elegantly, as ugly a creature as she could humanly conceive. "Then voice your rescension, Baroness. I will pass the message along to the Administers. I am sure they would like to prepare the next auspices on the basis of such information."

Administers prepared auspices—propitious rituals—among dozens of species associated with the mercantile consolidations. Non-humans especially had taken to the old Earth ritual of seeking signs in the patterns of nature. But none were like the auspices of the Aighor members of Hafkan Bestmerit. Anna had attended a ceremony once. It had sickened her. Still, she had a strong abhorrence of judging another species by human standards. If they wished to sacrifice their young and seek signs in their bowels, so be it. Human justice had no meaning for the Aighors.

"I deny the support of Hafkan Bestmerit, and the oath of noninterference thereby accrued. I will do everything in my power to prevent you and your associates from stripping Fairchild of his life and holdings. And I'll defend him with all my power. That's no small force, Kamon."

"The Baroness is influential," the Aighor said. He bowed as well as he was able and swung the lower third of his snake-like body into a coil around his thorax. "But not omnipotent—her weapons are registered. And she does have to answer to the Combine as all of us do. A most interesting challenge, however."

Anna was fuming at the reminder of her limitations. "I'll warn you further. Strike against me and you strike against my allies, United Stars. Hafkan Bestmerit, I understand, is extremely interested in establishing stronger relations with USC. You may alienate your own allies. You're sitting above a dark, dark singularity, Kamon. Beware losing momentum and falling in."

She turned and walked away, leaving the Aighor to watch the dance with expression unchanged.

2

Lady Edith Fairchild, after the final dance, made her way from the floor into the small gilded elevator, then up the marble stairs (edged with malachite) to her third floor bedroom. She looked around with her head moving jerk, jerk, nervous as a bird. Her hands were trembling. Her shoulders slumped and tiny rivulets glistened on her cheeks, spotting the shiny saffron robe. She reached down, pulled up the hem of her gown, and sat on the padded bar edging the sleep field as she undid her shoes. One finger reached for the sleep-field button. The bed hummed into action and she fell back, her hair fanning out.

Disjohn Fairchild stood over her, his entrance as quiet as the activation of the sleepfield. "What's wrong?" he asked.

"I saw the Aighor in the hallway," she said, her voice shaking with anger. "They could at least have the decency to hide themselves while they scheme!"

"They're too honest and aboveboard for that," Disjohn said, sitting beside her. He looked at the ceramic wall mural, then at his shelves of old books—all as familiar as his own hands. He had no official connections with the Centrum, but diplomacy worked in such devious ways that he'd used this office and billet on the Centrum world for twenty years. It was more than home, it was the repository of his life's work. Christ, he thought, it's my world and it can't save me.

But what was there to be immediately afraid of? The Aighors wouldn't do anything drastic to get to him. It would come some unspecified time when the opportunity presented itself, probably when he was called back to Shireport to deliver his personal lectures. Then they would declare the cultural insult and vendetta, commandeer his ship, and be done with him cleanly. There wasn't a thing Dallat or United Stars could do about it. There was complex diplomacy involved, and he wasn't so important a figure they'd risk the anger of the Centrum.

Of course, if he could reach Shireport safely, there were Crocerians who might consent to go with him from there—paid, say, in trade preference for two years. The Aighors wouldn't touch his ship from Shireport to Ansinger with their allies aboard. When he delivered his lectures at Ansinger, he could apply for a United Stars Zone immunity. Ansinger was the largest USC stellar province, ten systems. He could transfer his funds, or what part of them he could mobilize and take with him—not much, he knew—convert his lands and holdings to transferrable commodities—trade them for data and software, perhaps—and set himself up on a terraformed world. Buy a continent on Kresham Elak. Start a school there. "Get the HELL AWAY!" he shouted. His wife flinched and squinted at him.

"Sorry," he said. "Thinking about alternatives." But the alternatives meant the demolition of his life as he knew it, and of his wife's. Would she stand for such a change?

"Are they so vindictive they'd kill you for doing such a simple thing? Why not destroy the station and kill the personnel, too?" she asked.

He shook his head. "It's not so simple from their viewpoint." That had to be their reason: that he had pioneered and promoted the construction of the Precipice 5 Station. He could think of no other. The station studied black hole radio emissions coming from the Pafloshwa Rift. The Aighors called such emissions Thrina, and had built up extensive obeisance rituals around them. Thus in some way his personal action had violated a religious or cultural tabu—who could tell what human words applied, if any?—and he was accountable.

"They can't destroy the station," he said. "It's under United Stars jurisdiction now, thanks to Anna Nestor. If they attack USC personnel, then the Centrum has to intervene. That would result in severe restrictions which the Aighors would have to abide by if they wished to survive economically. It's pretty tight from that angle. But I'm under Dallat protection, and Dallat hasn't yet signed a full agreement with the Centrum. It's still a renegade consolidation. Until an agreement is signed, the Aighors can resort to old pre-human law and call a cultural vendetta." With their early half-grasp of human tongues, they had called it a "venging". The name had stuck in legal terminology.

"It's so damned complicated," Edith said, staring at the night-sky ceiling.

"Not really, once you've been around it for a while."

"You almost make it sound just."

"It kept interspecies conflict to a minimum for a thousand years before we came," Disjohn said quietly. "Roger Bacon was messing around with crude lenses when the original pact was established."

Edith stood up from the sleepfield and unhitched her gown in the back, letting the folds pile themselves automatically into a tight, square pile. At fifty she wasn't doing at all badly, he thought, and without yet relying on juvenates.

As if she were reading his mind in part, she said, "They don't have any way of staying young."

"What?"

"From what we know, they all die at about sixty years of age. They don't have any way to prevent it. Maybe that's why they cling to old religions and rituals. It means personal survival after death, or whatever their equivalent is."

"You mean, what I've done blocks their chances of surviving after death?"

"They bury their dead in black holes, don't they?"

"Yes, but before they die. Pilgrim ships of old and sick."

"Maybe studying the thing takes it out of religion and puts it into science. Science still says nobody survives after death. Maybe the conscious mind won't accept what the subconscious—"

"That's archaic," he said. "And they aren't even human, besides." She shrugged and lay back on the bed. He crawled in beside her and the lights automatically went out.

What if his actions had condemned some of the Aighors to eternal darkness? He shuddered and closed his eyes tight, trying not to think, not to empathize.

3

Kamon looked across the message spheres on the floor before him and crossed his eyes in irritation. This gave him a double view of the opposite sides of the octagonal room—*gepter* knives hung ceremoniously on one wall, over the receiver-altar which periodically reproduced the radio noise of the Thrina as sound; wooden tub next to another wall, filled with mineral water smelling of sulfur and iodine salts.

He picked up a sphere and put it in the depression in

his tape-pad, then instructed the little machine to record all the successive layers of information and display them linearly. The method tasted too much of human thought-patterns for his liking, but it had been adopted by Hafkan Bestmerit as a common method of using interculture information. It was disgusting that a single cultural method of writing—left to right, top to bottom—should control information techniques stretching halfway across the galaxy.

But such was the dominance pattern of the young humans.

The pad's read-out began immediately. The first message was from the council at Frain, the Aighor birthworld. The council had examined the theological and ethical problem of Fairchild and his sacrilege, and supported the judgement of the district priests. Not even Fairchild's alien background and influence could exempt him from the Venging.

He had condemned millions of Aighors to oblivion after death. He had profaned the major region of Thrina pilgrimage by treating it as an area of rational investigation, and not of deep reverence.

The death-ships could no longer drop the assembled dying pilgrims below the event horizons of their chosen black holes. They would no longer experience the redemption of Zero, or bathe themselves in the source of the Thrina song. Kamon seethed with the Venging. He was one of those potential pilgrims.

He had wanted so much to live forever.

4

"I think Fairchild has gotten himself into more than he can handle, but I see no way USC can interfere. We're conducting high-level talks with Hafkan Bestmerit, very delicate. If I were to start an incident I would forego my employment quick as that." Kiril Kondrashef snapped his fingers in demonstration and stared at Anna Sigrid-Nestor with large, woeful eyes. His jowly face was pale in the white light of his reading bureau.

"So I can expect no support from USC," Anna said, anger beginning to color her cheeks.

"At the moment, no."

"Then what do you suggest?"

"For Fairchild, finding his way to some immunity zone like Ansinger. He can seek USC support, but only by renouncing his associations with Dallat. As I understand it, that would mean giving up most of his wealth."

"I'm asking, what can *I* do to help him now."

"Keep your nose out of it. Give him the advice I've given you. But stay clear unless you want USC to renounce its connections with you."

"Kiril, I've known you for over a century now. We're about as friendly as two old wolves can be. You bailed me out of my doldrums after the death of my first husband. More even, we're both Abstainers and dedicated to our creed, that immortality is no desirable thing. Yet now you tell me you won't do anything to help a man who has done more good for colonists and the consolidations than anyone, Dallat association or no. You're incredibly two-faced, I think."

"Calling our relation friendship is a drastic misnomer. I don't like your tactics much and I never have. You're too forceful, when you should step softly. A good many fragile and important things hang in the balance. Do you have any idea—you must have, you're no idiot—how difficult it is for species to coexist when all they have in common is the fact they're alive? It's like standing on tiptoes all the time, for all concerned. Involve yourself and you might start a collapse you can hardly imagine."

She sat in front of his desk, hands gripping the edge as if to push it aside. Her forearms were rigid but her facial expression hadn't changed from the mild, grandmotherly smile she'd put on when she came in. "Besides," he continued in an undertone, "your weapons are registered whenever fired, in defense or otherwise, and the situation is recorded in stasis memory. You can't get around that. We'll have you on the carpet if you do anything that can't be strictly considered defensive."

"I've never been able to figure out a bureacrat," Anna said. "But you're right about one thing." She sighed and picked up her silk duffel bag to leave. "It hasn't been much of a friendship, after all."

She took a transit tube beneath the modular city as any pedestrian might have, nothing more than an old woman. In her bag were several pictures of young men, one of whom attracted her very much. She glanced at them several times as she rode, trying to lose herself in reverie and allow her limbic mind to feel its way through to an action. Gut-level thought had carried her through crises before.

She isolated one photograph and tapped it against her cheek as she left the tube. She was at an underground terminal beneath the Myriadne starport, largest on Tau Ceti II. Shuttles landed and departed dozens by the hour overhead, bronze and silver smooth bullets homing for their mother ships. One such bullet, small and utilitarian, waited for her. She rode a wheeled maneuvering tug out to it. In ten minutes it was off-planet.

Disjohn Fairchild was an intelligent man. He would already be implementing some of the suggestions Kiril had made to her. They were the only outs he had for the moment, with or without her help. She calmly analyzed her own reaction to the suggestions, watching sun, planets and stars form a glittering bow around her ship. Then she smiled grimly and went to sleep as the stars winked out.

When she came awake three hours later, dark still surrounded her. It grew muddied and started to take on form. There was a queasy moment, a tiny shiver, and the outer universe returned. Occasional wisps of color appeared and vanished streamer-like along the forty-five degree rotated starbow.

She began to wonder what Kamon had meant by the reminder that his kind were mortal without choice. Did it have something to do with Disjohn? She went to the ship's library to do research. On her way, she dropped the photograph into an unlabelled chute and told it, "Hire him." They would pick him up at Shireport.

5

Edith grew tired of the viewscreen's translation of what was happening outside the ship. She frowned and closed her eyes, trying to wipe her mind clear for a moment. The books in front of her ghosted and darkened, and she swam in a small red sea of interior designs.

After a moment, she no longer thought in words, and pictures came to her clearly.

Three large, very fast starships all moved across hyperspacial geodesics toward a common goal. They left tracks—she could see them in an allegorical fashion—in amorphous higher geometries. They were aware of each other's presence and direction. By deduction they would be aware of each other's purpose. Each carried an individual bent on accomplishing one task.

Edith wondered what Anna Sigrid-Nestor's purpose was, beyond friendship. They'd communicated briefly a few hours before, and Disjohn had told her to leave well enough alone. But Edith was sure she wouldn't.

Her concentration broken, she opened her eyes again and scanned the books.

One ship carried a being built very differently from any of the masters of the other ships. The being wasn't classifiable in terms of terrestrial biology, having aspects of many phyla, none completely imitated. He was called "he" by default—a cultural tendency to view the convex sexual form as male. But Kamon was neither a male nor a female in the reproductive process of his kind. He was a gestator of young. His children, by human standards, were not his children.

His neurological make-up was also different from a human's. The arrangement of his nervous system was central, nor dorsal, changing the position of his brain, which was located in three places around his esophagus. One of his brains was an evolutionary vestige, handling automatic and emotive functions. It was very powerful in influence despite its size, and was connected with the two other portions by fibers substantially larger than any human nervous connection—networks of medullae, each marvelously complex.

He could contemplate at least four different things at once while involved in a routine action. While driven by what humans might consider a mania, the Aighor could think as rationally as any calm human. He was a dangerous enemy, highly motivated and cunningly reinforced. In this match, Kamon had the upper hand. He would know everything they had planned—with benefit of manic certainty and calm intellection—and he'd act without hesitation.

But Kamon was not supernatural. He would have his faults, too. They could elude him. They could survive him.

Perhaps Sigrid-Nestor could help by distracting him. There was at least hope, and perhaps even a good chance. So why was she feeling so dark inside, and cold?

She closed her books, stood up slowly from the table, and went to join her husband on the bridge.

"A ship riding proto-geometry has three options in case of attack," Graetikin, the captain, was telling Fairchild as she entered. He nodded at her and continued. "It can drop into half-phase, that is, fluctuate between two geometries—" his finger lightly sketched an equation on the tapas pad—"or drop into status geometry, our normal continuum. Or it can dispatch part of its mass and create pseudo-ships like squid's ink. This happens to some extent during any transfer of geometries, to satisfy the Dirac corollaries, but the mass loss is on the order of fifty or sixty atomic units, randomly scattered."

"What about protection from shields?"

"Shields only operate in status geometry. They're electromagnetic and that implies charge-holes in hyperspacial manifolds."

"It would have been easier if we'd had a few Crocerians," Fairchild said wistfully. But they were a pragmatic species. When the ship had put in at Shireport, all the Crocerians he'd asked had politely refused, not wishing to gamble, or, if gambling, betting on the Aighor.

"I'd certainly never fight Aighors if I could avoid it," Graetikin said. "I would avoid it by not having them challenge me."

"We're still taking that risk, though."

"It's up to you to estimate that risk. Once committed to a proto-geometry vector we can't back down."

"How far ahead of us is he?"

"About four light-hours and matching course and velocity."

"How much of a jump can we get if we take one of these proto-geometries?"

"He'll receive signs of our jump about a tenth of a second status time after we make it. That gives us a good hour or two at the other end of the pierce."

"They might take that as an affront," Disjohn said, looking at Edith.

"Why, for God's sake?" Graetikin said. "We'd have to jump into some manifold or another anyway."

"But proto-geometry jumps are a waste of energy, unless one wants to gain a certain advantage." Fairchild pushed away fom the anchored chair and drifted across the cabin. "And if I give any clue that I think they're after me, they'll interpret it as a cultural insult. Kamon is sharper than I care to think about. He won't miss a trick."

Graetikin shrugged and doodled an equation among the others on the tapas. He had been working on it in his head for months, unaware he was so close to a solution. His eyes widened. He had just described what the Thrina were in terms of physics and mathematics, and how they operated. He branched off with another equation, and saw

that in any geometry outside of status—any universe beyond his own continuum—the Thrina would be ubiqui-
tous. He could describe it in mathematics, but he couldn't
put it into words. That, he idly thought, did qualify them
for godhood somewhat.

He would transmit it to Precipice 5 when he had a
chance, and see what they made of it. But for the moment, it wasn't relevant. He folded the tapas and put it
into his shirt pocket.

"We're four light-days out from Shireport, and sixty
parsecs from the Ansinger systems. We made it to Shireport without harassment, and that makes me suspicious.
So far we've only been tailed." Graetikin turned around to
look at Fairchild floating on his back in mid-air. "They're
usually more punctual."

7

The Aighor captain lay against the wall with his throat
and triplet brain smashed flat. He managed a final autonomic gasp of query before Kamon pressed the slammer
button again and laid his head out. The thorax and tail
twitched and the arms writhed slowly, then all motion
stopped. Kamon's mate-of-ship huddled against the back
of the cabin and croaked tightly, regularly, her face black
as blood with fear. Kamon put the slammer down and
sent his message to the Council at Frain.

"The diplomatic team has caused damage to the Venging," he said. The hazy, distorted image of the Auspiseer
chided him for his vehemence.

"They have called the meeting at Precipice 5 partly for
your advantage," the Auspiseer said. "The human Fairchild's ship has been notified en route to Ansinger, and he
cannot refuse."

"But I have already had several chances to attack—"

"The captain's reluctance to destroy the Fairchild ship
was part of his training. You should have been gentler
with him."

"He is of the governing breed. They've become almost human in the past centuries."

"The Council allowed the meeting at Precipice 5 to be called for a number of reasons. For one, it makes our relations with the humans easier temporarily. And for another, it puts you in a better position should the discussions be unsuccessful. So the Council cannot discount your premature release of Captain Liiank, without benefit of pilgrimage. Your mission has now become one of self-immolation upon completion."

"The release of Fairchild will sanctify the Rift Thrina, and I will take my end there."

"So be your course of action, wise and good."

"But I have lost the Fairchild ship now because of the Captain's reluctance. It will take time to regain an advantage."

"What else has offended besides Fairchild?"

"His station."

"Kamon, you are officially declared rogue and we are not answerable for your actions. We will broadcast suitable warnings to that effect."

"That is how I've planned, Auspiseer." He ended the communication and turned to speak to his mate. She had regained her composure and was adjusting her belts of pre-fertilized egg capsules. "We will gestate no more young," he said.

8

"So far, three things have gone wrong with the predictions," the Heuritex said. "I've calculated based on all known constants and variables, all options open, but the trend is against the predicted results. I must conclude that there are large portions of information unavailable to me, making the model inadequate."

"In short, you're useless," Anna told the machine.

"That is as it may be."

"I should replace you with my gigolo."

"He's a handsome bastard, I'll say that for him."

"What if we add the assumption that Kamon is going to behave erratically, say, deranged by being denied an after-life?"

"The results are open again and we have more options."

"Then that's our operating hypothesis. No, wait. Use this—Kamon will behave *as if* he is deranged, by human standards. And very probably will not be by his own. I never underestimate opponents."

"Do you wish that to be an hypothesis, or an assumption? There is a difference, you know."

"Whichever way it works out best. You know what you're doing better than I do, dearie."

"Incorporated. The resulting future-model indicates that the meeting at Precipice 5—course corrected for that destination, by the by—will not take place. The station will be destroyed. Kamon will probably be the destroyer, and the Aighors will allege insanity and rogue tactics to deny responsibility."

"There. That sounds satisfying, doesn't it? I think so." She paced in front of the panel, then asked for gravitation to be shut off, and floated at ease. "Warn Precipice 5 to be on full alert when Disjohn arrives."

"Done."

"And contact USC, division of Martial Aids, at Shireport. Tell them there is going to be a confrontation in the Pafloshwa Rift, co-ordinates unknown."

"Such an action will mark you as a rogue agent as well," the machine said, a speculative tone in its voice.

"Whatever for?"

"First, it isn't . . . kosher . . . to expect a supposedly friendly non-human ship to attack. It indicates a willingness to engage in battle, since you are heading toward the Rift and not backing out, and going there of your own free will."

"Not exactly *my* free will. USC doesn't know I'm aboard this vessel, so they'll assume—will have to assume, and believe me are smart enough to assume—that the captain of this ship is not playing with a full deck of cards."

"You are the captain."

"Nonsense. You are. I shall have you overhauled when we get back to Ansinger."

"That will be a good time to install the new Parakem function modules. Where are you, since you're not here?"

"On Tau Ceti II. I made an appointment with Jessamyn Negras for a business talk, and she hates me enough to keep me waiting for at least a month. She will refuse to believe anyone would miss out on the blessed chance to talk to her. And appropriately deluded recorders are going at all times in my apartments. I'm there, that's certain."

"I see," said the Heuritex.

9

Kamon regretted killing the captain before learning all there was to know about ship operation. The Aighors who crewed the vessel were all competent in their special tasks, and the computers were helpful, but an overall cohesion was, if not lacking, at least shaky. Kamon absorbed the captain's library rapidly.

He was gratified to know an Aighor pilgrimage fleet was forming on the borders of the Rift. His kind cheered him on, and the government—diplomats and rulers alike—had not yet sent a ship to stop him. It would be useless if they did.

Coldly, precisely, he used his triplet brain to figure where difficulties would arise. First would be the protection of Precipice 5—negligible defenses, all things considered. Second would be the presence of Anna Sigrid-Nestor, whom of all the humans he'd met he most admired. Third—the final battleground would not be Precipice 5. He would have to chase Fairchild across the Rift.

The station would be destroyed before the human ships arrived.

10

Fairchild's ship saw the dead ruin, issued a distress signal on the station's behalf, and headed at full power for deep space. It was away from the major gravitational effects of the small system in hours and shamelessly relied on proto-geometry jumps to take it deep into the Rift. It shut down all activities not connected with life-support, went into half-phase, and laid ghost images of itself across a wide range of continua.

Graetikin silently cursed the Dallat conventions which made all private ships carry nothing more offensive than meteoroid deflection shields. He had spent his first thirty years in space as an apprentice commander in the Centrum Astry, helping to command ships armed to their nodes with all conceivable weapons, from rocket projectiles to stasis-shielded neutronium blocks which, when warped into the center of another vessel, quickly gravitated everything into super-dense spheres. Now he was facing a violent confrontation with nothing more offensive than flare rockets and half-phase warps.

It was like the final charge of an old lion against assegai-wielding warriors. Fairchild's motives and the Aighor's motives didn't concern him. Both in their own ways were altruistic and noble, concerned with good tasks. But he was concerned with survival to captain another ship, or at least continue captaining this one. He didn't mind Fairchild's employ. The man was reasonably sharp and knew how to provide for the upkeep of his own ships. If he had the tact of a young bull in dealing with alien cultures, that was usually not Graetikin's province.

Between and around these concerns, he re-worked his equations describing the Thrina. There was a cool, young hypothesis on the horizons of his mind, and it tantalized him. In reworking the single expression on his notepad, he found four connections with Parakem functions which he hadn't noticed earlier. They implied that the Thrina, though ineffectual in a cause-effect relation in most geometries, had interesting properties in coincidence-controlled geometries. They could influence certain aspects of status-geometry, where cause-effect and synchronicity operated in struggling balance. And that implied . . .

He raised his eyebrows.

11

"There is a good possibility we can contact Fairchild if he chooses to coast free within the next thirty-five hours," the Heuritex said.

Anna grumbled out of a light doze at the pronouncement. "What was that?"

"We can join forces with him at points I have calculated along geodesics meeting in higher geometries."

"Translate for us mortals, please." She straightened up in her command chair and rubbed her face with her hands.

"I think we can join with Fairchild's ship before Kamon reaches it. Here is our condition: fifth standard day of flight; all three ships are deep into the Rift. Fairchild is inert, following a least-energy geodesic in half-phase. Kamon is matching the most likely direction of that geodesic, though I'm certain he had no clear picture of the ship's present position along such a path. We follow Kamon closely. And we are constantly correcting our charts with observations of the Rift pulsars and singularities."

"Yes, but what's this about joining Fairchild?"

"His vessel alone is not sufficient to propel itself away from Kamon. He has little or no chance of escape in the long run. But with our two ships linked, we can create a broader affect-beam in proto-geometry—"

"You can arrange this in more than just theory?"

"I think so, madame. I can contact Disjohn Fairchild's

ship in a code only it can understand, and arrange for the rendezvous without the Aighor knowing."

"You're a maker of wonders, and you draw my curiosity like a magnet . . . into areas I'm sure will baffle me. But explain the code."

"It would mix a standard Centrum code with keys and message vectors linked to Fairchild's position and frequency of interspatial . . . excuse me, I grow technical. Simply, those peculiar characteristics of Fairchild's ship along its world line would enable it to quickly decode such a standardized message. Since only one ship occupies its peculiar position, only it can have any chance of decoding."

"I'll think on it," she said. Why did she hesitate? she asked herself. Because now, faced with the possibility of doing what she had started out to do—save Disjohn Fairchild at any cost—a miserable, cold sense started to creep in. She needed to think about it, long and hard. There were too many considerations to weigh for a hasty decision.

She made her way to the ship's observation chamber. Far out on the needle-like boom which extended from the crew ball, an isolated multi-sense chamber seemed to hang in dark space. But its walls were transparent only by illusion. Millions of luminous cells provided adjustable images of anything within range of the ship's sensors, down to the finest detail a human eye could perceive. Images could be magnified, starbows undistorted into normal starfields for quick reference, or high-frequency energy shifted into visual regions. If need demanded, such subtle effects as light distortion in higher geometries could be brought within human interpretation. The sphere could also synthesize programmed journeys and sound effects, or any combination of fictions and synasthesias.

Anna requested a tour of the nearby singularities. "Will there be a specific sequence, madame?" the media computer asked.

"Only an introductory tour. Explain what I'm seeing."

The visual journey started.

"Some singularities are made obvious by surrounding nebulae," the voice-over began. "These are veils of super-nova dust and gas that have been expanding at tens of thousands of miles per second for hundreds of millions of years." Fading in, wisps like mare's-tail clouds in a sunset, backdropped by velvet space. Hidden within, a tiny spinning and glowing cloud, a pinprick, not worth noticing . . . geometric jaws gaping wide, tides deadly as any ravening star-furnace.

"Others are companions to dim red stars, and thus are heavy x-ray sources. They suck in matter from their neighbors, accelerate and heat it through friction, and absorb it in bottomless wells.

"There is no comprehensive explanation why the majority of the Rift stars supernovaed within ten million years of each other, half an eon ago, but the result is a treacherous graveyard of black holes, dwarfs and a few dim giants. They all affect each other across their close-packed Rift in incalculable patterns.

"Some can be seen through observation of the stellar background. The rings of stars around a black hole show the effects of gravitational lensing. Light is captured and orbited above the event horizons any number of times depending on the angle of incidence, producing two primary images and a succession of subsidiary images caused by anomalies in the spinning singularity. The glowing gas-clouds falling into the holes produce central points of high-energy radiation, red-shifted into the visual spectrum by the enormous gravitational fields. These are surrounded by rings of stars reddened through clouds of gas, images of stars from every angle—every visible object, including those behind the observer. There are gaps of darkness and then succeeding rings of stars like the bands on an interferometer plate, finally blending into star-images undeviated by the singularity."

She was reminded of electronic Christmas ornaments from her childhood. The splendor was heightened by the sphere's adaptation to human vision, but only in part. Anna knew what she saw was very close to what existed outside, perhaps only a few million miles away in any direction, so close her ship could reach out to touch it in mere minutes . . .

"Dear God," she murmured. To fall into one of those things would be to transcend any past experience of death. They were miracles, intrusions into reality, jesters of space-time. Her eyes filled with tears which nearly broke their tension bonds to drift away in free-fall.

"Where no such diffractions and reflections are visible, perhaps absorbed in dark nebulosities, and where no X-ray or Thrina sources give clues, naked singularities stripped of their event horizons lurk like invisible teeth. These have been charted by evidence obtained in proto-geometry warps. There is no other way to know they exist."

The Thrina song of a near singularity was played to her. It sounded like the wailing of lost children, sweetly mixed with a potent bass *boum,* an echoing cave-sound, ghost-sound, preternatural mind-sound. "No reason is known for the existence of the Thrina song. It is connected with singularities as an unpredictable phenomenon of radiating and patterned energy, perhaps in some way directed by intelligence."

Nestor left the sphere and drifted quickly back through the extension to the crew-ball. Her hands were shaking. Her cheeks were wet.

12

Kamon followed and waited. A ship could remain in half-phase only so long before its unintentional mass loss (how easily he had spotted and avoided the ghosts!) reached a critical level. His shipmate meditated and fasted alone in her cabin. Kamon was left with the silent computers—it was blasphemous for an Aighor machine to have a voice—and a few aides to see to his food and

wastes. He preferred it that way. At one point he even ordered them to clear away the smashed captain's body so
he might be more alone.

The Venging was close. He had had no further contact
with the Council at Frain or any other Aighor agencies.
He had spotted and charted the ship of Anna Sigrid-Nestor, and felt his own sort of appreciation at the intuition
she was following him personally. She was on her own
Venging.

Such was the dominance pattern of humans.

13

"Four minutes thirty seconds before critical point," Graetikin said softly. Lady Fairchild gripped her husband's
arm tighter. For a society woman she was holding up
remarkably well, Graetikin thought. He'd never had a
chance to talk to her and see what she was like.

The worst was yet to come. Kamon would inevitably
chase them down, and there was only one chance left. His
equation implied their survival if they took that chance. It
was a terrifying prospect, even so.

"We have to leave half-phase," Fairchild said. "And
we have to outrun him. There's no other way." Edith
nodded and turned away from the bridge consoles.

"Have you ever wondered why he called a Venging?"
she asked, turning away from the two men.

"What?" Fairchild asked, not paying much attention to
her. He was focusing on the blank viewers, as if to strain
some impossible clue from them. It was useless giving
glimpses of half-phase exteriors, however. The eye interpreted them as if they weren't there, and indeed half the
time they weren't.

"No other way," Fairchild repeated, his voice quiet as
Graetikin's.

"Kamon has to have a reason," Edith said, louder.

"I'm sure he does," Graetikin said.

"I've been trying to find out what that reason is. I might have a clue."

"That doesn't concern us now," Fairchild said, irritated. "Reason or no, we have to get away from him."

"But doesn't it help to know what we're going to die for?" Edith cried, her voice cracking. "You know damn well we can't outrun him! Graetikin knows it, too. Don't you?"

Graetikin nodded. "But I wouldn't say we're going to die. There might be another way."

"You know of one?" Fairchild asked.

Graetikin nodded. "First, I want to know what Lady Fairchild has to say about Kamon's motive." Disjohn took a deep breath and held up his arms. "Okay," he said to his wife, "Lady Ethnographer, tell us."

"It's all in the library, for whoever cares to look it up. Some of it is even in the old books. We've known about it for a century at least—the basic form of the Aighor pilgrimage. They have three brains, that's well-known—but we've ignored the way they use those brains. One is for rational purposes, and it can do everything a computer can do, but it isn't the strongest. Another is for emotive and autonomic purposes, and that's where the seat of their religion is. We don't know exactly what the third brain does. But I have an idea it's used for preparing the other two brains for a proper death. It has to balance them out, mediate. If the rational brain has an edge, the pilgrim won't be prepared for death. I think the research conducted by the station gave the Aighors a dilemma they couldn't face—the rational treatment of subjects hitherto purely religious to them. It gave their rational minds an edge and caused an imbalance. So the pilgrims couldn't be delivered to the black holes without wholesale failure in proper rituals of dying."

"And?" Graetikin asked, fingering his stylus. It seemed there was another foot to drop in the matter, and she wasn't dropping it.

"And that's it. I can't go any further. I'm not really an

ethnographer. But sometimes I wish to hell you had been, dear husband!" There was no bitterness in her voice, only a loving rebuke. Fairchild said nothing, staring at the empty screens.

"You have another way?" he asked finally.

"It's possible," Graetikin said. He began to outline his alternative. From the ninth word on Fairchild was pale, convinced his Captain had broken under the strain.

14

Anna lay in the half-dark and watched him dress. For the first time in years she felt guilt that her emotional needs should draw her away from constant alertness. But this was the first time she'd been with the handsome lad she was employing for anything more than companionship. He had proven serviceable enough and charming, as though her aging frame didn't bother him. He was a professional and perhaps more than that, a sympathetic human being.

"I don't understand all you've told me," he said. His well-browned Polynesian physique shone in the golden sanitoire lamps. "But I think what you're asking me is, do you have a right to put your whole crew in danger. Well, I'm part of that, but you're the captain, and I signed on——"

"Not as a crew-member," she reminded him.

"No, but I signed on with the understanding there might be hazards involved in deep-space travel."

"These aren't the normal hazards."

"But if it serves your purpose to link up with the other ship, then how can I or anyone else persuade you not to?"

"Not by discussion, of that I'm sure," she said. "But maybe by your presence. I have responsibilities toward the people who work for me." She was reminded of what Kondrashef had said to her. Even if they could link up with the Fairchild ship, what guarantee did she have that the Heuritex's predictions were completely accurate? They didn't know precisely what Kamon's ship was capable of. Already they'd been surprised several times. And her first lieutenant, Nilsbaum, had worked the problem out on an alternate computer, a human-manufacture Datapak. It had given them an eighty percent chance of hitting a singularity if they linked and performed a proto-geometry jump. The Heuritex had disagreed. But still, the dichotomy existed.

"I can't blast the bastard," Anna said, "because every potshot is registered by the tattling machines I had to hook up to pass USC regulations. I can't tamper with them—they retreat into stasis whenever they're not registering."

She looked sharply at the kanaka. He looked back at her, his face blank and expectant. "Go take a shower," she said. Then, softer, "Please. You helped me very much." She turned over and relaxed to the sounds of the door closing and water running.

She was staring at the drifting colors on the nacreous ceiling when the intership chimed. She reached over to depress the switch and listened half-drowsily. The voice of the Heuritex brought her fully awake.

"Madame, we've contacted Fairchild's ship. First Lieutenant Nilsbaum requests your presence on the bridge."

"I'll be there. Any message from Disjohn?"

"He refuses to allow a link-up. He says he has two reasons—first, that he will not jeopardize your life; and second, that his computers predict failure if such a plan is carried out. I don't understand these machines of human construction."

"Did he say anything else?"

"He just warned you to leave."

She sat up in bed and put her chin in her hands. The shower was still running. "Another question," she said.

"Yes, madame."

"What happens if we hit a black hole?"

"Depending on the angle of impact, we have several

varieties of doom. If we go straight in, perpendicular to a tangent, we pass through two or more event horizons, depending on the theoretical geometry you subscribe to—"

"What are event horizons?"

"Simply the horizons beyond which no further events can be seen. The gravitational field at that point has accelerated any particle approaching it close to the speed of light. From an outside point of view, the particle's time has slowed to almost nothing, no motion at all, so it will take an infinite time to hit the singularity below the event horizon. But from our point of view—if we are the hypothetical particle—we will hit it. Not that it will matter to us, though. Long before we pass through the inner event horizon tidal forces will strip us down to subatomic particles."

"Not too pleasant."

"No, but there are other options. At a lesser angle, we might pass through an outer event horizon at a speed sufficient to propel us into another geometry, and out again someplace else—a different place and time in our own universe, perhaps, or in another full-continuum universe. We might survive that, if certain theoretical conditions prove true—though it would be a rough trip and the ship might not emerge in one piece."

"How can there be more than one event horizon?"

"Because black holes rotate. May I draw you a comparison of two Kruskal-Szekeres diagrams?"

"By all means," Anna said, activating the display screen on the intership.

But the mosaic-like charts did little to help her comprehension. She had forgotten most of her physics decades before.

15

"Out of half-phase," Kamon said to himself, "now!"

The image reappeared. He had misjudged the geodesic

slightly. The ship was a light-hour further away than he had predicted, which meant the ship's appearance was an hour off from actual emergence. He felt a brief confusion. Fairchild had pulled it out of half-phase an hour early, then, since the appearance had happened according to Kamon's schedule. But the ruse—if ruse it was—had gained them a very small advantage. He immediately switched to sub-space sensors.

Fairchild's ship was over four light-hours away. More disturbing, it was heading toward a nebulosity which charts said contained three collapsars, two of them black holes. Kamon deftly probed the nebula with his proto-geometry sensors. None of these singularities had ever been used for pilgrimages, thus they did not radiate Thrina songs. The area had not been thoroughly charted except on visual and radio levels from thousands of light-years away, where the patterns of the roiling gas-clouds had given away the presence of hidden collapsars. His new scanning revealed another member in the family, elusive and sacred: a naked singularity. The very presence of humans in such a region was sacrilege—but if they were choosing suicide over destruction at his hands, the danger was unthinkable.

A shudder racked his entire body. He had heard of humans going insane under stress, but if they fell into a singularity *here,* the Venging was a failure and the Rift would never be sacred again.

He forced himself to be calm. They wouldn't know how to prepare themselves for the Fall. They knew nothing about the mental ritual involved. It would be, in effect, nothing more than a suicide. Or it would be something worse, for them.

But his instinct told him to destroy them before they ever reached the cloud. For the first time he felt anxiety that he might fail, even fear.

16

"It can't be done!" Lady Fairchild shouted. "Disjohn, I'm not ignorant! I know what those things are. Graetikin has to be insane to think we can survive that!"

"I've heard him explain it. The computers back him up."

"Yes, on his assumptions!"

"He's on to something new. He knows what he's talking about—and he's right. We don't have any other choice. The Aighor has every advantage over us, including religious zeal—as you pointed out. We've tested event-models on the computers again and again. We have one chance in a thousand of coming out alive. With Graetikin's plan, our chances are at least ten times greater."

"We're going to die, is what you're saying, either way."

"Probably. But there's something grander about this way of going. It robs Kamon of his goal. We hold the upper hand now."

"You know what will happen if we suicide in one of the singularities?" Edith asked.

"We don't plan on suiciding."

"Just going down one, we make this entire region useless to them for their pilgrimages. Mixing souls is anathema to them, just like mixing meat and milk is to an orthodox Jew."

"There was a hygienic reason not to mix meat and milk. It spoils faster."

"Are we so bloody materialistic that we can't see a reason for this kind of tabu?"

Fairchild swung his hands out and turned away from her, talking loudly to the wall. "Damn it, Edith, we have to use Occam's razor! We can't multiply our hypotheses until we avoid stepping on cracks for fear of killing our mothers. We're rational beings! Kamon has that advantage over us—he is not acting rationally. He's on a Venging, just like a Goddam berserker, and he's got a faster, better armed ship. We're doomed! What should we do, bare our breast to him and shout 'mea culpa?' "

Edith shook her head. "I don't know. I just feel so lost."

Fairchild was shivering. His teeth knocked together and he wrapped his arms around himself. "You're not alone. I'm petrified. We're about to do something no one else has ever done."

"Except Aighors," Edith reminded him. "And they've always been prepared for it."

17

"He won't let us dock with him, he's turning toward the singularities—there's nothing more I can do," Anna said. "He's choosing suicide rather than giving in. Or is he up to something else?"

"I can offer no explanation, madame. Either something has malfunctioned or they have gone insane."

"I hate Kondrashef," Anna said quietly. "He has always been right, has always given advice I could never follow—and he's always been so damned, irrefutably correct. But I've got to follow my own wyrd." She sighed and leaned back in her chair. "Can they receive any messages now?"

"They are in the cloud. There's too much interference."

"Veer off. Circle to the opposite side of the nebula and see if anything emerges that end. I've met Fairchild's captain—he may have more up his sleeve than we can know from this perspective."

Dumbfounded, Anna watched the final act on her sensors and tapped her fingers on the Heuritex.

18

Probability fell apart at the ergosphere interface of a singularity. Whether the same conditions applied to a naked singularity or not, he didn't know—he guessed they would. But they wouldn't have to face the danger of the tidal forces—there would be no event horizons, no overt indication of in-rushing space-time. The singularity ahead had collapsed from a star oblated by the presence of other stars, and the result was a hole in space-time stretched out into a line. If conditions still applied here, he'd have to figure their chances of survival on a near-intuitive hunch.

It was clear to Graetikin now. Inter-universe connections of necessity were devoid of probabilities. They were truce zones between regions of differing qualities, differing constants. Hence, somewhere above the singularity, reshaping of in-falling material had to take place.

Perhaps the Aighors weren't far wrong after all.

He worked all his findings into a single tight-packed signal on several media, and broadcast it to space in general. When he was finished he turned to Disjohn and Edith and said, "Feels good to toss out a bottle, anyway. If someone picks it up, well and good. If not, we've lost a few mega-watts."

19

Kamon could either back off, let them escape and hope for an encounter later, or he could pursue to the very end. But he was becoming fatalistic. It seemed the Fairchild ship was behaving not with human insanity, but with divine irrationality—a shield to his Venging. That could imply they were operating in the Grace of the Thrina, not against it. He wished he could consult the Council with his new intuition, but there was no time. Whether he was correct or not, it made him reluctant to interfere. That small reluctance made him hesitate.

"No!" he shouted, pounding his thorax in disgust. "They are only insane! There is no Grace upon them!"

But it was too late. He had followed the Fairchild ship into the nebulosity on a matching course. They could only construe that as an intention to continue the chase. Since they were insane, they would destroy themselves.

In his self-rage, he considered destroying the Nestor ship for personal satisfaction. But he had other things to do. He had to prepare himself mentally for the Fall. He told the others to begin their rituals. They would follow all the way.

20

"Course plotted," the computer told Graetikin. "There will be a proper configuration at these points on the chart. We can meet the singularity's affect-field here, or here— that is, at these points in our future-line. If we fail within any width of time measurably in quantum jump intervals, we will come in at a closer angle, and the warp-wave of our approach will create a temporary event horizon which will destroy us. These are our options."

"Initiate the action and test it on a closed loop. Then choose the best approach and put us there. Kamon hasn't left our tail?"

"No, he still follows. And still jams."

"Then my message didn't get through." Somehow it didn't matter much.

Fairchild gave the final order. Edith watched from his side with a small, knowing smile. She was trying to remember her childhood. There had been so many pleasant things then. She'd married Disjohn, in fact, because he reminded her of the strength of her father. She needed that strength now. She wished she had the strength of a father near.

The ship was otherwise empty. Her corridors echoed as the impact of the nebula's clouds bucked her and made her groan.

The tiny neutron star was pulsating regularly. It was surrounded by a halo of accelerated particles, a natural generator of radio energy. The two normal singularities orbited each other, half a light-hour apart. The violet influx of gases outlined them clearly. Like two whirlpools whose surfaces have been smeared with oil, they glowed in disparate, shimmering mazes of light. Starlight ran in rings around them. Ghost images of each other flickered in the rings, and the ghosts carried rings of stars, and images of other ghosts.

Here time and space rushed into multi-dimensional holes so rapidly that an object had to move at the speed of light to stay in one place. It was Red Queen's race on cosmic and cosmological proportions.

In drawing diagrams of what happens in the singularity below the event horizons, space and time axes cross and replace each other. The word "singularity" itself is a phrase of no more significance than "boojum." It implies points in any mathematical manifold where results start coming out in impossible terms, zeroes or infinities or imaginary numbers. Thus, Graetikin knew, they were soon to step off the pages of one book which had told their lives until now, leave that book behind and everything associated with it, and risk a plunge into null.

God's universe was being twisted into ridiculous failures and inconceivable alterations.

The naked singularity invisibly approached.

21

Kamon's thoughts grew fuzzy and uncoordinated. He bristled with rage as one portion of his mind came unbalanced in the ritual, and kicked out with his tail at the bulkhead before him. He dented the inch-thick steel. Then he regained his balance.

The holiday display of the black holes dominated everything.

He was ready. A tiny reserved part of him set his weapons for a last-ditch attempt, then vanished into the calm pool of his prepared being.

22

Disjohn Fairchild felt a giddiness he'd never known before. It was analogous to being spun on a carnival toy, but every part of him felt it differently.

"I'm expanding," Lady Fairchild said. "I'm getting bigger. Alice down the rabbit hole—"

Still the ship fell. And fell.

Edith gasped. The bridge darkened for the blink of an eye, then was suddenly aglow with scattered bits of ghost lightning. She held her hands in front of her eyes and saw a blue halo around them like Cherenkov radiation. Expansion. Alteration. The desk in front of her, and her arms on the desk, broke into color-separated images and developed intricate networks of filigree, became crystalline, net-like, tingled and shimmered and pulsed, then repeated in reverse and became solid again. Everything smelled of dust and age, musty like vast libraries.

Both ships ended their existence in status geometry at the same moment. Kamon followed at a different angle and hit the affect-field at the same instant the Fairchild ship did. As he had known and expected, his warp-wave created a temporary event horizon and he was divested of his material form.

The Fairchild ship survived its fall. Graetikin's equations, thus far, were wholly accurate.

None of them could conceive of what happened in the interface. It was not chaos—it was instead a sea of quiet, an end to action. The destruction and rearrangement of rules and constants led to a lassitude of space-time, an endless sargasso of thought and event, mired and tangled and grey.

Then each experienced that peculiar quality of their world-line which made them unique. Fairchild, stable and strong, did not see much to surprise him. Graetikin marvelled at the insight into his work. For Edith, still wrapped in her childhood, she had a nightmare and woke far in her past, a little child screaming for her father.

Again the darkness. The ouroboros of the hole spat them out. The computers triggered a lengthy jump, as best as they were able, for the actions of their smallest circuits were still not statistically reliable. This was the chance Graetikin knew they all had to take.

They escaped. The ship rattled and shivered like a dog shaking after a swim. The howl of metal made Fairchild's scalp prickle and his arm-hair stood on end. The bridge cabin was swept by a rush of wind. Edith Fairchild wept quietly and Disjohn, beside her, trembled.

They came together to hold each other, panicked like wild beasts, sweat dripping and noses flaring. Graetikin bounced his fingers clumsily over the screen controls, then corrected his foul-up and gave them a view of what lay outside.

"I don't see anything," Fairchild said.

"I'm astonished we even made it," Graetikin whispered. Disjohn gave him a wild look. With adjustment, the screen still showed darkness.

"Give me a scan and chart all radiating sources," the captain instructed the computer.

"Standard H-R distribution shows nothing. There is only an average temperature," it said.

"What's the temperature?"

"Two point seven one degrees Kelvin."

Graetikin slammed his scriber onto the panel. "Any white hole activity? Any sign of the singularity we just came through?"

"Nothing."

"We had to come out of something!"

"Undefined," the machine said cryptically.

"What does it mean?" Edith asked, holding her chin in her hands.

"It means we're in a region of heat-death."

"Where's that?"

"Undefined," the computer said again.

" 'Where' is meaningless now," Graetikin explained. "Everything's evenly distributed. We've come into a dead universe. We're at the top of a beat between expansion and collapse."

"What can we do?" Disjohn asked. He felt an intense ache for his wife, and wished she were at his side. It seemed he had lost her only recently, the grief was so strong. He looked at Edith. She resembled her mother so much his throat ached. He patted his daughter on the head, but felt none of the reassurance he was trying to give.

"We might be able to go into stasis and wait it out. But we'd have to have a timer, something measuring the progress of the universe outside us. I don't think any of our instruments would last that long."

"There has to be a way!" Fairchild said.

"I told you, Father," Edith said. "We were the offenders." She did a mad little dance. "I told you. We weren't prepared. Why—"

Graetikin thought of them waiting until the ship ran out of energy and food and breathable air. Years, certainly. But years with a burnt-out old politician and his pre-pubescent daughter, a triangle of agonizing possibilities. Even could they survive, they would have no basis for a new life.

"Why," Edith went on, her face white and distorted, "we're in hell!"

23

They rounded the nebula and waited. Anna asked the Heuritex several times if anything had been sighted, and each time it replied in the negative. "There is no sign," it said finally. "We would do well to return home."

"Nothing left," Anna said. She couldn't convince herself she had done all she could.

"One moment, madame," the Heuritex said. "This region was devoid of Thrina before."

"So?"

"There is a signal emerging from the black holes. A single Thrina tone, very strong."

"That's what started this whole thing," Anna said quietly. "Ignore it, and let's go home."

On the edges of the Rift, the pilgrims received the Thrina, and there was rejoicing.

The death-ships resumed their voyages.

IN THE BEGINNING . . .

Jerry Pournelle

This was written hours after the experience it describes; and it has not needed revision. It may be a strange title for the final essay in a book, but it is not inappropriate.

First, let me establish something. When I go to Cal Tech I do *not* expect an experience out of H. P. Lovecraft. Horror may be interesting at the proper time and place, but it's not very pleasant as a total surprise.

It started peacefully enough. Dr Robert Forward, the Hughes Research gravity expert you've heard of here and other places, called to ask if I would be interested in meeting Stephen Hawking. Since Hawking is considered by important physicists to possibly rank alongside Newton and Einstein, it took perhaps five milliseconds to think over the proposition. I didn't even need to look at my calendar; nothing I had planned could be that important.

A week later Larry Niven and I drove over to the California Institute of Technology. It was a bright spring afternoon ...

In order properly to tell this story I must now give some personal details about Professor Hawking. I've consulted his friends, who assure me that he doesn't mind.

Stephen Hawking is quite young, early thirties at the oldest. He is a resident theoretician at Cambridge University, and he yearly produces marvels in astronomical theory, particularly in the field of black-hole dynamics.

GALAXY readers will recall a column in which I described Hawking's fiery marriage of quantum mechanics to Einstein's classical relativity theories, to produce the startling prediction that black holes are unstable. (FUZZY BLACK HOLES HAVE NO HAIR, *GALAXY* Jan. 1975 present volume, pp 89/96). He is also responsible in large part for the so-called "laws of black-hole dynamics". An important man indeed.

Alas, Professor Hawking suffers from a nervous-system disorder which severely impairs his speech and confines him to a wheel chair. Those who attend his lectures are warned that they must listen closely; he can be understood, but only with difficulty and concentration. Of course, given the subject matter, this would be true if he spoke with the oratorical clarity of a William Jennings Bryan to such bards of the sciences as Larry and me; we were prepared to be doubly confused.

Cal Tech's architecture is a neat blend of Old California and modern LA; arched thick-walled Monterrey-style buildings with large shaded porches alternate with steel-and-glass towers and clean-lined functionalism. It sounds horrible, but the effect is actually quite pleasing. It's a nice place to be, especially if you're looking forward to hearing one of the truly great men of our time.

The lecture was in a small modern slant-floored room of the type sometimes called lecture theaters; the sort of classroom lecturers like. The tiered seats let everyone have a good view of the speaker and his materials, and give the speaker a good view of the audience.

It was only partly filled: graduate students, several undergraduates, a sprinkling of faculty, one or two of the top names in theoretical physics. It was a room of serious women and men, mostly younger than I, all expectantly quiet. At the bottom of the well, the focus of attention on the stage, was an incredibly thin, very young-appearing man seated in a high-backed motorized chair of Victorian design; the chair had no flavor of the hospital about it. He wore a light suit, dark shirt, and flowered tie, and he kept his hands folded carefully in his lap as he was introduced.

The chairman gave his credits and spoke wonderingly of how privileged we were to hear a man of this stature. No one disagreed. Not, of course, than anyone would have said anything no matter what he thought, but the total silence in the room was an obvious sign of unanimous assent.

Hawking began to speak. Everyone leaned slightly forward, straining to hear. Except for the heavily slurred voice there was absolutely no sound; you could quite literally hear a pen drop, for I dropped mine and it clattered loudly on the cement floor.

This is the scene, then: a lecture room partly filled with very bright people, a few extremely well known in theoretical physics, others students at one of the world's most prestigious institutions. They all strain to hear a wizened young man who makes awkward gestures and speaks with a thick slur that keeps his words just at the edge of intelligibility.

He grins like a thief. He's obviously not in pain and he doesn't feel sorry for himself. And he tells that room of bright, highly educated people that everything they thought they knew is nonsense. And he chuckles.

He tells us that the pudding that ate Chicago may some day exist; that duplicates of each one of us may one day wander the universe; that *anything* can, and probably will, happen. He tells us that the universe isn't lawful, never will be lawful, never *can* be lawful; that we *cannot ever* know enough to predict the totality of events in this universe; that at best we study local phenomena that may be predictable for an unspecifiable time.

And he laughs.

He tells us that Cthulthu may exist after all.

As I said, it was an afternoon of Lovecraftian horror. Larry and I escaped with our sanity, after first, in the question period, making certain that Hawking really did say what we thought he'd said.

He had.

Stephen Hawking's lecture had originally been entitled "The Breakdown of Physics in the Region of Space-Time Singularities." The title was flashed on the screen; then another slide took its place, and Hawking chuckled. The new slide:

THE BREAKDOWN OF PHYSICISTS
IN THE REGION OF
SPACE-TIME SINGULARITIES

He began simply enough. The principle of equivalence, he said, is well established. This is the principle that states that *inertial* mass, that is, the resistance of objects to being moved by an outside force, is exactly equivalent to *gravitational* mass, that is, the gravitational force a given mass will exert: there is only one kind of mass.

This was Galilieo's Principle, and the source of the famous if apocryphal story of his dropping a cannon-ball and a musket-ball from the Leaning Tower of Pisa and observing them striking the ground at the same time. Obviously if gravitational and inertial mass were different, heavy objects would *not* fall at the same speed as light ones.

So far so good. Next, gravity affects light. It can bend light rays, as predicted by Einstein and observed several times in solar eclipses.

Now in short order: the energy-momentum tensor of gravity is positive; gravity is universally attractive, not repellent. Therefore, enough mass will create a field from which no light can escape.

The Special Theory of Relativity says that nothing can travel faster than light.

And *therefore* sufficient mass must create a space-time singularity—a place which cannot be observed.

A singularity is therefore inevitable; that is, one must exist, provided only: (1) that Einstein's general relativity is correct; (2) gravity is truly attractive and never repellant and (3), enough mass has ever been collected together.

And *therefore* at least one singularity exists in our universe, since at the time of the Big Bang all the conditions certainly prevailed; and also, it's very likely that other singularities have been created by collapse of stars, since many stars have more than enough matter and don't have enough energy to throw that matter away as they die.

Okay so far? Nothing startling here. Bit dry, but all we've proved is that singularities must exist, and heck, nearly everyone accepts the idea now. They're hidden away inside black holes, of course, and observers are now very nearly certain that we can *observe* a black hole.

Well, not observe the hole itself; but Cygnus X-1, an x-ray emitting star in the constellation Cygnus, has an invisible companion and the pair of stars, the one we can see and the one we can't, together act very like what Cal Tech's Kip Thorne predicted such a pair would act like if one were a black hole.

So what else is new? We've proved black holes can exist, and lo, the observers think they've found one. What's scary about *that*?

Nothing, so far. Holes aren't scary unless you're about to fall into one. We even understand them. We know they "have no hair," that is, that they can be completely described given their mass, M; angular momentum, J; and electric charge, Q. Given these data we can describe their shape, and predict what effect they'll have on nearby objects, and play all kinds of fascinating scientific-theory games.

We can talk about black hole bombs, and toy with ideas on how to extract energy from them: take one rotating black hole, throw garbage into it, and you not only get rid of the garbage, but can get useful energy back out. There are speculations (not SF; just plain science) about extremely advanced civilizations using black holes for precisely that purpose.

There's just no end to the nice things you could do with black holes, and although not many years ago they were no more than toys for theoreticians to play mental games with, black holes have become household-word objects now.

Black holes don't make us nervous.

Ah, but inside each black hole there lurks a singularity. This is the little beastie that breaks down physics in the nearby regions. By definition they do things we can't predict. They behave in strange ways. Up close to them time reversals can happen. How, then, can we avoid this breakdown of our nice predictable universe?

Hawking discussed several theoretical alternatives, and dismissed each. A couple of the cases seemed to startle one of the big-name theoreticians listening to the lecture. When Hawking was finished, though, the singularities were back and inevitable. I won't pretend to have understood all of this part of the lecture; and I wouldn't bore readers with it if I had. If you appreciate that sort of thing you'll read Hawking's paper.

For the rest of us I sum up by saying that he found no

good alternatives; eliminating General Relativity doesn't eliminate the singularities, or else lands you in an even worse theoretical soup.

Therefore, let us look at General Relativity; but let us add quantum theory to it. Hawking recently published that work, and I described it here.

The important fact is that the quantum effects violate cosmic censorship. The Law of Cosmic Censorship, you may recall, states that there shall be no naked singularities; every singularity shall be decently clothed with an event horizon that prevents us from ever being able to observe it directly, and thus prevents us from observing the region in which physics breaks down.

Thus we needn't fear the singularity. It can't affect our lives, because nothing it does can get out of that black hole "around" it.

But adding quantum effects to General Relativity repeals cosmic censorship. Black holes evaporate. Big ones slowly, small ones rapidly, all inevitably. And what of the singularity that MUST have been created by the Big Bang of creation?

Evaporation of black holes produces naked singularities. We may play about with the concept of quantizing relativity, and Hawking did; but the conclusion was inescapable. Again I don't pretend to have followed every step, nor did most of the rest of us in that room; but several did, and they weren't pleased.

Because now comes the punch-line. The singularities emit matter and energy. And "they emit all possible configurations with equal probability. Perhaps this is why the early universe from the Big Bang singularity was in thermal equilibrium, and was very nearly homogeneous and isotropic; thermal equilibrium would represent the largest number of configurations."

But since that time the universe has changed, and we have stars and planets and nematodes and comets and great whales (for a little while longer) and people; but the singularity must still be around. It emits. And what comes out is completely random, absolutely uncorrelated. This fundamental breakdown in prediction—Hawking is saying not only that we can't predict *now,* but that in principle we can *never* predict, no matter how much we know or how smart we get or how large a computer we build—is a "consequence of the fact that General Relativity allows fundamental changes in the topology of space-time; that is, allows holes.

"Matter and information can fall into these holes—or can come out. And what comes out is completely random and uncorrelated."

The hole can emit anything. Anything at all.

"No," I thought. I looked to Niven. "No," he was thinking. Surely we misunderstood.

And the thin chap grinned ever more broadly. "Of course we might have to wait quite a while for it to emit one of the people here this afternoon, or myself, but eventually it must—"

Hawking chuckled and waited expectantly, and after a long and very silent pause first one, then another joined him in laughter, but it had a rather hollow sound, or so I thought. Larry agreed when we could talk about it later.

So far as we can tell, we've just heard one of the top people in theoretical physics tell us that we don't know anything and can't know anything; that causality is a local phenomenon of purely temporary nature; that time travel is possible; that Cthulthu might emerge from a singularity, and indeed is as probable as, say, H. P. Lovecraft.

Hawking concluded by reminding us that Albert Einstein once said "God does not play dice with the universe."

"On the contrary," Hawking said, "it appears that not only does God play dice, but also that he sometimes throws the dice where they cannot be seen!"

Lovecraftian horror indeed. Our rational universe is crumbling. Western civilization assumes reason; that *some things are impossible, that's all,* and we can know that;

that werewolves don't exist, and there never was, never could be, a god Poseidon, or an Oracle that spoke truly; that the universe is at least in principle discoverable by human reason, is *knowable*.

That, says one of the men we believe best understands this universe, is not true. It's not very probable that Cthulthu will emerge from the primeval singularity created in the Big Bang, or that Poseidon will suddenly appear on Mount Olympus, but neither is it *impossible*; and for that matter, this world we think we understand, which seems to obey rational laws we can discover, isn't very probable either—isn't, in fact, in the long run, any more probable than a world that includes Cthulthu, or the pudding that ate Chicago.

Well, of course I don't believe that; not in the sense that I'm going to alter my life to conform to a lawless and unpredictable universe. But I am now reduced to an act of faith: an irrational belief that the world and universe are, must be, lawful, and rational.

This is not "faith in science" or believing in science; not any more. It never was, actually; but Hawking has laid bare the hidden flaw. So long as science itself concluded that the universe was lawful, few of us were tempted to ask *why* this should be so, or to realize that this is the one question science can never answer.

Now, though, science itself says the universe is not lawful. If you want a lawful universe, you've got to take a leap of faith; you've got to hold fast to an irrational belief. While you're doing that, why not also believe there's a higher purpose to it all?

Is it harder to believe the universe is lawful and purposeful than to believe it is lawful but without purpose?

In the Beginning, the Big Bang emitted Chaos; and the Chaos was without form, and void, for it was homogeneous and isotropic. And the Singularity moved upon the face of the Chaos and emitted light; and the Universe was no longer homogeneous, for the light was divided from the darkness.

And there came forth firmaments and dry land and seas and stars and moons; and the worlds brought forth grass, the herb yielding seed, and the fruit trees yielding fruit after his kind, whose seed is in itself.

It is quite literally true that if you can believe that, you can believe anything; more, you *must* believe anything. To exclude anything you must make an act of faith.

As we drove away from Pasadena, Larry remarked that if we ever had proximity to a singularity, he could well imagine people praying to it. After all, their prayers probably wouldn't influence what came out of it—but they might, and certainly nothing else would. I even had an idea for a flippant story to be entitled "The Oracle."

I don't think I'll write that story.

If this new work of Hawking's holds up—and if we've correctly interpreted what we heard—there are going to be some changes in the fundamentals of Western Civilization.

Will philosophy once again become the "Queen of Sciences?" I don't know; I suspect, though, that what we heard during our Lovecraftian afternoon will have a long reach. We either need some fundamental new breakthroughs in theoretical physics—and I've heard no hint of what they may be—or we'll have to start thinking about faith again.